Sources for the History of Cyprus

Volume VII

Greek Texts of the
Fourth to Thirteenth Centuries

Sources for the History of Cyprus

Edited by

Paul W. Wallace and Andreas G. Orphanides

Volume VII

Greek Texts of the Fourth to Thirteenth Centuries

Selected and Edited by

HANS A. POHLSANDER

(University at Albany, State University of New York)

Greece and Cyprus Research Center
1999

ISBN: 0-9651704-7-0

ISBN set: 0-9651704-0-3

TABLE OF CONTENTS

Preface

Like preceding volumes in this series, this volume endeavors to make original source material on the history of Cyprus available in English translation to those who might have a serious interest in the subject but limited or no knowledge of Greek (or other pertinent languages). Those who read Greek may find this volume a convenient first step in further research. In the anticipation that this volume will be used as a reference source rather than for sustained reading, I have provided detailed indices.

The Byzantine period of Cyprus, as far as its external history is concerned, is usually reckoned from the year 330, when Constantine I dedicated his new capital of Constantinople, to the year 1191, when Richard the Lionheart arrived in Cyprus. It has seemed expedient, however, to extend the limits of the present work at both ends. At the beginning the first three decades of the fourth century have been encompassed; this allows for continuity with Volume I of this series and for the inclusion of Eusebius of Caesarea. At the far end another century has been added to allow for the inclusion of Nikephoros Kallistos Xanthopoulos. But such major sources as Leontios Machairas, George Bustrone, Ephraim, patriarch of Jerusalem, and the archimandrite Kyprianos, given their much later dates, have been excluded; for these only references and brief descriptions have been provided.

Other collections of sources have been made in Greek; they differ from this one in arrangement and in chronological parameters. Much but by no means all of the material found in the present work is also found in Kyriakos Hadjiioannou, Η ΑΡΧΑΙΑ ΚΥΠΡΟΣ ΕΙΣ ΤΑΣ ΕΛΛΗΝΙΚΑΣ ΠΗΓΑΣ (*Ancient Cyprus in the Greek Sources*), vols. 1–2, Nicosia 1985, hereafter abbreviated ΑΚΕΠ; and in B. Nerantze-Barmaze, ΣΥΝΤΑΓΜΑ ΒΥ-ΖΑΝΤΙΝΩΝ ΠΗΓΩΝ ΚΥΠΡΙΑΚΗΣ ΙΣΤΟΡΙΑΣ (*Collection of Byzantine Sources for the History of Cyprus*), Nicosia 1996, hereafter abbreviated ΣΒΠΚΙ. Some passages cited in the former work have been omitted from the present collection, especially in the area of mythology, while a great many passages have been added in order to extend the coverage beyond ancient Cyprus to the limits of the present work. The last two segments of the latter work, covering the 14th and 15th centuries, have been excluded, as they are not within the chronological parameters set to the present work. Wherever a passage adduced in ΑΚΕΠ and/or ΣΒΠΚΙ overlaps or coincides with a passage adduced here the appropriate reference has given in brackets. All quotations, however, are based not on the text provided by Hadjiioannou or Nerantze-Barmaze, but on the best available editions and translations (see Editions and Translations Consulted).

Some of the texts which have been excerpted are available only in older editions which do not meet the standards of modern scholarship. Therefore I have found it necessary in a few cases to emend the Greek text; such emendations have been marked in my translation. And in one case the text is so corrupted that my translation has, by necessity, remained rather tentative.

Following the practice adopted for Vol. I of this series, I have arranged the authors quoted in this source book, as far as possible, in their chronological order. Each author's dates are given directly after his name. For the chronological information I have generally relied on the *Oxford Dictionary of Byzantium.* I have also made extensive use of Johannes Karayannopulos and Günter Weiß, *Quellenkunde zur Geschichte von Byzanz (324–1453)* (Wiesbaden 1982).

Greek names may be found in a variety of forms which reflect Greek, Latin, and English practice. To achieve a measure of uniformity I have again let the *Oxford Dictionary of Byzantium* be my guide. Thus I have written, for example, "Kedrenos, George" rather than "Georgius Cedrenus," "Alexios Komnenos" rather than "Alexius Comnenus," and "Kosmas Indikopleustes" rather than "Cosmas Indicopleustes." This should be to the advantage of those readers who might want to use the *Oxford Dictionary of Byzantium* as a companion to the present work (as I certainly would recommend). At the same time I have taken care to list significant variants as cross-references in the indices. On the other hand I have given many Greek names of the classical period in the Latinized or Anglicized forms which have long been familiar. Thus I have written "Aeschylus," "Andocides," or "Isocrates," not "Aischylos," "Andokides," or "Isokrates."

Wherever possible I have used translations already published elsewhere; in those cases I have retained, of course, whatever spellings I found. A number of publishers have kindly granted permission to quote copyrighted materials (see Acknowledgments). For quite a few translations I am indebted to the editor of this series, Professor Paul W. Wallace. Where no translator is credited the translation is mine. For a few documents of unusual length I have provided summaries rather than translations.

Interpolations in the text, providing useful information, especially dates, are set off by square brackets.

Acknowledgments

The following publishers have kindly given permission to use copyrighted materials:

American Philosophical Society, Philadelphia
Australian Association for Byzantine Studies, Melbourne
E. J. Brill, Leiden
Cambridge University Press, New York City
Columbia University Press, New York City
Gerald Duckworth & Co., London
Dumbarton Oaks Research Library and Collection, Washington, D.C.
Loeb Classical Library and Harvard University Press, Cambridge, Massachusetts
University of Pennsylvania Press, Philadelphia
Wayne State University Press, Detroit

Gratitude is expressed to these, and to all editors and translators, living or deceased, whose work has made this volume possible.

Editions and Translations Consulted

Abbreviations

AASS	*Acta Sanctorum Bollandistarum*, Brussels.
ACO	*Acta Conciliorum Oecumenicorum*, ed. Eduard Schwartz et al., Berlin and Leipzig, 1914 ff.
ACW	*Ancient Christian Writers*, New York.
Auct.	*Auctarium Bibliothecae Hagiographicae Graecae*, *Subsidia Hagiograpica* 47, ed. François Halkin, Brussels 1969.
BHG	*Bibliotheca Hagiographica Graeca*, *Subsidia Hagiographica* 8A, 3rd ed., ed. François Halkin, Brussels 1957.
BT	*Bibliotheca Teubneriana*, Leipzig and Stuttgart.
Budé	*Collection des Universités de France*, Paris.
BZ	*Byzantinische Zeitschrift*.
CCSG	*Corpus Christanorum, Series Graeca*, Turnhout.
CFHB	*Corpus Fontium Historiae Byzantinae*.
CSHB	*Corpus Scriptorum Historiae Byzantinae*, Bonn.
Cramer, *Anecd. Gr. Oxon.*	John Anthony Cramer, *Anecdota Graeca e codicibus bibliothecarum Oxoniensium*, Oxford 1835–1837.
Cramer, *Anecd. Gr. Paris.*	John Anthony Cramer, *Anecdota Graeca e codicibus manuscriptis bibliothecae regiae Parisiensis*, Oxford 1839–1841, repr. Hildesheim 1967.
DOP	*Dumbarton Oaks Papers*.
FAC	*The Fragments of Attic Comedy*, ed. John Maxwell Edmonds, Leiden 1957–1961.
FC	*Fathers of the Church*, New York.
FGrH	*Fragmente der griechischen Historiker*, ed. Felix Jacoby, Berlin and Leiden 1923 ff.
FHG	*Fragmenta Historicum Graecorum*, ed. Carl Müller, Paris 1841–1870, repr. Frankfurt 1975.
GCS	*Die griechischen christlichen Schriftsteller der ersten* [*drei*] *Jahrhunderte*, Leipzig and Berlin.
GGM	*Geographi Graeci Minores*, ed. Carl Müller, Paris 1855–1861, repr. Hildesheim 1965.
Hackett	J. Hackett, *A History of the Orthodox Church of Cyprus*, London 1901.
Halkin	François Halkin, ed., *Douze récits byzantins sur Saint Jean Chrysostome*, *Subsidia Hagiographica* 60, Brussels 1977.
LCL	*Loeb Classical Library*, Cambridge, Massachusetts, and London.
Mansi	Giovanni Domenico Mansi, *Sacrorum Conciliorum Nova et Amplissima Collectio*, ed. Paris 1901; repr. Graz 1960.
Migne, *PG*	J. P. Migne, *Patrologia, Series Graeca*, Paris.
NPNF	*A Select Library of the Nicene and Post-Nicene Fathers of the Christian Church*, New York.

Orat. Attici	*Oratores Attici,* edd. Johann Georg Baiter and Hermann Sauppe, Zürich 1850, repr. Hildesheim 1967.
RE	Pauly-Wissowa, *Real-Encyclopädie der Klassischen Altertumswissenschaft,* Stuttgart 1893 ff.
REB	*Revue des Études Byzantines.*
SC	*Sources Chrétiennes,* Paris.
SVF	*Stoicorum Veterum Fragmenta,* ed. Johannes von Arnim, Leipzig 1905–1924, repr. Stuttgart 1964.
TGF[2]	*Tragicorum Graecorum Fragmenta,* 2nd ed., ed. August Nauck, Leipzig 1899, repr. Hildesheim 1964.

Texts and Translations

Achilles Tatius, *Leucippe et Clitophon*
> Ed. Ebbe Vilborg, Stockholm 1955.
> Ed. and French trans. Jean Philippe Garnaud, *Budé* 1991.
> Ed. and trans. Stephen Gaselee, *LCL* 1917.

Acts of St. Barnabas (apocryphal)
> Ed. *AASS* Iunii II, pp. 431–36.
> Ed. Maximilian Bonnet in Richard Adalbert Lipsius and Maximilian Bonnet, edd., *Acta Apostolorum Apocrypha* II.2, Leipzig 1903, repr. Darmstadt 1959. Summary of contents in Richard Adelbert Lipsius, *Die apokryphen Apostelgeschichten und Apostellegenden* II.2, Leipzig 1884, pp. 280–85.

Acts of the Synod of 1157
> Ed. Migne, *PG* 140, cols. 177–97.
> Ed. Ioannes Sakellion, Πατμιακὴ Βιβλιοθήκη, Athens 1890, pp. 316–28.

Acts of the Synod of 1170
> Ed. Louis Petit, "Documents inédits sur le concile de 1166 et ses derniers adversaires," *Vizantijskij Vremennik* 11 (1904) 465–93 at 479–89.

Acts of the Synod of 1209
> Ed. K. Chatzopsaltes, Ἡ ἐκκλησία Κύπρου καὶ τὸ ἐν Νικαίᾳ Οἰκουμενικὸν Πατριαρχεῖον, ΚΥΠΡΙΑΚΑΙ ΣΠΟΥΔΑΙ 28 (1964) 135–68 at 141–44.

Akolouthia of St. Philo
> Ed. ΚΥΠΡΙΑΚΑΙ ΣΠΟΥΔΑΙ 11 (1947) 3–28.

Alexander the Monk, *De Inventione Sanctae Crucis*
> Ed. Migne, *PG* 87.3, cols. 4015–76.

Alexander the Monk, *Laudatio in Apostolum Barnabam*
> Ed. *AASS* Iunii II, pp. 436–52.
> Ed. Peter van Deun in *Hagiographica Cypria, CCSG* 26, 1933, pp. 82–122.

Anastasios Sinaites, Ἐρωτήσεις καὶ ἀποκρίσεις (*Quaestiones et Responsiones*)
> Ed. Migne, *PG* 89, cols. 329–824.

Arethas, Archbishop of Caesarea, *Scripta Minora*
> Ed. L. G. Westerink, *BT* 1968–1972.

Aristenos, Alexios, *Interpretation of the Canons*

    Ed. Georgios A. Rhalles and Michael Potles, Σύνταγμα τῶν θείων καὶ ἱερῶν κανόνων, Athens 1852–1859, repr. 1966, vol II.

Aristides, Aelius, *Panathenaicus*

    Ed. James H. Oliver, *The Civilizing Power, Transactions of the American Philosophical Society,* new ser. 58:1 (1968).

Aristotle, Fragments

    Ed. Valentin Rose, Leipzig 1886, repr. Stuttgart 1967.

Athanasios of Alexandria, *Contra Gentes*

    Ed. and trans. Robert W. Thomson, Oxford 1971.

    Ed. and French trans. Pierre Thomas Camelot, *SC* 18, 2nd ed., 1977.

    Trans. Archibald Robertson, *NPNF,* 2nd ser., vol. IV, 1891.

    Trans. E. P. Meijerling, Leiden 1984.

Athanasios of Alexandria, *Apologia Secunda* or *Apologia contra Arianos*

    Ed. Hans-Georg Opitz, *Athanasius: Werke* II.1, Berlin 1940.

    Trans. Archibald Robertson, *NPNF,* 2nd ser., vol. IV, 1891.

Balsamon, Theodore, *Interpretation of the Canons*

    Ed. Georgios A. Rhalles and Michael Potles, Σύνταγμα τῶν θείων καὶ ἱερῶν κανόνων, Athens 1852–1859, repr. 1966, vol II.

Basil the Great, *Letters*

    Ed. and trans. Roy J. Deferrari, *LCL* 1939.

    Ed. and French trans. Yves Courtonne, *Budé* 1957–1966.

    Trans. Sister Agnes Clare Way, *FC* 1951.

Basilakes, Nikephoros, *Encomium of Nicholas Mouzalon*

    Ed. Antonius Garzya, *BT* 1984.

Blemmydes, Nikephoros, Γεωγραφία συνοπτική (*Concise Geography*)

    Ed. Carl Müller, *GGM* II 458–68.

Choiroboskos, George, *Orthographia*

    Ed. Cramer, *Anecd. Gr. Oxon.* II, pp. 167–281.

Choniates, Niketas, *History* or *Annals*

    Ed. Jan-Louis van Dieten, *CFHB* XI.1–2, Berlin and New York 1975.

    Trans. Harry J. Magoulias, *O City of Byzantium: Annals of Niketas Choniates,* Detroit 1984. Quoted by permission of Wayne State University Press.

Chrestomathiae (*Epitome of Strabo*)

    Ed. Carl Müller, *GGM* II, pp. 529–636.

Chronica Byzantina Breviora

    Ed. Peter Schreiner, *Die byzantinischen Kleinchroniken* I, *CFHB* XII.1, Vienna 1975.

Church Councils, *acta,* subscriptions, and canons

    Mansi.

    ACO.

    Périclès-Pierre Joannou, *Discipline générale antique* (Pontificia commissione per la redazione del codice di diritto canonico orientale, *Fonti* IX), Rome 1962–1964.

Constantine (VII) Porphyrogennetos, *De Thematibus*
>Ed. Migne, *PG* 113, cols. 63–140.
>Ed. A. Pertusi, Vatican City 1952.

Constantine (VII) Porphyrogennetos, *De Ceremoniis Aulae Byzantinae*
>Ed. Migne, *PG* 112, cols. 73–1446.

Constantine (VII) Porphyrogennetos, *De Administrando Imperio*
>Ed. and trans. Gyula Moravcsik and R. J. H. Jenkins, Budapest 1949; rev. ed., *CFHB* 1, Washington, D.C., 1967.

Continuator of George Hamartolos *or* George the Monk, *Vitae Recentiorum Imperatorum*
>Ed. Migne, *PG* 109, cols. 823–984.

Cyril of Alexandria, *Commentarius in Isaiam*
>Ed. Migne, *PG* 70, cols. 9–1450.

Dionysios Periegetes, Οἰκουμένης Περιήγησις (*Orbis Descriptio*)
>Ed. Carl Müller, *GGM* II, pp.103–76.

Doxopatres, Neilos, Τάξις τῶν πατριαρχικῶν θρόνων (*Notitia Thronorum Patriarchalium*)
>Ed. Migne, *PG* 132, cols. 1083–1114.
>Greek and Armenian ed. Franz Nikolaus Finck, Marburg 1902.

Epiphanios, *Adversus Haereses* or *Panarion*
>Ed. Karl Holl, *GCS* 1915–1933. Rev. ed. Jürgen Dummer, II 1980 and III 1985.
>Trans. Frank Williams, *Nag Hammadi and Manichaean Studies* 35 and 36, Leiden 1987 and 1994. Quoted by permission of E. J. Brill.
>Trans. (selected passages) Philip R. Amidon, Oxford 1990.

Epiphanios, *De Mensuris et Ponderibus*
>Ed. Paul Anton de Lagarde, *Symmicta*, Göttingen 1880, II, pp. 149–216.
>Trans. (from the Syriac) James Elmer Dean, Chicago 1935.

Etymologium Genuinum
>Cited fom *FGrH.*

Etymologium Magnum
>Ed. Thomas Gaisford, Oxford 1848, repr. Amsterdam 1965.

Eusebios of Caesarea, *Chronicon*
>Armenian version (in Latin translation) and Greek fragments, ed. Alfred Schoene, Berlin 1866–1875.
>German trans. Josef Karst, *GCS* 1911.

Eusebios of Caesarea, *Commentarius in Isaiam*
>Ed. Joseph Ziegler, *GCS* 1975.

Eusebios of Caesarea, *De Martyribus Palestinae*
>Ed. Theodor Mommsen, *GCS* 1908.
>Trans. Hugh Jackson Lawlor and John Ernest Leonard Oulton, London 1927.

Eusebios of Caesarea, *Historia Ecclesiastica*
>Ed. Eduard Schwartz, *GCS* 1903–1909.
>Ed. and trans. Kirsopp Lake (vol. I) and John Ernest Leonard Oulton (vol. II), *LCL* 1926–1932.

Eusebios of Caesarea, *Onomasticon*
 Ed. Erich Klostermann, *GCS* 1904.

Eusebios of Caesarea, *Praeparatio Evangelica*
 Ed. Karl Mras and Édouard des Places, *GCS* 1982.
 Trans. Edwin Hamilton Gifford, Oxford 1903.

Eustathios of Antioch, *Commentarius in Hexaemeron*
 Ed. Migne, *PG* 18, cols. 707–94.

Eustathios of Thessalonike, *Commentary on Dionysos Periegetes*
 Ed. *GGM* II, pp. 201–407.

Eustathios of Thessalonike, *Commentary on Homer's Iliad*
 Ed. Gottfried Stallbaum, Leipzig 1827–1829, repr. Hildesheim 1960.
 Ed. Marchinus van der Valk, Leiden 1971–1987.

Eustathios of Thessalonike, *Commentary on Homer's Odyssey*
 Ed. Gottfried Stallbaum, Leipzig 1825–1826, repr. Hildesheim 1960.

Galenos, John, Deacon, *Allegories to Hesiod's Theogony*
 Ed. Hans Flach, *Glossen und Scholien zur Hesiodischen Theogonie mit Prolegomena,* Leipzig 1876, pp. 295–365.

George Hamartolos *or* George the Monk, *Chronicon*
 Ed. Carl de Boor, *BT* 1904, rev. Peter Wirth 1978.

George of Alexandria, Life of St. John Chrysostom
 Ed. Halkin, pp. 69–285.

George of Cyprus, *Descriptio Orbis Romani*
 Ed. Heinrich Gelzer, Leipzig 1890.
 Ed. Ernst Honigmann, *Le Synekdèmos d'Hiéroklès et l'opuscule géographique de Georges de Chypre*, Brussels 1939, pp. 49–70.

George the Synkellos, *Ecloga Chronographica*
 Ed. Alden A. Mosshammer, *BT* 1984.

Germanos II, patriarch of Constantinople, Letters to the clergy of Cyprus
 Ed. Migne, *PG* 140, cols. 601–22.
 Summary in J. Hackett, *A History of the Orthodox Church of Cyprus*, London 1901, pp. 91–93.

Glykas, Michael, *Annales*
 Ed. Immanuel Becker, *CSHB* 1836.
 Ed. Migne, *PG* 158, cols. 1–624.

Goudeles, Theodosios, *Encomium on St. Christodoulos*
 Ed. Eras L. Branouses, Τὰ ἁγιολογικὰ κείμενα τοῦ ὁσίου Χριστουδούλου, ἱδρυτοῦ τῆς ἐν Πάτμῳ μονῆς, Athens 1966.

Gregory of Cyprus, Autobiography
 Ed. and French trans. William Lameere, *La tradition manuscrite de la correspondance de Grégoire de Chypre, Patriarche de Constantinople (1283–1289)*, Brussels 1937, pp. 176–91.

Gregory of Cyprus, Letter to the King of Cyprus
 Ed. William Lameere (see previous entry), pp. 93–94.

Gregory of Nyssa, *Contra Fatum*
> Ed. Migne, *PG* 45, cols. 145–74.
> Ed. Jacobus A. McDonough in J. Kenneth Downing, Jacobus A. McDonough, and Hadwiga Hörner, edd., *Gregorii Nysseni Opera Dogmatica Minora* II = *Gregorii Nysseni Opera* III.2, Leiden 1987, pp. 29–63.

Hesychios of Alexandria, *Lexicon*
> Ed. Moritz Schmidt, Jena 1858–1868.
> Ed. Kurt Latte, Copenhagen 1953–1966 (A–O only).

Hierokles, *Synekdemos*
> See George of Cyprus.

Iveron Monastery (Mt. Athos), MS. 4501 (381)
> Ed. Spyridon Lampros, *Catalogue of the Greek Manuscripts on Mount Athos* II, Cambridge 1900.

Joel, *Chronographia*
> Ed. and Italian trans. Francesca Iadevaia, Messina 1979.

John Chrysostom, *Homilies on the Acts of the Apostles*
> Ed. Migne, *PG* 60, cols. 13–384.
> Trans. J. Walker, J. Sheppard, and H. Browne, *NPNF*, 1st ser., vol. XI, 1889.

John Chrysostom, *Letters*
> Ed. Migne, *PG*. 52, cols. 529–791.

John Lydos, *De Mensibus*
> Ed. Richard Wünsch, *BT* 1898, repr. 1967.

John Lydos, *De Magistratibus Populi Romani*
> Ed. Richard Wünsch, *BT* 1903, repr. 1967.
> Ed. and trans. Anastasius C. Bandy, Philadelphia 1983. Quoted by permission of the American Philosophical Society.
> Trans. Thomas F. Carney, Lawrence, Kansas, 1972.

John of Damascus, *Oratio Tertia de Imaginibus*
> Ed. Migne, *PG* 94, cols. 1317–1420.
> Ed. Bonifatius Kotter, *Die Schriften des Johannes von Damaskos* III, Berlin and New York 1975.

John the Almoner (Eleemon)
> See vita of St. Tychon.

Julian "the Apostate," *Epistulae* and *Orationes*
> Ed. and French trans. Joseph Bidez, Gabriele Rochefort, and Christian Lacombrade, *L'Empereur Julien: Oeuvres complètes*, 2 vols. in 4, *Budé* 1924–1972.
> Ed. and trans. Wilmer Cave Wright, *The Works of the Emperor Julian*, 3 vols., *LCL* 1913–1923.

Justinian I, *Novellae*
> *Corpus Iuris Civilis* III, edd. Rudolf Schoell and Wilhelm Kroll, 8th ed., Berlin 1963.

Kaminiates, John, *The Capture of Thessalonike*
> Ed. Gertrud Böhlig, *CFHB* 4, Berlin and New York 1972.
> German trans. Gertrud Böhlig, Graz, Vienna, and Cologne 1975.

Kedrenos, George, *Compendium Historiarum*

    Ed. Emmanuel Becker, *CSHB* 1838–1839.

    Ed. Migne, *PG* 121, col. 23–122, col. 368.

Kekaumenos, Λόγος νουθετικὸς πρὸς βασιλέα (*Advice to the Emperor*; appended to the author's *Strategikon*)

    Ed. and Russian trans. Gennadii Gregorovich Litavrin, *Cekaumeni Consilia et Narrationes*, Moscow 1972.

    German trans. Hans-Georg Beck, *Vademecum des byzantinischen Aristokraten,* 2nd. ed., Graz, Vienna, and Cologne 1964, pp. 135–51.

Kinnamos, John, *Epitome*

    Ed. August Meineke, *CSHB* 1836.

    Ed. Migne, *PG* 133, cols. 309–678.

    Trans. Charles M. Brand, *Deeds of John and Manuel Comnenus*, New York 1976. Quoted by permission of Columbia University Press.

Komnene, Anna, *Alexiad*

    Ed. and French trans. Bernard Leib, *Budé* 1937–1945, repr. 1967.

    Trans. Elizabeth A. S. Dawes, London 1928, repr. New York 1978.

    Trans. E. R. A. Sewter, Harmondsworth, England, 1969.

Kosmas Indikopleustes, *Topographia Christiana*

    Ed. E. O. Winstedt, Cambridge 1909.

    Ed. and French trans. Wanda Wolska-Conus, *SC* 141, 159, and 197, 1968–1973.

    Trans. J. W. McCrindle, London 1897.

Leo VI, *Taktika*

    Ed. Migne, *PG 107*, cols. 669–1120

Leontios of Neapolis, Life of St. John the Almoner

    Ed. Heinrich Gelzer, Freiburg and Leipzig 1893.

    Ed. and French trans. André-Jean Festugière, Paris 1974.

    Trans. Elizabeth Dawes and Norman H. Baynes, *Three Byzantine Saints*, Oxford 1948, pp. 195–270.

Libanios, *Epistulae*

    Ed. Richard Förster, *BT* 1921–1922.

    Ed. and trans. (selection) A. F. Norman, *LCL* 1992. Quoted by permission of the Loeb Classical Library and Harvard University Press.

Libanios, *Orationes*

    Ed. Richard Förster, *BT* 1903–1908.

Malalas, John, *Chronographia*

    Ed. Ludwig Dindorf, *CSHB* 1831.

    Ed. Migne, *PG* 97, cols. 64–718.

    Trans. Elizabeth Jeffreys, Michael Jeffreys, and Roger Scott, Melbourne 1986. Quoted by permission of the Australian Association for Byzantine Studies.

Manasses, Constantine, *Hodoiporikon* (*Journey to Jerusalem*)

    Ed. Konstantin Horna in *BZ* 13 (1904) 313–55.

Menaion

    Ed. P. P. Paraskeuopolos, Athens 1904.

Ed. Georgios G. Gegle, Athens 1926.

Anonymous ed., Athens 1970.

Menologion of Basil II

Ed. Migne, *PG* 117, cols. 19–614.

Facsimile ed. Pio Franchi de' Cavalieri, Turin 1907.

Neophytos, Archbishop, Letter to the Emperor

Ed. Spyridon Lampros, Κυπριακὰ καὶ ἄλλα ἔγγραφα. Νέος Ἑλληνομνήμων 14 (1917) 14–50 at 41–43, no. 28.

Neophytos Enkleistos, *Encomium of St. Theosebios*

Ed. Hippolyte Delehaye, "Saints de Chypre," *Analecta Bollandiana* 26 (1907) 161–297 at 181–97.

Neophytos Enkleistos, *Encomium of St. Gennadios*

Ed. Hippolyte Delehaye, "Saints de Chypre," *Analecta Bollandiana* 26 (1907) 161–297 at 221–28.

Neophytos Enkleistos, Ἐγκώμιον εἰς τὸν τίμιον καὶ ζωοποιὸν σταυρόν (*Encomium of the Venerable and Life-giving Cross*; Cod. Paris. gr. 1189, fol. 29v–38v). Cited from Benedict Englezakis, *Studies on the History of the Church of Cyprus, 4th–20th Centuries,* Aldershot, Hampshire, 1995, pp. 168–69 with n. 60.

Neophytos Enkleistos, *Letter Concerning the Misfortunes of the Land of Cyprus*

Ed. Ioannes P. Tsiknopoullos in *Byzantion* 39 (1969) 336–39.

Ed. and trans. William Stubbs, *Itinerarium peregrinorum et gesta regis Ricardi* (Rolls Series 38.1; London 1864), pp. CLXXXIII–CLXXXIX.

Ed. and trans. Claude Delaval Cobham, *Excerpta Cypria: Materials for a History of Cyprus,* Cambridge 1908, pp. 9–13. Trans. quoted by permission of Cambridge University Press.

Neophytos Enkleistos, *Oratio de Terrae Motibus*

Ed. Hippolyte Delehaye, "Saints de Chypre," *Analecta Bollandiana* 26 (1907) 161–297 at 207–12.

Neophytos Enkleistos, *Typike Diatheke* (Ritual Ordinance, A.D. 1214)

Ed. Ioannes P. Tsiknopoullos, Κυπριακὰ Τυπικά, Nicosia 1969, pp. 69–104.

Nicholas I Mystikos, Patriarch of Constantinople, *Letters*

Ed. and trans. R. J. H. Jenkins and L. G. Westerink, *CFHB* 6, Washington, D.C. 1973. Quoted by permission of Dumbarton Oaks Research Library and Collection.

Nicholas IV Mouzalon, Patriarch of Constantinople, Στίχοι (poem)

Ed. Sophia I. Doanidou in Ἑλληνικά 7 (1934) 109–50.

Nikephoros, Patriarch of Constantinople, *Historia Syntomos, Breviarium,* or *Short History*

Ed. Carl de Boor, *BT* 1880, repr. New York 1975.

Ed. and trans. Cyril Mango, *CFHB* 13, Washington, D.C., 1990.

Niketas of Ankyra, Λόγος ἀντιρρητικὸς πρὸς τοὺς λέγοντας μὴ δεῖν παρατείσθαι (*On the Right of Resignation*)

Ed. Jean Darrouzès, *Documents inédits d'ecclésiologie byzantine, Archives de l'Orient* 10, Paris 1966, pp. 250–65.

Nonnos of Panopolis, *Dionysiaca*
>> Ed. and French trans. Francis Vian et al., *Budé* 1976 f.
>> Ed. and trans. W. H. D. Rouse, *LCL* 1940.

Notitiae Episcopatuum Ecclesiae Constantinopolitanae
>> Ed. Jean Darrouzès, Paris 1981.

Ὀνομασία Μηνῶν (*The Names of the Months*)
>> Ed. Cramer, *Anecd. Gr. Oxon.* III, pp. 402–403.

Oracula Sibyllina
>> Ed. Johannes Geffcken, Leipzig 1902.

Oribasios
>> Ed. J. Raeder, *Oribasii Collectionum Medicarum Reliquia*, Leipzig 1928–1933,
>>> repr. Amsterdam 1964.

Palladas, *Epigrams*
>> Ed. and trans. W. R. Paton, *The Greek Anthology* III, *LCL* 1915.
>> Ed. and French trans. Pierre Waltz and Guy Soury, *Anthologie Grecque* VIII, *Budé*
>>> 1974.

Palladios, *Dialogue on the Life of St. John Chrysostom*
>> Ed. Migne, *PG* 47, cols. 5–82.
>> Ed. P. R. Coleman-Norton, Cambridge 1928.
>> Trans. Robert T. Meyer, *ACW* 45, 1985.

Περὶ μεταθέσεων (*On Transfers*)
>> Ed. Jean Darrouzès, *REB* 42 (1984) 147–214.

Περὶ Νικηφόρου τοῦ ἄνακτος (*On the Lord Nikephoros*)
>> Ed. François Halkin, *Inédits Byzantins d'Ochrida, Candi et Moscou, Subsidia
>>> Hagiographica* 38, Brussels 1963, pp. 255–56.

Περὶ προβολῆς καὶ ψήφου καὶ ἐκλογῆς καὶ καταστάσεως καὶ προνομίων μητροπολιτῶν
καὶ ἀρχιεπισκόπων καὶ ἐπισκόπων (*On the Nomination, Election, Appointment,
and Prerogatives of Metropolitans, Archbishops, and Bishops*)
>> Ed. Jean Darrouzès, *Documents inédits d'ecclésiologie byzantine, Archives de
>>> l'Orient* 10, Paris 1966, pp. 116–59.

Περὶ Σιβύλλης (*On the Sibyl*)
>> Ed. Cramer, *Anecd. Gr. Paris.* I, pp. 332–35.

Philostorgios, *Historia Ecclesiastica*
>> Ed. Migne, *PG* 65, cols. 459–624.
>> Ed. Joseph Bidez and Friedhelm Winkelmann, *GCS* 1981.

Philotheos, Protospatharios, *Kletorologion*
>> Ed. J. B. Bury, *The Imperial Administrative System in the Ninth Century, With a
>>> Revised Text of the* Kletorologion *of Philotheos,* London 1911, repr. New
>>> York 1958, pp. 131–79.
>> Ed. and French trans. Nicolas Oikonomides, *Les listes de préséance byzantines de
>>> IXe et Xe siècles,* Paris 1972, pp. 65–235.

Photios, Patriarch of Constantinople, *Bibliotheca*
>> *FGrH* nos. 100–8 (Dexippus), 115–103 (Theopompus), and 688–7 (Ctesias).
>> Ed. and French trans. René Henry, *Budé* 1959–1991.

Trans. (selection) N. G. Wilson, London 1994. Quoted by permission of Gerald
Duckworth & Co.

Photios, Patriarch of Constantinople, *Epistulae*

Ed. B. Laourdas and L. G. Westerink, *BT* 1983–1988.

Photios, Patriarch of Constantinople, *Lexicon*

Ed. S. A. Naber, Leiden 1864–1865.

Ed. Christos Theodoridis, vol. I only, Berlin 1982.

Τὰ πραχθέντα ἐπὶ τῇ καθαιρέσει τοῦ πατριάρχου ἐκείνου τοῦ Μουζάλων (*Acts of the
Deposition of the Patriarch Mouzalon*)

Ed. Jean Darrouzès, *Documents inédits d'ecclésiologie byzantine*, *Archives de
l'Orient* 10, Paris 1966, pp. 310–31.

Prokopios of Caesarea, *De Aedificiis*

Ed. Jacob Haury, corr. Gerhard Wirth, *BT* 1964.

Ed. and trans. H. B. Dewing with Glanville Downey, *LCL* 1940.

Ed. and German trans. Otto Veh, *Prokop*, Vol. V, Munich 1977.

Prokopios of Gaza, *Epistulae et Declamationes*

Ed. Antonio Garzya and Raymond Joseph Loenertz, *Studia Patristica et Byzantina*
IX, Ettal 1963.

Scholia

Aeschylus, *Persians*

Ed. Wilhelm Dindorf, *Aeschyli Tragoediae* III, Oxford 1851, repr. Hildesheim 1962.

Aristides, Aelius

Ed. Wilhelm Dindorf, Aristides, *Opera* III, Leipzig 1829.

Aristophanes, *Plutus*

Ed. Friedrich Dübner, Paris 1877, repr. Hildesheim 1969.

Demosthenes

Ed. *Orat. Attici*, pp. 49–126.

Ed. M. R. Dilts, *BT* 1983–1986.

Dionysios Periegetes

Ed. *GGM* II, pp 427–57.

Euripides, *Andromache*

Cited from *FHG* III, p. 340, fr. 18.

Hesiod, *Theogony*

Ed. Lamberto di Gregorio, Milan 1975.

Homer, *Iliad*

Ed. Hartmut Erbse, Berlin 1969–1988.

Homer, *Odyssey*

Ed. Wilhelm Dindorf, Oxford 1855, repr. Amsterdam 1962.

Isocrates

Orat. Attici, pp. 3–11.

Ed. George Mathieu and Émilè Brémond, Isocrates, *Discours* II, *Budé*
1967.

Lycophron, *Alexandra*
>Ed. Gottfried Kinkel, Lycophron, *Alexandra*, *BT* 1880.
>Ed. Eduard Scheer, *Lycophronis Alexandra,* Berlin 1881–1908.

Pindar
>Ed. Anders Bjorn Drachmann, *BT* 1903–1927, repr. Amsterdam 1964.

Plato
>Ed. William Chase Greene, Haverford, Pennsylvania, 1938.

Theocritus
>Ed. Carl Wendel, *BT* 1967.

Tzetzes, John
>Ed. P. A. M. Leone, *Ioannis Tzetzae Historiae*, Naples 1968.

Sergios, Archbishop of Cyprus, Letter to Pope Theodore I
>Ed. Mansi X, col. 913–916.

Simokattes, Theophylaktos
>Ed. Carl de Boor, *BT* 1887, rev. Peter Wirth 1972.
>Trans. Michael and Mary Whitby, Oxford 1986.

Skoutariotes, Theodore, Σύνοψις Χρονική
>Ed. K. N. Sathas, Μεσαιωνικὴ Βιβλιοθήκη VII, Athens, Venice, and Paris 1894, repr. Hildesheim 1972, pp. 1–556.

Skylitzes, John, *Synopsis Historiarum*
>Ed. Ioannis Thurn, *CFHB* 5, Berlin and New York 1973.

Sokrates Scholastikos, *Historia Ecclesiastica*
>Ed. Robert Hussey and William Bright, Oxford 1893.
>Trans. A. C. Zenos, *NPNF,* 2nd ser., vol. II, 1890.

Souda
>Ed. Ada Adler, Leipzig 1928–1938.

Sozomenos, *Historia Ecclesiastica*
>Ed. Joseph Bidez and Günther Christian Hansen, *GCS* 1960.
>Trans. Chester D. Hartranft, *NPNF*, 2nd ser., vol. II, 1890.

Stephen, Deacon of Hagia Sophia
>See vita of St. Stephen the Younger.

Stephen of Byzantium, *Ethnica*
>Ed. August Meineke, Berlin 1849.

Stephen (unknown), Scholia to Aristotle's *Rhetoric*
>Ed. Cramer, *Anecd. Gr. Paris* I, pp. 245–312.
>Ed. Hugo Rabe, *Commentaria in Aristotelem Graeca* XXI.2, Berlin 1896, pp. 263–322.

Symeon Magistros, Logothete, *Chronographia*
>Ed. Immanuel Becker, *CSHB* 1842.

Symeon Metaphrastes, Life of St. Spyridon
>Ed. Migne, *PG* 116, cols. 417–68.

Symeon Metaphrastes, Life of St. John the Almoner
>Ed. Migne, *PG* 114, cols. 895–966.

Synaxarion of Constantinople
>Ed. Hippolyte Delehaye, *AASS*, Propylaeum Novembris, Brussels 1902.

Synesios of Cyrene, *Epistulae*
>Ed. Rudolf Hercher, *Epistolographi Graeci*, Paris 1873, pp. 638–739.
>Ed. A. Garzya, Rome 1979.
>Trans. Augustine Fitzgerald, Oxford 1926.

Synodikon of Orthodoxy, The
>Ed. Jean Gouillard, *Le Synodikon de l'Orthodoxie, Travaux et Memoirs* 2 (1967) 1–316.

Taktikon Escurial or *Escorialense*
>Ed. and French trans. Nicolas Oikonomides, *Les listes de préséance byzantines de IXe et Xe siècles,* Paris 1972, pp. 255–77.

Taktikon Uspenskij
>Ed. and French trans. Nicolas Oikonomides, *Les listes de préséance byzantines de IXe et Xe siècles,* Paris 1972, pp. 41–63.

Theodore Lector or Anagnostes, *Historia Ecclesiastica*
>Ed. Günther Christian Hansen, *GCS* 1971.

Theodore of Paphos, Panegyric of St. Spyridon
>See Vitae of St. Spyridon.

Theodore of Tremithous, Life of St. John Chrysostom (*BHG* 872b)
>Ed. Migne, *PG* 47, cols. LI–LXXXVIII.
>Ed. Halkin, pp. 7–44.

Theodoret of Cyrrhus, *Interpretatio* or *Commentarius in Ezechielem*
>Ed. Migne, *PG* 81, cols. 807–1256.

Theodoret of Cyrrhus, *Interpretatio in Jeremiam*
>Ed. Migne, *PG* 81, cols. 495–806.

Theodoret of Cyrrhus, *Historia Ecclesiastica*
>Ed. Léon Parmentier and Felix Scheidweiler, *GCS* 1954.

Theophanes the Confessor, *Chronographia*
>Ed. Carl de Boor, Leipzig 1883–1885.
>Trans. Harry Turtledove (for the years A.D. 602–813), Philadelphia 1982. Quoted by permission of University of Pennsylvania Press.
>Trans., with commentary, Cyril Mango and Roger Scott, Oxford 1997.

Theophrastus, fragments
>Ed. William W. Fortenbaugh et al., *Theophrastus of Eresus: Sources for His Life, Writings, Thought and Influence,* 2 vols., Leiden 1993.

Typicon of the Monastery of St. John Chrysostom at Koutsovendi (Cod. Paris. gr. 402)
>Cited from Cyril Mango and Ernest J. W. Hawkins in *DOP* 18 (1964) 332, nn. 58 and 59.

Tzetzes, John, *Historiae* or *Chiliades*
>Ed. P. A. M. Leone, Naples 1968.

Tzetzes, John, Scholia to Lycophron
>Ed. Eduard Scheer, Lycophron, *Alexandra*, vol. II, Berlin 1908.

Vitae of St. Athanasios the Athonite
>Ed. Jacques Noret, *CCSG* 9, 1982.

Vita of St. Auxibios
>   Ed. Athanasios Papageorgiou, Ἀπόστολος Βαρνάβας 30 (1969) 13–24.
>   Ed. Jaques Noret in *Hagiographica Cypria, CCSG* 26, 1993, pp. 176–202.

Vita of St. Constantine the Jew
>   Ed. *AASS* Nov. IV, pp. 628–56.

Vita of St. Demetrianos
>   Ed. Henri Grégoire, *BZ* 16 (1907) 217–37.

Vita of St. Epiphanios (with continuation)
>   Ed. Migne, *PG* 41, cols. 23–114.
>   Ed. Wilhelm Dindorf, *Epiphanii episcopi Constantiae opera* I, Leipzig 1859, pp. 1–77.

Vita of St. Herakleides
>   Ed. François Halkin, "Les actes apocryphes de Saint Héraclide de Chypre, disciple de l'apôtre Barnabé," *Analecta Bollandiana* 82 (1964) 133–169.
>   Summary of contents Felix Nau, "La légende des saints évêques Héraclide, Mnason et Rhodon, ou l'apostolocité de l'église de Chypre," *Revue de l'Orient chrétien* 12 (1907) 125–38 at 129–36.

Vitae of St. John Chrysostom
>   *BHG* 872d, 873e, and 874d, ed. Halkin, pp. 45–68, 287–301, and 303–383.
>   See also Theodore of Tremithous and George of Alexandria.

Vita of St. John the Almoner
>   See Leontios of Neapolis.

Vita of St. John the Almoner (anonymous)
>   Ed. Hippolyte Delehaye, "Une vie inédite de S. Jean l'Aumonier," *Analecta Bollandiana* 45 (1927) 19–73.

Vita of the blessed Petros of Atroa
>   Ed. and French trans. Vitalien Laurent, *Subsidia Hagiographica* 29, Brussels 1956.

Vitae of St. Spyridon
>   Ed. Paul van den Ven, *La légende de S. Spyridon évêque de Tremithonte*, Louvain 1953.

Vita of St. Stephen the Younger, by Stephen, deacon of Hagia Sophia
>   Ed. Migne, *PG* 100, cols. 1067–1186.

Vita of St. Therapon.
>   Ed. *AASS* Maii VI, pp. 681–92

Vita of St. Triphyllios
>   Ed. *AASS* Iun. II, p. 681–84.

Vita of St. Tychon, by John the Almoner (Eleemon)
>   Ed. Hippolyte Delehaye, "Saints de Chypre," *Analecta Bollandiana* 26 (1907) 161–297 at 229–32.

Vita of St. Zeno
>   Ed. M. Sauget, "S. Zenon de Chypre," *REB* 25 (1967) 147–53.

Xanthopoulos, Nikephoros Kallistos, *Historia Ecclesiastica*
>   Ed. Migne, *PG* 145, cols. 55–1332; 146, cols. 9–1274; and 147, cols. 9–448.

Xanthopoulos, Nikephoros Kallistos, *Enarratio de episcopis Byzantii et de patriarchis omnibus Constantinopolitanis*
    Ed. Migne, *PG* 147, cols. 449–68.
Ὑποτύπωσις γεωγραφίας ἐν ἐπιτομῇ (*A Concise Outline of Geography*)
    Ed. *GGM* II, pp. 494–509.
Zonaras, John, *Chronicon*
    Ed. Moritz Pinder, *CSHB* 1841–1897.
    Ed. Ludwig Dindorf, *BT* 1868–1875.
Zonaras, John, *Interpretation of the Canons*
    Ed. Georgios A. Rhalles and Michael Potles, Σύνταγμα θείων καὶ ἱερῶν κανόνων, Athens 1852–1859, repr. 1966, vol II.
Zosimos, *Historia Nova*
    Ed. and French trans. François Paschoud, *Budé* 1971–1989.
    Trans. Ronald T. Ridley, Sydney 1982. Quoted by permission of the Australian Association for Byzantine Studies.

TEXTS

1. ACHILLES TATIUS (2nd c., not 4th–6th c. as previously believed)

1. *Leucippe et Clitophon* 2.15.3 [AKEΠ II 164.7]

  For the Egyptian ox is especially favoured, both in bulk and in colouring; he is of very great size, with a brawny neck, a broad back, a great belly, horns neither small like those of the Sicilian cattle, nor ugly like those from Cyprus.   (trans. S. Gaselee)

2. COUNCIL OF NICAEA (First Ecumenical Council) (325)

1. Subscriptions (in Latin only; Mansi II, col. 696)

  Cyril of Paphos. Gelasios of Salamis.

2. From a letter of Photios, Patriarch of Constantinople (ca. 810–after 893), to Michael, prince of Bulgaria (Mansi II, col. 749) [AKEΠ I 121.6α]

  [There were present at the Council of Nicaea] a great many others who were conspicuous by their apostolic gifts and who had suffered as confessors; among them were Paphnoutios and Spyridon.

3. EUSTATHIOS of Antioch (d. before 337)

1. *Commentaries in Hexaemeron* (spurious) (Migne, *PG* 18, col.756A.) [AKEΠ I.35.3; II 150.1]

  There were three sons of Iooua [Javan]: Elisasa [Elishah], the father of the Alisaioi, now the Aioleis; Tharses [Tarshish], the father of the Tharseis, now the Kilikes, for so Cilicia was called of old (even now its metropolis is called Tharses); Khatheim [Kittim], who lived on the island Khatheima, which they now call Cyprus, from which the Jews call every island and the seacoast Eththo. [cf. Genesis 10:4]   (trans. P.W.W.)

4. EUSEBIOS of Caesarea (ca. 260–339/340)

1. *Historia Ecclesiastica* 1.12.1

No list of the Seventy is anywhere extant. It is said, however, that one of them was Barnabas, and of him the Acts of the Apostles has also made special mention, and so also has Paul when writing to the Galatians [2:1 and 9].

(trans. K. Lake)

2. *Historia Ecclesiastica* 2.3.3

It was at that moment and in that place [Antioch], when so many of the prophets from Jerusalem were also present, and with them Barnabas and Paul, and a number of the other brethren besides them, that the name of Christian was first given [cf. Acts 11:26], as from a fresh and life-giving fountain. Agabus also, one of the prophets with them, made predictions that there was to be a famine, and Paul and Barnabas were sent to give assistance to the ministry of the brethren.

(trans. K. Lake)

3. *Historia Ecclesiastica* 2.12.2

You would find that this [report of a famine] too agrees with the writing of the Acts of the Apostles [11:28–30], which records how the disciples in Antioch, each according to his several ability, determined to send to the relief of the dwellers in Judaea, which they did, sending it to the elders by the hand of Barnabas and Paul.

(trans. K. Lake)

4. *Historia Ecclesiastica* 3.25.4

Among the books which are not genuine must be reckoned the Acts of Paul, the work entitled the Shepherd, the Apocalypse of Peter, and in addition to them the letter called of Barnabas and the so-called Teachings of the Apostles.

(trans. K. Lake)

5. *Historia Ecclesiastica* 6.14.1

And in the *Hypotyposeis*, to speak briefly, he [Clement of Alexandria] has given concise explanations of all the Canonical Scriptures, not passing over even the disputed writings, I mean the Epistle of Jude and the remaining Catholic Epistles, and the Epistle of Barnabas, and the Apocalypse known as Peter's.

(trans J. E. L. Oulton)

6. *Historia Ecclesiastica* 7.25.15–16 [ΑΚΕΠ I 110.14α]

So then, there is also another John in the Acts of the Apostles, whose surname was Mark, whom Barnabas and Paul took with themselves, concerning whom also the Scripture says again: 'And they had also John as their attendant' [Acts 13:5]. But as to whether it were he who was the writer [of the Book of Revelation], I should say No. For it is written that he did not arrive in Asia along with them, but 'having set sail,' the Scripture says, 'from Paphos Paul and his company came to Perga in Pamphylia; and John departed from them and returned to Jerusalem' [Acts 13:13]. But I think that there was a certain other [John] among them that were in Asia, since it is said both that there were two tombs at Ephesus, and that each of the two is said to be John's.

(trans. J. E. L. Oulton)

7. *Onomasticon* (ed. E. Klostermann, p. 174) [АКЕП I 35.9]

Chettieim: The land of the Chettieim is Cyprus, where he [?] founded the city of Louza.

8. *De Martyribus Palestinae* 13.1–2 [АКЕП I 119]

A seventh year of the conflict against us [A.D. 310] was nearing its end, and our affairs having taken a quieter and more peaceful turn—a state of things which continued until the eighth year—in the neighbourhood of the copper mines in Palestine no small number of confessors was gathered together, who used great boldness, so as even to build houses for church assemblies. But the ruler of the province (a cruel and wicked person, as bad a man as his acts against the martyrs proved him to be), having come to stay there and learning the manner of their life, communicated everything he thought fit to the emperor in a letter that was meant to slander. Next came on the scene the superintendent of the mines, and acting, apparently, on the emperor's orders he divided the body of the confessors, assigning to some a place of abode in Cyprus, to others in Lebanon, scattering some here and some there in the districts of Palestine; and ordered that they all should be oppressed with various kinds of labour. (trans. H. J. Lawlor and J. E. L. Oulton)

9. *Commentarius in Isaiam* 23:1 [АКЕП I 35.13]

They are no longer coming from the land of the Kittieians, or from the land of the Chettieim, according to the other interpreters. It is said that Cyprus is so known and that Citium is a city in it, which those who sail from Tyre passed by. (trans. P. W. W.)

10. *Chronicon,* Armenian version, ed. A. Schoene, I, col.157; trans. Karst, p. 73

And he himself (Sethos) departed for Cyprus and the land of the Phoenicians.

11. *Chronicon,* Armenian version, ed. A. Schoene, I, col. 163; trans. Karst, p. 76

Around the tenth year of his rule he [Ptolemy IX Soter II, Lathyrus] killed the friends of his father [Ptolemy VIII Euergetes II, Physkon] and of his mother [Cleopatra III], was toppled from power on orders from his mother because of his cruel disposition, and fled to Cyprus. [107 B.C.]

12. *Chronicon,* Armenian version, ed. A. Schoene, I, col. 163; trans. Karst, p. 76

The younger brother [Ptolemy X Alexander] ruled together with his mother, [counting the years of his reign] from the time when he had assumed the rule over the Cypriots.

13. *Chronicon,* Armenian version, ed. A. Schoene, I, col. 163 and 165; trans. Karst, p. 76

They (mutinous soldiers) . . . drove him [Ptolemy X Alexander] to flight . . . with his wife and daughter; he reached a city of the Lycians, Mira; from there he fled to Cyprus.

14. *Chronicon*, Armenian version, ed. A. Schoene, I, col. 165; trans. Karst, pp. 76–77

After he had fled, the Alexandrians sent messengers to the older brother, Ptolemy [IX] Soter [II], and returned the kingdom to him as he sailed back from Cyprus.

15. *Chronicon*, Armenian version, ed. A. Schoene, I, col. 209; trans. Karst, p. 98

In the 144th Olympiad: Heraclides from Salamis on the island of Cyprus [winner] in the stadium.

16. *Chronicon*, Armenian version, ed. A. Schoene, I, col. 225; trans. Karst, p. 107 [ΑΚΕΠ I 32]

Of those who ruled the seas after the Trojan War . . . the sixth were the Cypriots, for 33 years.

17. *Praeparatio Evangelica* 2.3.12–15 [ΑΚΕΠ II 47.2]

For never will I be cajoled by that Cyprian islander Cinyras, who dared to transfer the lewd orgies of Aphrodite from night to day, in his desire to deify a harlot of his own country . . . And I shall proclaim the hidden secrets openly, and not let modesty hinder me from speaking of things which you are not ashamed to worship. First then, the daughter of the foam, the Cyprus-born, the beloved of Cinyras, Aphrodite I mean, 'Enamour'd of the source from which she sprang,' those mutilated members of Uranus, those lustful members, which after their excision did violence to the waves, how wanton the members of which your Aphrodite becomes the worthy fruit! (From Clement of Alexandria, *Protrepticus* 2.12–13)   (trans. E. H. Gifford)

18. *Praeparatio Evangelica* 4.16.2–3 [ΑΚΕΠ II 122]

And in what is now called Salamis, but formerly Coronia [more correctly Koronis], in the month Aphrodisius according to the Cyprians, a man used to be sacrificed to Agraulos, the daughter of Cecrops and a nymph of Agraule. This custom continued until the times of Diomedes; then it changed, so that the man was sacrificed to Diomedes; and the shrine of Athena, and that of Agraulos and Diomedes are under one enclosure. The man to be sacrificed ran thrice round the altar, led by the youths: then the priest struck him in the throat with a spear, and so they offered him as a burnt-sacrifice upon the pyre that was heaped up.

But this ordinance was abolished by Diphilus, king of Cyprus, who lived in the times of Seleucus the theologian, and changed the custom into a sacrifice of an ox: and the daemon accepted the ox instead of a man; so little is the difference in value of the performance. (From Porphyry, Πρὸς ἀποχῆς ἐμψύχων or *De Abstinentia* 2.54–55)   (trans. E. H. Gifford)

5. COUNCIL OF SERDICA (SARDICA) (343)

1. Mansi III, cols. 65 and 69 (AKEΠ I 121.9; II 134)

See Athanasios of Alexandria **7.**2.

6. JULIAN "the Apostate" (332–363)

1. *Epistulae* 17 (ed. Wright) or 58 (ed. Bidez) 426A-C

To Zeno [physician at Alexandria and native of Cyprus]:
There is indeed abundant evidence of other kinds that you have attained to the first rank in the art of medicine and that your morals, uprightness and temperate life are in harmony with your professional skill . . . This is the reason for putting an end to your exile, and with very great distinction for yourself. For if it was owing to George [Arian bishop of Alexandria] that you were removed from Alexandria, you were removed unjustly, and it would be most just that you should return in all honour and in possession of your former dignity. And let the favour that I bestow be credited to me by both parties in common, since it restores Zeno to the Alexandrians and Alexandria to you. [362] (trans. W. C. Wright)

2. *Epistulae* 50 (ed. Wright) or 82 (ed. Bidez) 446A [AKEΠ I 14.33β]

And yet I am well aware that it is said that even the sandal of Aphrodite was satirised by Momus [? possibly for Monimos the Cynic?]. But you observe that though Momus poured forth floods of criticism he could barely find anything to criticise in her sandal. Even so may you grow old fretting yourself over things of this sort, more decrepit than Tithonus, richer than Cinyras, more luxurious than Sardanapalus [Ashurbanipal], so that in you may be fulfilled the proverb, "Old men are twice children." (trans. W. C. Wright)

3. *Orationes* (*To King Helios*) 4 (ed. Wright) or 11 (ed. Lacombrade) 135D [AKEΠ II 91]

But if he [Helios] has nothing in common with those other gods except his beneficent energy, and of this too he gives them all a share, then let us call to witness the priests of Cyprus who set up common altars to Helios and Zeus. (trans. W. C. Wright)

4. *Orationes* (*To King Helios*) 4 (ed. Wright) or 11 (ed. Lacombrade) 143D

And the creative power of Zeus also coincides with him [Helios], by reason of which in Cyprus, as I said earlier, shrines are founded and assigned to them in common. (trans. W. C. Wright)

5. *Orationes* (*Against the Uneducated Cynics*) 6 (ed. Wright) or 9 (ed. Rochefort) 185C

Now truth is one and philosophy is one, and they whom I just now spoke of are its lovers one and all; and also they whom I ought in fairness to mention now by name, I mean the disciples of the man of Citium [Zeno the Stoic].

(trans. W. C. Wright)

7. ATHANASIOS of Alexandria (295–373)

1. *Contra Gentes* 9 E–F [AKEΠ II 12.12]

But others, straining impiety to the outmost, have deified the motive of their invention of these things and of their own wickedness, namely pleasure and lust, and worship them, such as their Eros, and the Aphrodite at Paphos.

(trans. A. Robertson)

2. *Apologia Secunda* or *Apologia contra Arianos* 48.1 and 50.2 [AKEΠ I 121.9; II 134]

48.1 Thus wrote the Council of Serdica [the modern Sofia; 343], and it sent word also to those who had not been able to attend, and they, too, became signatories to the decisions made. The names of those who signed at the council and of the other bishops are as follows:

50.2 From Cyprus: Auxibios, Photios, Gerasios, Aphrodisios, Irenikos, Nounechios, Athanasios, Makedonios, Triphyllios, Spyridon, Norbanos, and Sosikrates.

8. BASIL THE GREAT (ca. 329–379)

1. Letter 258

To Bishop Epiphanius: . . . For surely no ordinary proof of charity it is, first, that you were mindful of us who are so insignificant and of no account, then that you also sent brethren to visit us, men fitting to be ministers of letters of peace. For there is no sight rarer than this, when all are now disposed to be suspicious of all. For nowhere is there mercy, nowhere compassion, no brotherly tear for a brother in distress. No persecutions for truth's sake, no churches whose entire membership groans, not this long series of misfortunes that encompass us, can move us to solicitude for one another. Nay, we leap upon the fallen, we irritate their wounds, we intensify the spitefull abuse that comes from the heretics, we who are supposed to share the same opinions, and those who are in harmony on the most important points are sure to be utterly at variance with one another on at least one matter. How, then, shall we help admiring him who is in such circumstances manifests a pure and guileless love towards his neighbours, and who, over so great a space of sea and land which separates us in body, graciously offers to our souls all possible care?

(trans. R. J. Deferrari)

9. FIRST COUNCIL OF CONSTANTINOPLE (381–382)
(Second Ecumenical Council)

1. Subscriptions (in Latin; Mansi III, col. 570

From the province of Cyprus: Julius of Paphos, Theopompos of Tremithous, Tychon of Thamasos, and Mnemios [Mnemonios] of Kition.

10. LIBANIOS (314–ca. 393)

1. *Epistulae* 366. [ΑΚΕΠ I 128.1; ΣΒΠΚΙ 1]

I think of Kyrinos [friend of Libanios, governor of Cyprus], whom the records seat on the throne of the sophist and Tyche brought to the throne of rulers. I speak of him who was attendant to Philip [correspondent of Libanios, general] did service to Lycia, saved Pamphilia, and governed Cyprus.

(trans. P.W.W.)

2. *Epistulae* 1221.5 (121.5 ed. Norman) [ΑΚΕΠ I 14.31α]

I shall not demand any payment from you, for I have it already—not in silver or gold, but something that far surpasses all the treasures of Croesus, Gyges, and Cinyras, the friendship of a noble man, and particularly, of one endowed with eloquence.

(trans. A. F. Norman)

3. *Epistulae* 1400.3 (108.3 ed. Norman) [ΑΚΕΠ I 14.31α]

Among those who perform civic duties among us the Syriarch enjoys a prestigious title for the huge amount he expends. Pactolus and the wealth of Cinyras and of Gyges are a mere nothing to him.

(trans. A. F. Norman)

4. *Epistulae* 1537.4 [ΑΚΕΠ II 59.6]

The gods sent forth the man, as the mother of the Erotes shows. For he did not come to her island seeing . . .

5. *Orationes* 11 (*Antiochicus*) 54–57 [ΑΚΕΠ I 7]

Now with greater deliberation he [Kasos] tried to secure for his city [Kasiotis] the goodwill of the Cypriots and married the daughter of Salaminos, who ruled the Cypriots. A flotilla accompanied the young woman on her voyage, making a naval parade (?) for his bride. When they tasted of our land they left their island and became a part of our city. One could take as proof that Kasos was celebrated for his virtue the fact that the ruler of such an island gladly gave him his daughter in marriage; and as proof of the gentleness of Kasos the fact that those who accompanied the girl chose his protection instead of their loved ones . . . Let one consider the nobility, and how that whatever was best in other places has flowed together here [Antioch], as to a place chosen by the better as a receptacle for the most admirable men; only for us the roots have brought together what was grand elsewhere into one place, the antiquity of the Argives, the good laws of Crete, the royal line from Cyprus, the emanation of Herakles.   (trans. P.W.W.)

6. *Orationes* 11 (*Antiochicus*) 111–112 [AKEΠ II 99.1]

The gods honored in Cyprus, from wherever they had their lot in Cyprus, desired this country [Antioch] and were eager to change their habitation. Submitting the city to the service of the oracle at Pytho they persuaded Apollo to accept one solution to their difficulties: the removal of the gods in Cyprus to us. And the king sent to the island those through whom he hoped to accomplish this. But since it was not possible to remove them openly nor to dig tunnels unobserved, they devised something like this. They said they wanted to make exact replicas of their gods. When they were given permission, with great labor they carved night and day, and the priests were unconcerned (?). The artisans made copies of such exactness that, taking down the originals and replacing them with the copies, they entered into their ships before the eyes of the Cypriots, carrying out the old ones as newly made and leaving those which had just received art in the appearance of ancient statues.   (trans. P.W.W.)

7. *Orationes* 25.23 [AKEΠ I 14.31α]

They are always talking about money, just as people thirsting talk about fountains. They deem happy not Nestor, not Argathonios (for their age), not Peleus for his marriage, not Adonis for his beauty, not Herakles for his immortality, but Kallias, Gyges, Kinyras, and Croesus.

8. *Orationes* 63.6 [AKEΠ I 14.31α]

Not even if he were to surpass the wealth and the money of Midas, Croesus, and Kinyras, would he be able to satisfy this powerful desire of so many men.

9. *Orationes* 64.107 [AKEΠ II 20.8ζ]

Anyone who has surrendered himself to the pleasures of the table has changed from a bird to lead. If then "Cypris is in being sated, not in being hungry" [Euripides, fr. 895 *TGF* [2]], those who are close to a perfect dance are far from the pleasures of love.

11. GREGORY of Nyssa (335/340–after 394)

1. *Contra Fatum*, pp. 54–55 ed. McDonough [AKEΠ I 129.8; ΣBΠKI 2]

Some people believe that in the destruction brought by earthquakes the conjunctions of the stars determine the fates of cities. How unreasonable this belief is anyone can see from the following: Who does not know that such natural disasters occur not only in inhabited places but also in uninhabited places? Such has been also the unfortunate experience of the country of the Paphlagonians: there are places where the dwellings of people have been destroyed by such chasms, and in many places the country appears deserted by the inhabitants in such disaster. What need is there to relate in detail what happened to the Cypriots, Pisidians, and Achaeans, among whom there are many proofs of what I have said?

12. ORIBASIOS (ca. 325–after 395/96)

1. *Collectionum Medicarum Reliquiae* 14. 61.1 (ed. Raeder II, p.231) [ΑΚΕΠ II 173.15γ]

   Cypriot ashes . . . are astringent.

13. PALLADAS (4th c.)

1. *Palatine Anthology* 9.487 [ΑΚΕΠ II 163.1α]

   You served me the food of the fig-fattened pigs from Cyprus, dry and thirst-provoking. But when you find me sufficiently fig-fattened, either kill me at once or quench my thirst with Cypriot wine.
   (trans. W. R. Paton)

14. EPIPHANIOS of Salamis (ca. 315–403)

1. *Adversus Haereses* or *Panarion,* title of the letter written in 376 to Epiphanius by Acacius and Paul, presbyters and archimandrites

   . . . to Epiphanius of Palestine and Eleutheropolis, some time abbot in the district of Eleutheropolis, now bishop of the city of Constantia in the province of Cyprus . . .
   (trans. F. Williams)

2. *Adversus Haereses* or *Panarion* 5.1.4

   Zeno was the founder of their Stoa, and there is much confused chatter about him. Some have said that he was a son of Cleanthes of Tyre. But others claim that he was a Citean, a Cypriote islander, and that he lived at Rome for a while, but later offered this doctrine at Athens, at the Stoa as it is called.
   (trans. F. Williams)

3. *Adversus Haereses* or *Panarion* 30.18.1

   Ebion too preached in Asia and Rome, but the roots of these thorny weeds come mostly from Nabataea and Banias [Panias, Paneas, or Caesarea Philippi, in northern Palestine], Moabitis, and Cocabe in Bashanitis [a district of northern Palestine] beyond Adrai [Adraa or Edrei in northern Palstine]—in Cyprus as well.   (trans. F. Williams)

4. *Adversus Haereses* or *Panarion* 30.25.6 [AKEΠ I 110.1]

For that matter, scripture also says that Barnabas—once he was called Joseph, but his name was changed to Barnabas, or "son of consolation" [Acts 4:36]—was a Cypriote Levite. And it is by no means true that, beause he was a Cypriote, he was not descended from Levi. Just so, even though St. Paul came from Tarsus, he was not foreign to Israel.   (trans. F. Williams)

5. *Adversus Haereses* or *Panarion* 30.25.8–9 [AKEΠ I 31; I 35.12; II 150.3]

Thus, because of the frequency, with which Israel had to flee from its enemies, the holy Jeremiah [2:10] said of it, "And if thou passest over to the Citians, there also shalt thou have no rest." Now anyone can see that Citium means the island of Cyprus, for Citians are Cypriotes and Rhodians. Moreover, the Cypriote and Rhodian stock had settled in Macedonia; thus Alexander of Macedon was Citian. And this is why the [First] Book of the Maccabees [1:1] says, "He came out of the land of the Citians;" Alexander of Macedon was of Citian descent.   (trans. F. Williams)

6. *Adversus Haereses* or *Panarion* 31.7.2

But on reaching Cyprus—and really having an actual shipwreck—he [Valentinus] departed from the faith and became perverted in mind. Before this, in those other places, he was thought to have a bit of piety and right faith. But on Cyprus he finally reached the last degree of impiety, and sank himself in this wickedness which he proclaims.   (trans. F. Williams)

7. *Adversus Haereses* or *Panarion* 42.1.2

The sect [the Marcionites] is still to be found even now, in Rome and Italy, Egypt and Palestine, Arabia and Syria, Cyprus and the Thebaid,—in Persia too, moreover, and other places.
                                                                                              (trans. F. Williams)

8. *Adversus Haereses* or *Panarion* 42.11.17, Elenchus 12b

How many persons say any number of things of Homer? Some claim he was Egyptian—others, that he was from Chios; others from Colophon; others a Phrygian. Others, Meletus and Critheidus, say that he came from Smyrna. Aristarchus [of Samothrace, 3rd/2nd c. B.C.] declared him an Athenian, others a Lydian from Maeon, others, a Cypriote from Propoetis, a district near Salamis. Yet Homer was a man, surely! But because of his visits to many countries, he has impelled many to give different descriptions of him.   (trans. F. Williams)

9. *Adversus Haereses* or *Panarion* 51.24.1 [AKEΠ II 166.3β]

For Christ was born in the month of January, that is, on the eighth before the Ides of January—in the Roman calendar this is the evening of January fifth, at the beginning of January sixth. In the Egyptian calendar it is the eleventh of Tybi. In the Syrian or Greek it is the sixth of Audynaeus. In the Cypriote or Salaminian it is the fifth day of the fifth month. In the Paphian it is the fourteenth of July . . . In the Athenian it is the fifth of Maemacterium. And in the Hebrew calendar it is the fifth of Tebeth.

(trans. F. Williams)

10. *Adversus Haereses* or *Panarion* 51.24.3

This had to be fulfilled first by the Hebrew reckoning, by the following of which many of the gentiles, I mean the Romans, observe the fifth day in the evening preceding the sixth. But the Cypriotes keep the fifth of the month itself; and the native Egyptians, and the Salaminians, observe that month as the fifth, just as the Hebrews make it the fifth month from their New Year.

(trans. F. Williams)

11. *Adversus Haereses* or *Panarion* 51.24.4–5 [ΑΚΕΠ II 166.2]

Christ . . . came to John in about the eleventh month, and was baptized in the river Jordan in the thirtieth year following his birth in the flesh, on the sixth before the Ides of November. That is, he was baptized on the twelfth of the Egyptian month Athyr, the eighth of the Greek month of Dius, the sixth of third Choiak in the Salaminian, or Constantinian calendar, the sixteenth of Apogonicus in the Paphian . . . the seventh of Metagitnium in the Athenian, and the seventh of Marcheshvan in the Hebrew.

(trans. F. Williams)

12. *Adversus Haereses* or *Panarion* 77.22.5

By this time I had become glad, for I had heard from some of those youngsters who came to me on Cyprus that he [Vitalius] did not believe that Christ's flesh was from Mary at all.

(trans. F. Williams)

13. *Mensuris et Ponderibus* 21.13–4 ed. de Lagard [ΑΚΕΠ II 167]

The *mnasis,* however, is used as a measure among the Cyprians and other peoples; and it is 10 *modii* of wheat or barley by the *modius* of 17 *xestai* among the Cyprians. But the *medimnos* varies among the Cyprians; for the people of Salamis, that is to say, of Constantia, have a *medimnos* of 5 *modii,* while those of Paphos and the Sicilians measure it at as 4½ *modii.*

(trans. J. E. Dean)

15. VITA OF ST. EPIPHANIOS (with continuation) (after 403)

1. 1 (318A) [ΑΚΕΠ I 135]

Epiphanios was by nationality a Phoenician from the district of Eleutheropolis, living three milestones away from it. His father was a farmer, and his mother's occupation was that of a weaver. They had two children, Epiphanios and a daughter named Kallitropos.

2. 2 (319C) [ΑΚΕΠ I 135]

Jacob said to Epiphanios, "Of what religion are you?," and Epiphanios said, "I am a Jew."

3. 4–6 (321B–323B) [ΑΚΕΠ I 135.1]

4. There was a certain Jewish lawyer in Eleutheropolis, an amazing man and a faithful observer of the law of Moses. This man owned property in the village in which Epiphanios had been born . . . This man came to inspect his property and said to Epiphanios' mother, "Lady, do you wish to give me your son for a son?" . . . When Epiphanios' mother heard these words from the lawyer, she rejoiced greatly, took Epiphanios, and gave him at once (to the lawyer) for a son. The lawyer's name was Trypho. He had a single daughter and wanted her to marry Epiphanios.
5. When Trypho had taken Epiphanios for a son he instructed him carefully and zealously in the law and in the doctrines of Judaism. Now Trypho's daughter died, and Epiphanios was alone in his house, prospering in in his youth and in the wisdom of the Jews. And it happened that Trypho also died and left all his property to Epiphanios . . . And Epiphanios went to the village of his birth, where he also had property left to him by Trypho. There he encountered a certain Christian, a remarkable and learned man by name of Lucian, who lived the life of a monk . . .
6. Then Epiphanios took Lucian into the house which he had inherited, showed him all the things in the house, and said, "These things are mine, father. I wish to become a Christian and follow the monastic life" . . . But the blessed Lucian said to Epiphanios, "My son, you cannot follow the monastic life while you own all this substance" . . . And Epiphanios said to Lucian, "First make me a Christian, father. Then I shall do all things enjoined upon me by you." And Lucian said to Epiphanios, "I cannot make you a Christian without the bishop."

4. 7–9 (323C–325B) [ΑΚΕΠ I 135.2]

7. And the bishop said to Lucian, "Go and teach him and as we enter the church make him supplicate the benevolent God."
8. And after the reading of the Gospel the bishop entered the baptistry and bade Epiphanios and his sister enter, and with them Lucian, who also became their father at the holy baptism. And the bishop taught them the entire liturgy and baptized them . . . And Epiphanios . . . left the city with Lucian, because Lucian had established a monastery for himself and had ten monks with him . . . And Epiphanios was sixteen years old when he became a monk.
9. There was in the monastery of Lucian a certain monk by name of Hilarion, second in rank after Lucian, a young man, endowed with many wondrous gifts. And another monk, a certain Claudius, emulated him in his life. And seeing them Epiphanios was zealous for goodness. And the great Lucian entrusted Epiphanios to the great Hilarion, so that he might teach him the divine scriptures. Epiphanios took great care and was surrounded by the good teachings of Hilarion, and thus he prospered in the grace of Christ and in every good art. And it happened that Lucian died and Hilarion ruled the assembly of monks . . . The food of the blessed Hilarion was bread and salt and ordinary water. He ate every other day, often only every third day, and very often

every fourth or every seventh day. And Epiphanios chose and followed this way of life for all of his life.

5. 26 (340A) [ΑΚΕΠ I 135.3]

Many people came to the monastery and did not allow Epiphanios to live in solitude. Therefore he intended to leave the place and to travel to Egypt; and he said to me, "My son, follow me."

6. 30 (344A–B) [ΑΚΕΠ I 135.3; 134.2]

But Epiphanios became famous throughout Egypt, and the bishops sought to make him a bishop. And God guided Epiphanios. For Epiphanios knew this and said to me, "Come, my son, let us return to our country." And we returned to our own country and entered the monastery of the great Hilarion. But the great Hilarion had left the monastery because of the considerable annoyance which he suffered and had sailed to Cyprus, to the places around Paphos.

7. 32–34 (346B–348 D) [ΑΚΕΠ I 135.5; 134.4; 124; 12; II 147; 163β; 140)

32. And God guided Epiphanios to Cyprus. During that night he took me and Polybios, and we left the monastery and traveled to Jerusalem to venerate the venerable cross, our life. And when we had reached the city we remained for three days. And then Epiphanios said to me and to Polybios, "Come, let us leave, so that we might be blessed by our father, the great Hilarion; for I have heard that he lives in Cyprus." And God guided Epiphanios.

33. When we had reached Caesarea we found there a Cypriot ship from Paphos. And Epiphanios inquired of the master of the ship about the great Hilarion and where he lives. He (the master of the ship) reported that (Hilarion lives) in the area of Paphos in a cave and that our ship was bound to that place. That night we boarded the ship and sailed to Paphos. When we had debarked from the ship and inquired we met the great Hilarion. And when we had entered there was great joy at our being together, and we remained in this place two months. But Hilarion suffered much tribulation from those who came to see him. And when Epiphanios decided that we should leave Paphos Hilarion said to Epiphanios, "Where are you going, my son?" And Epiphanios replied to Hilarion, "To Ascalon, Gaza, and beyond." And Hilarion said to Epiphanios, "Go to Salamis, my son, and there you will find a place to dwell." But Epiphanios was not willing to listen to the words of Hilarion. Then Hilarion spoke again to Epiphanios, "I have told you, my son, that you must go there and dwell there. Do not strive against my word, and you will encountrer no danger at sea. And when we had said our farewells and had come to the shore we found two ships, one crossing to Ascalon (in Palestine), the other sailing to Salamis. And when we had embarked on the ship that was supposed to sail to Ascalon there arose a great storm and the ship was in danger of being wrecked. We remained at sea for three days, despairing of ourselves. On the fourth day the winds drove us in the direction of the waves and propelled us to the city of Salamis. And when they had debarked from the ship all collapsed on the ground [nearly] dead from exhaustion and hunger . . . After we had stayed for three days conditions improved,

through the grace of God, and again Epiphanios wanted to sail from this place. But the bishop of this place, I mean the city of Salamis, had died.

34. Now all the bishops of the island were gathered for the purpose of ordaining someone who would be able to be a shepherd to the flock of Christ. For several days they were intent on the same purpose and prayed to Christ that he should reveal to them the man who would be able to serve in the priestly office. There was among the bishops a certain holy man who had been ordained bishop in a miserable city named Kythrea and located twenty-five milestones away from the city of Salamis. Of him it was said that he held the office of bishop for fifty years. This man was judged worthy of martyrdom and when he had suffered much for Christ's sake he was released, still confessing the Son of God. Of this man it is said that he was seized with Gelasios, the bishop of the city of Salamis, to suffer martyrdom. His name was the one given to him by his parents, Pappos, and he was with the bishops. All the bishops regarded him as their father, both because he had confessed Christ and because of the number of years he had served as bishop. And he had the gift of prophecy. And to him it was revealed that Epiphanios should be ordained bishop of the church of Salamis. And it was the summer season which brings grapes. And when Epiphanios had decided to sail from the city of Salamis he said to me and to Polybios, "My son, let us go to the market place to buy grapes for the voyage" . . . Then the holy Pappos appeared, attended by two deacons. And three bishops were with him. And when they approached Epiphanios he had in his hands the grapes and the money to pay for them. And some of the bystanders said, "Look, the bishops are here." And Pappos said to Epiphanios, "Return the grapes to the seller, Abbas, and follow us unto the church." And when he remembered the scripture which reads, "I was gladdened by those who said to me, 'We shall go into the house of the Lord'" [Psalms 122:1], he followed them into the church. And Pappos said to Epiphanios, "Say a prayer, father." And these things Pappos said to Epiphanios so that he might make himself known to the clergy. And Epiphanios said to Pappos, "Forgive me, father; for I am not a member of the clergy." But Pappos said to Epiphanios, "Look, my son, do not, in the presence of these holy fathers, deny yourself and do not allow yourself to be found like one who has hidden his talent." But Epiphanios said to Pappos, "I do not, father, I am not ordained." When Epiphanios had said these things Pappos granted peace. But one of the deacons seized Epiphanios by the head and led him by force to Pappos at the altar, and most of the others joined, so as to save him at the altar. And Pappos ordained Epiphanios a deacon, again granted peace, and then ordained him a presbyter. And a service was held, and then Pappos ordained Epiphanios a bishop. And after the service had been dismissed we went into the bishop's residence. [367]

8. 40–42 (354B–356B) [ΑΚΕΠ I 135.6; II 145]

40. When Epiphanios had fallen on his face to call upon God that it might be given to him to build unto God a church in his name (for the first church was too small for those who wished to enter) and when he was on his face beseeching God about the need for a church, the voice of God came to him, calling him, "Epiphanios." But Epiphanios was used to often hearing such a voice. Thus without being disturbed, he said, "What is it, my God?" and [the voice spoke] again, "Begin to build the house." And Epiphanios at once, without hesitation, went out, said a prayer, dedicated the ground, and engaged workmen. There were sixty construction foremen and a large

number [of workmen] working under them. But there were at that time rich pagans in the city with money and possessions at their disposal.

41. There was a certain man named Drakon, called great Drakon by many; this man had a son by the same name. This son suffered from a terrible burning sensation on the right side [of his body] . . . But Epiphanios approached, courteously greeted these men [the rich men seated on their chairs], and seized young Drakon by the hand, saying, "Drakon, be whole." And at once, upon Epiphanios' word, Drakon was whole . . . The next morning he [the elder Drakon] took five thousand coins and brought them to Epiphanios. But Epiphanios said to him, "My son, one cloak for my body, ordinary bread, and potable water suffice for my needs. Why do you bring me a burden when I do not want you to be burdened? But, if you desire glory, go and stay at the church of God and offer these coins to those who labor and toil there. And Drakon did just that, which pleased Epiphanios. And Epiphanios baptized Drakon and his wife.

42. There was a certain other rich man, Synesios by name, a pagan. This man had an only son, thirteen years old. This boy attracted a disease which affected his neck all-round and choked him, and thus he died . . . But Epiphanios approached the bed, touched the boy's neck, rubbed it, and said to him with a cheerful countenance, "Eustorgios." And the boy at once opened his eyes and sat up on his bed, so that all in the house were amazed. Then, when Eustorgios' mother saw what had happened to the boy thanks to Epiphanios, she took three thousand coins and brought them to Epiphanios. But Epiphanios said to her, "I have no need of those, lady. Let Synesios your husband take these and go the the house of Him who has raised your son and let him give these to the workmen. And this is what Synesios did. And he was baptized, and so was his wife, and also his son, whom Epiphanios had raised from the dead.

9. 44 (357B) [ΣΒΠΚΙ 4.1.1]

We [Epiphanios and Polybios] sailed from Cyprus to Caesarea Philippi [erroneously for Caesarea Maritima?]. And from there we went to Jerusalem.

10. 46 (359A) [ΣΒΠΚΙ 4.1.2]

When we [Epiphanios and Polybios] left the city to sail to Cyprus, there were two scoffers in that place.

11. 46 (359C) [ΣΒΠΚΙ 4.1.3]

And when we [Epiphanios and Polybios] had returned to Caesarea we sailed to Cyprus, and our brethren received us with great joy.

12. 48–52 (359D–363D) [ΑΚΕΠ I 135.7; 136; II 136; ΣΒΠΚΙ 4.2–4]

48. The emperors Arkadios [395–408] and Honorius [395–423], had a sister [Galla Placidia?] who was living in Rome and became ill. Since she had heard that God was healing the sick through Epiphanios, she summoned Epiphanios from Cyprus to Rome . . .

49. Those who had been sent by the emperors made Epiphanios sail to Rome. There was among the teachers a certain cleric by name of Philo, a holy man. And there was a need to fill the vacant see of the city of Karpass. Then Epiphanios, under divine inspiration, ordained him a bishop (and placed him) on the throne of the city and the church of Karpass. Then, when Epiphanios needed to reside in Rome, he appointed Philo, of whom we have just spoken, as bishop and gave to him the responsibility for the church of Constantia, so that, if a need for clerics should arise, he himself might perform ordinations. Epiphanios took Isaac and me, and we sailed to Rome . . . 50. Epiphanios approached the bed on which the emperors' sister was reclining and spoke to her with a kind countenance, "Do not despair because of your ailment, my daughter. Have hope in the living God, and you will see your health [restored] this hour. Believe in the Son of God, who was crucified, and you will be walking this hour. The pain has been lifted from your body. Glorify God, who is granting you his grace. Keep him in your thoughts unceasingly, and he will be a shield to you at all times." With these words Epiphanios took the lady's hand, placed a seal [made the sign of the cross] upon her three times, and at once she was relieved of her pains . . . 52. We remained in Rome for an entire year . . . After we had departed from Rome we reached Cyprus in forty days, and our brethren received us with much joy.

13. 53 (364A–C) [ΑΚΕΠ II 93.8; ΣΒΠΚΙ 4.5.1]

Once there was a great famine [in Salamis], no bread could be found in the market-place . . . and there was dire need in the city. Then Epiphanios went into the cemetery one night and beseeched God to nourish all those who were suffering. There was in this place an ancient temple, which was called a sanctuary of Zeus. According to tradition anyone approaching this temple would immediately be seized by death. But when Epiphanios was praying to God on behalf of those who were suffering, God's voice came to him and said, "Epiphanios, do not be disturbed." And he said, "Lord, what is it?" And the voice said to him, "Go to the temple which is called the sanctuary of Zeus, the seals of its doors will be loosed, and upon entering you will find a large amount of gold. Take it, purchase all the wheat and barley of Phaustinianos [a dealer, who was withholding grain from the people], and give it for food to those in need."

14. 54 (365A–B) [ΣΒΠΚΙ 4.5.2]

When the ships were sailing and had been filled with grain and other supplies they sailed in four months' time, with the grain. A hundred stadia from Constantia, opposite the place called Dianeuterion, a mighty storm arose at sea.

15. 57 (367B–368B) [ΑΚΕΠ I 135.8; 136.1; ΣΒΠΚΙ 4.6]

At this time the emperor Theodosios [I, 379–395], for some reason which I do not know, suffered from an ailment of his feet, and his entire body from the knees down was paralyzed, and he was bedfast for seven months. So he sent word to Epiphanios in Cyprus asking him to come to the capital of Constantinople and help him in his sufferings . . . And when Epiphanios had sent for the bishop Philo, most beloved of God, he enjoined upon him to take care of the needs of the church. When all the fathers and brothers and those who had been instructed by Epiphanios were gathered we all embraced one another and then we sailed for the capital. And when we had reached Constantinople the arrival of Epiphanios was announced to the emperor. And when the emperor had invited us to come to the palace Epiphanios went with great confidence . . . And when he had approached the emperor, touched his feet, and set a seal upon him three times he said to the emperor, "My son, rise from your bed, for your feet have been healed." Upon hearing these words the emperor forthwith rose from his bed and no longer had any trouble with his feet.

16. 58 (368D–369D) [ΣΒΠΚΙ 4.7]

On orders of the emperor some men brought Phaustinianos from the island of Cyprus to the capital, where he was to be charged with having insulted the emperor, and he was put under guard by orders of the emperor. When Epiphanios heard this he went to the place where Phaustinianos was detained . . . But Phaustinianos said to Epiphanios: "Be off to Cyprus!" . . . And when Phaustinianos had thus spoken to Epiphanios, insulting him, Epiphanios took me and together we went to the emperor's palace, so that with his permission we might sail to Cyprus . . . But in the morning a messenger came to the palace to report that Phaustinianos the Cypriot had died . . . But we, in nine days' time, sailed for Cyprus.

17. 59 (370B–D) [ΑΚΕΠ Ι 135.9; ΣΒΠΚΙ 4.8.1]

At one time Epiphanios addressed a message to Aetios the bishop of the Valentinians. There were many in Constantia who adhered to this heresy . . . There were also in the land of Cyprus many other heresies, namely these: Ophites [reading Ὀφῖται for Σοφισταί], Sabellians, Nicolaitans, Simonians, Basilidians, and Carpocratians. Concerning these Epiphanios wrote a letter to the emperor Theodosios [I, 379–395] asking him to drive them from the island by imperial decree. For there were wealthy men among them who had been entrusted with public affairs and were humiliating the orthodox. When the emperor had received Epiphanios' letter he issued the following rescript: "If anyone does not obey Father Epiphanios, the bishop of the land of Cyprus, and his divine words, let him leave the island and live wherever he wants to. But those who are willing to repent and to recognize the common father, saying, 'We have erred but are willing to return to the path of the truth,' shall remain on the island and shall be taught by the common father." Then, when the edict was delivered by a military officer and was made public, many of them obeyed Epiphanios, but those who did not obey were at once expelled from the island.

18. 62 (373A–374C) [ΑΚΕΠ Ι 135.11γ]

When Theophilos [bishop of Alexandria] learned that the empress [Eudoxia] wished to exile John [Chrysostom, ca. 347–407; bishop of Constantinople 398–404] he became exceedingly active. Thus he sent many letters to Epiphanios accusing John of being an Origenist and saying that the empress was provoked to exile him. Epiphanios at once followed Theophilos' instructions, but he did not know that Theophilos hated John. It so happened that Epiphanios for good reason wanted to travel to the capital, and when he had heard such things from Theophilos he was all the more anxious to get there, not to harm John but to help him. So he took Isaac and me, and we sailed to Constantinople. And when we had arrived in the city [we found that] there was much confusion about John, because he was much beloved by the citizens. But there were some monasteries and chapels which received contributions from the empress and did not recognize John. And when we had entered one of the monasteries [at Hebdomon] they [the monks] forced Epiphanios to perform an ordination because there was an ecclesiastical need for it. And when Epiphanios had done this John learned about it, became very upset with Epiphanios, and wrote a letter to him voicing his complaint; and Epiphanios responded similarly to John's letter. And the empress heard that John was angry at Epiphanios. She summoned Epiphanios and said to him, "Father Epiphanios, the whole Roman empire is mine, and all the priesthood of the churches within my empire is yours. And since John has violated the good order of the priesthood and is behaving himself unseemingly towards the emperors and is said to entertain some heresy, therefore my thinking has been for some time to hold a council concerning him, to depose him from the priesthood as being unworthy, and to place on the throne another man, one capable of holding the priesthood, so that my empire might enjoy peace everywhere." And when the empress said these things to Epiphanios she waxed quite emotional and spoke to him again, "Since your holiness is here with the help of God, there is no need to trouble the other fathers. But appoint as bishop whomever God reveals to you and expel John from the church." But Epiphanios spoke to the empress, "My daughter, listen patiently to your father." And the empress said to Epiphanios, "If there is anything that your priestly office demands let me know, and I shall take care of my father."

But Epiphanios said to the empress: "If John is found guilty of the heresy with which he is charged and if he does not admit his error he is not worthy of the priestly office. And if there is anything that your authority orders I shall do it. But if you seek to oust John from the church because he has offended you, then your Epiphanios will not consent to it. And, my daughter, it is especially given to kings to be offended and to forgive, since you, too, have a king in heaven, against whom you sin routinely and who forgives you if you, too, forgive those who offend you; as is written in the gospels, be merciful, as is our father in heaven" [Luke 6:36]. But the empress said to Epiphanios, "If you will stand in the way of John being exiled I shall open the pagan temples and I shall make people worship there and I shall make the last worse than the first" [Matthew 12:45]. And as she bitterly said these things she poured forth tears from her eyes. But Epiphanios said, "My daughter, I have no part of this judgement."

19. 63 (374D–375B) [AKEΠ I 135.12ζ]

And a rumor circulated through the entire city to the effect that the great priest Epiphanios, bishop of Cyprus, had called upon the empress and had brought about the exile of the great John . . . And John was convinced that Epiphanios had agreed to his (John's) exile. He took a tablet and wrote to Epiphanios, "Wise Epiphanios, you have agreed to my exile. You will no longer sit on your throne." Similarly Epiphanios wrote back to John, "Athlete, be beaten and win. Because you have believed that I agreed to your exile you will not reach the place of your exile." I have recorded these things, brethren, so that no one will assign guilt in this matter to Epiphanios. Would a man who did so many good deeds stoop so low? May it never come to pass!

20. 63 (375B–C) [ΑΚΕΠ I 135.13α]

When Epiphanios was asked by the emperor Arkadios [395–408] how old he was he replied, "I am 115 years old minus three months. I became a bishop at the age of sixty and have been in office for fifty-five years minus three months." This conversation took place on the day when we boarded the ship.

21. 63–64 (375C–376A) [ΣΒΠΚΙ 4.8.2]

He [Epiphanios] began to weep and said to us: . . . "What evils I have suffered in Phoenicia from the haughty Simonians, in Egypt from the foul Gnostics, and in Cyprus from the lawless Valentinians and other heresies!"

22. 65 (377C–D) [ΑΚΕΠ I 135.14]

On the third day [of a storm] Epiphanios said to me, "My son Polybios." I said to him, "What is it, Father?" And he said to me, "Speak to the sailors and have them kindle wood and make a charcoal fire. Then take incense and bring it here." . . . Then he said a prayer as he lay down and after the prayer he greeted us and said, "You are saved, my sons. For Epiphanios will no longer see you in this life." And forthwith he gave up his spirit, and at once the storm of the sea abated. [403]

23. 66 (378A) [ΑΚΕΠ I 135.14; ΣΒΠΚΙ 4.9]

When we had reached Constantia at the place which is called Dianeuterion the sailors debarked from the ship, circulated through the city, and shouted with a loud voice, "Brethren, you who dwell in the populous capital of Constantia, come to the shore at the place called Dianeuterion and receive the venerable remains of your holy father Epiphanios. For he has ended his earthly life."

16. JOHN CHRYSOSTOM (340/350–407)

1. *Homilies on the Acts of the Apostles,* Homily 28 on Acts 13:4–5 (Migne, *PG* 60, cols. 209–10)

As soon as they were ordained they [Paul and Barnabas] went forth, and hastened to Cyprus, that being a place where there was no ill-design hatching against them, and where moreover the Word had been sown already . . .

"And when they were come to Salamis," the metropolis of Cyprus, "they preached the word of God" [Acts 13:5].

(trans. J. Walker, J. Sheppard, and H. Browne)

2. Letter 221, to the presbyter Constantius [ΣΒΠΚΙ 3]

In matters of Salamis, a place located in Salamis and besieged by the heretic Marcionists, I was conversing with the proper people and setting everything in order, but then I was sent into exile.

17. SYNESIOS of Cyrene (ca. 370–ca. 413)

1. *Epistulae* 148 [ΑΚΕΠ II 163.1]

They seek the lightest wine, the thickest honey, the thinnest oil, and the heaviest wheat. They are always singing the praises of the places where these products may be obtained, such as Cyprus, a certain Hymettus, Phoenice and Barathra.

(trans. A. Fitzgerald)

18. PALLADIOS (successively bishop of Helenopolis and Aspona) (ca. 363–ca. 431)

1. *Dialogue on the Life of St. John Chrysostom* 16 (p. 99 ed. Coleman-Norton) [ΑΚΕΠ I 135.13]

Why do you not recognize from his letters [the letters of Bishop Theophilos of Alexandria] how they contradict one another? For he maligns Epiphanios, the blessed bishop of Constantia in Cyprus, who presided over his church for thirty-six years, as heretic or schismatic. This was at the time of [Pope] Damasus [I, 366–384] or the blessed Siricius [384–399]; but later, in his letter to Pope Innocent [I, 401–417], in which he slanders the blessed John [Chrysostom], we find that he refers to Epiphanios as most holy.

2. *Dialogue on the Life of St. John Chrysostom* 17 (p. 110 ed. Coleman-Norton)

What need is there to mention Amphilochios [bishop of Ikonion 374–ca. 397], Optimus [bishop of Antioch in Pisidia], Gregory [bishop of Constantinople for one month in 381], Peter [bishop of Sebaste 380–392], the brother of Basil [the Great, 329–379, bishop of Caesarea in Cappadocia], and Epiphanios of Cyprus, to all of whom she [Olympias] donated real property and money?

19. COUNCIL OF EPHESUS (Third Ecumenical Council) (431)

1. Πρᾶξις Πρώτη (Mansi IV, col. 1125; *ACO* I.1.2, p. 6)

Saprikios of Paphos in Cyprus, Zeno of Kourion in Cyprus, Rheginos of Constantia, Evagrios of Soloi, and Caesarius, *chorepiscopus*.

2. Canon 8 (Mansi IV, col. 1469; *ACO* I.1.7, p. 122; Joannou I.1, pp. 63–64) [ΣΒΠΚΙ 8]

The holy synod has spoken: An innovation which has been introduced contrary to the ecclesiastical constitutions and the canons of the holy fathers and which touches upon the liberty of all has been reported by the most pious bishop Rheginos and by the most pious bishops Zeno and Evagrios from the province of Cyprus who are with him. Common injuries call for the greater remedy, because they cause the greater damage, especially if they do not follow ancient traditions. These most pious men, who are attending this holy synod, have informed the holy synod both in writing and with their own voices that the bishop of the city of Antioch is performing ordinations in Cyprus. [It is now ordained that] those who preside over the holy churches of Cyprus shall have the undiminished and inviolate right, according to the canons of the holy fathers and ancient custom, to ordain their own pious bishops. The same principle shall be applied also in other dioceses and in all provinces: none of the holy bishops shall seize another province which previously and from the beginning has not been under his or his predecessors' authority. But if anyone has seized [another bishop's province] and brought it under his control, let him surrender it, lest the canons of the Fathers be violated and lest, under the pretense of divine service, the illusion of wordly power might take hold among the bishops and lest we might lose little by little, without realizing it, the freedom which our Lord Jesus Christ, the savior of all men, has given to us by his own blood. Therefore this holy and ecumenical council has ruled that in each province the rights which belong to it from the very beginning and according to long-standing custom shall be preserved inviolate and undiminished. And each metropolitan is given permission to receive a copy of the resolution for his own safety. But if anyone should produce a document which is not in agreement with the present rulings, it shall be invalid; this is the will of the entire holy and ecumenical council.

20. PHILOSTORGIOS (ca. 368–ca. 439)

1. *Historia Ecclesiastica* 11.6 [ΣΒΠΚΙ 5.1]

At once he (the emperor Arkadios, 395–408) stripped Eutropios of all his honors, confiscated his property, and banished him to Cyprus. Not much later some people charged that, when he was made consul, he had used those insignia of rank which are reserved for the emperor. He was then recalled from Cyprus. [399]

2. *Historia Ecclesiastica* 11.8 [ΣΒΠΚΙ 5.2]

In addition to these calamities the tribe of the Isaurians inflicted various disasters [on the Romans]. To the East they invaded Cilicia and neighboring Syria, not only Syria Coele, but all the rest, as far as Persia. To the West and Northwest they invaded Pamphylia and plundered Lycia. They also laid waste the island of Cyprus and led the Lykaonians and Pisidians into captivity.

21. SOKRATES Scholastikos (ca. 380–after 439)

1. *Historia Ecclesiastica* 1.8

There were among the bishops [at the Council of Nicaea] two of extraordinary celebrity, Paphnutius, bishop of Upper Thebes, and Spyridon, bishop of Cyprus. (trans. A. C. Zenos)

2. *Historia Ecclesiastica* 1.12 [ΑΚΕΠ Ι 121.3α; ΣΒΠΚΙ 6]

With respect to Spyridon, so great was his sanctity while a shepherd, that he was thought worthy of being made a Pastor of men; and having been assigned the bishopric of one of the cities in Cyprus named Trimithus, on account of his extreme humility he continued to feed his sheep during his incumbency of the bishopric. Many extraordinary things are related of him . . . Such characters as these adorned the churches in the time of the emperor Constantine [I, 306–337]. These details I obtained from many inhabitants of Cyprus. I have also found a treatise composed in Latin by the presbyter Rufinus, from which I have collected these and some other things which will be hereafter adduced. (trans. A. C. Zenos)

3. *Historia Ecclesiastica* 5.24

But if anyone should be desirous of knowing the names of the various sects, he may easily satisfy himself, by reading a book entitled *Ancoratus,* composed by Epiphanius, bishop of Cyprus. (trans. A. C. Zenos)

4. *Historia Ecclesiastica* 6.10 [ΑΚΕΠ Ι 135.10]

He [Theophilus of Alexandria] moreover renewed his friendship with Epiphanius bishop of Constantia in Cyprus, with whom he had formerly been at variance. For Theophilus accused Epiphanius of entertaining low thoughts of God, by supposing him to have a human form. Now although Theophilus was really unchanged in sentiment, and had denounced those who thought that the divinity was human in form, yet on account of his hatred of others, he openly denied his own convictions; and he now professed to be friendly with Epiphanius, as if he had altered his mind and agreed with him in his views of God. He then managed it so that Epiphanius by letter should convene a Synod of the bishops in Cyprus, in order to condemn the writings of Origen. Epiphanius being on account of his extraordinary piety a man of simple mind and manners was easily influenced by the letters of Theophilus; having therefore assembled a council of bishops in that island, he caused a prohibition to be therein made of the reading of Origen's works. He also wrote to John, exhorting him to abstain from the study of Origen's books, and to convoke a Synod of decreeing the same thing as he had done. Accordingly when Theophilus had in this way deluded Epiphanius, who was famous for his piety, seeing his design prosper according to his wish, he became more confident, and himself also assembled a great number of bishops. In that convention, pursuing the same course as Epiphanius, he caused a like sentence of condemnation to be pronounced on the writings of Origen, who had been dead nearly two hundred years; not having this as his first object, but rather his purpose of revenge on Dioscorus and his brethren. John [Chrysostom, bishop of Constantinople] paying but little attention to the communications of Epiphanius and Theophilus, was intent on instructing the churches; and he flourished more and more as a preacher, but made no account of the plots which were laid against him. As soon, however, as it became apparent to everybody that Theophilus was endeavoring to divest John of his bishopric, then all those who had any ill-will against John, combined in calumniating him. And thus many of the clergy, and many of those in office, and of those who had great influence at the court, believing that they had found an opportunity now of avenging themselves upon John, exerted themselves to procure the convocation of a Grand Synod at Constantinople, partly by sending letters and partly by dispatching messengers in all directions for that purpose.

(trans. A. C. Zenos)

5. *Historia Ecclesiastica* 6.12 and 14 [ΑΚΕΠ I 135.11 and 12ε]

12. Not long after this, at the suggestion of Theophilus, the bishop Epiphanius again came from Cyprus to Constantinople; he brought also with him a copy of the synodical decree in which they did not excommunicate Origen himself, but condemned his books. On reaching St. John's church, which is seven miles distant from the city [at Hebdomon], he disembarked, and there celebrated a service; then after having ordained a deacon, he again entered the city. In complaisance to Theophilus he declined John's courtesy, and engaged apartments in a private house. He afterwards assembled those of the bishops who were then in the capital, and producing his copy of the synodical decree condemnatory of Origen's works, recited it before them; not being able to assign any reason for this judgment, than that it seemed fit to Theophilus and himself to reject them. Some indeed from a reverential respect for Epiphanius subscribed the decree; but many refused to do so; among whom was Theotimus bishop of Scythia, who thus addressed Epiphanius:—'I neither choose, Epiphanius,' said he, 'to insult the memory of one who ended his life piously long ago; nor dare I be guilty of so impious an act, as that of condemning what our predecessors did not reject; and especially when I know of no evil doctrine contained in Origen's books.' Having said this, he brought forward one of that author's works, and reading a few passages therefrom, showed that the sentiments propounded were in perfect accordance with the orthodox faith. He then added, 'Those who speak evil of these writings are unconsciously casting dishonor upon the sacred volume whence their principles are drawn.' Such was the reply which Theotimus, a bishop celebrated for his piety and rectitude of life, made to Epiphanius.

14. John was not offended because Epiphanius, contrary to the ecclesiastical canon, had made an ordination in his church; but invited him to remain with him at the episcopal palace. He, however, replied that he would neither stay nor pray with him, unless he would expel Dioscorus and his brethren from the city, and with his own hand subscribe the condemnation of Origen's books. Now as John deferred the performance of these things, saying that nothing ought to be done rashly before investigation by a general council, John's adversaries led Epiphanius to adopt another course. For they contrived it so that a meeting was in the church named *The Apostles*, Epiphanius came forth and before all the people condemned the books of Origen, excommunicated Dioscorus with his followers, and charged John with countenancing them. These things were reported to John; whereupon on the following day he sent the appended message to Epiphanius just as he entered the church:

'You do many things contrary to the canons, Epiphanius. In the first place you have made an ordination in the churches under my jurisdiction; then without my appointment, you have on your own authority officiated in them. Moreover, when heretofore I invited you hither, you refused to come, and now you take that liberty yourself. Beware therefore, lest a tumult being excited among the people, you yourself should also incur danger therefrom.'

Epiphanius becoming alarmed on hearing these admonitions, left the church; and after accusing John of many things, he set out on his return to Cyprus. Some say that when he was about to depart, he said to John, 'I hope that you will not die a bishop'; to which John replied, 'Expect not to arrive at your own country.' I cannot be sure that those who reported these things to me spoke the truth; but nevertheless the event was in the case of both as prophesied above. For Epiphanius did not reach Cyprus, having died on board the ship during his voyage; and John a short time afterwards was driven from his see, as we shall show in proceeding.

(trans. A. C. Zenos)

22. SOZOMENOS (d. after 443)

1. *Historia Ecclesiastica* 1.11.1 [ΑΚΕΠ I 121.4; ΣΒΠΚΙ 7.1.1]

Spyridon, bishop of Trimythun in Cyprus, flourished at this period. To show his virtues, I think the fame which still prevails about him suffices. The wonderful works which he wrought by Divine assistance are, it appears, generally known by those who dwell in the same region. I shall not conceal the facts which have come to me.

He was a peasant, was married, and had children; yet he was not on this account without spiritual attainments.

(trans. C. D. Hartranft)

2. *Historia Ecclesiastica* 1.11.8–9 [ΑΚΕΠ I 125.3α; ΣΒΠΚΙ 7.1.2]

It is said that on one occasion thereafter, the bishops of Cyprus met to consult on some particular emergency. Spyridon was present, as likewise Triphyllius, bishop of the Ledri [Leukosia], a man otherwise eloquent, who on account of practicing the law, had lived alone while at Berytus [Beirut]. When an assembly had convened, having been requested to address the people, Triphyllius had occasion, in the middle of his discourse, to quote the text, "Take up thy bed and walk" [Matthew 9:6] and he substituted the word "couch" (σκίμπους) for the word "bed" (κράββατος). Spyridon was indignant, and exclaimed, "Art thou greater than he who uttered the word 'bed', that thou art ashamed to use his words?"

(trans. C. D. Hartranft)

3. *Historia Ecclesiastica* 3.14.21 and 26–27 [ΑΚΕΠ I 134; 134.5; ΣΒΠΚΙ 7.2.1]

The same species of philosophy was about this time cultivated in Palestine, after being learned in Egypt, and Hilarion the divine then acquired great celebrity. He was a native of Thabatha, a village situated near the town of Gaza. . . . It is remarkable that he was first interred in the island of Cyprus, but that his remains are now deposited in Palestine; for it so happened, that he died during his residence in Cyprus, and was buried by the inhabitants with great honor and respect. But Hesychas, one of the most renowned of his disciples, stole the body, conveyed it to Palestine, and interred it in his own monastery.

(trans. C. D. Hartranft)

4. *Historia Ecclesiastica* 5.10.4 [ΑΚΕΠ I 134.3; II 140; ΣΒΠΚΙ 7.2.2]

Eventually he [Hilarion] sailed for the island of Cyprus, but touched at Paphos, and, at the entreaty of the bishop of Cyprus, he loved the life there and practiced philosophy at a place called Charburis . . . Here he only escaped martyrdom by flight; for he fled in compliance with the Divine precept which commands us not to expose ourselves to persecution [Matthew 10:23]; but that if we fall into the hands of persecutors, to overcome by our own fortitude the violence of our oppressors.

(trans. C. D. Hartranft)

5. *Historia Ecclesiastica* 6.32.1–5 [ΣΒΠΚΙ 7.3]

Many monastical institutions flourished in Palestine. Many of those whom I enumerated under the reign of Constantius were still cultivating the science. They and their associates attained the summit of philosophical perfection, and added still greater reputation to their monasteries; and among them Hesycas, a companion of Hilarion, and Epiphanius, afterwards bishop of Salamis in Cyprus, deserve to be particularly noticed. Hesycas devoted himself to a life of philosophy in the same locality where his master had formerly resided; and Epiphanius fixed his abode near the village of Besauduc, which was his birthplace, in the government of Eleutheropolis. Having been instructed from his youth by the most celebrated ascetics, and having on this account passed the most of his time in Egypt, Epiphanius became most celebrated in Egypt and Palestine by his attainments in monastic philosophy, and was chosen by the inhabitants of Cyprus to act as bishop of the metropolis of their island. Hence he is, I think, the most revered man under the whole heaven, so to speak; for he fulfilled his priesthood in the concourse of a large city and in a seaport; and when he threw himself into civil affairs, he conducted them with so much virtue that he became known in a little while to all citizens and every variety of foreigner; to some, because they had seen the man himself, and had experience of his manner of living; and to others, who had learned it from these spectators. Before he went to Cyprus, he resided for some time, during the present reign, in Palestine.

(trans. C. D. Hartranft)

6. *Historia Ecclesiastica* 7.19.2 [ΣΒΠΚΙ 7.4]

For exactly similar traditions on every point are [not] to be found in all the churches, even though they hold the same opinions. There are, for instance, many cities in Scythia, and yet they all have but one bishop; whereas, in other nations a bishop serves as priest even over a village, as I have myself observed in Arabia, and in Cyprus, and among the Novatians and Montanists of Phrygia.

(trans. C. D. Hartranft)

7. *Historia Ecclesiastica* 7.27.1 [ΣΒΠΚΙ 7.5.1]

Epiphanius was at this period at the head of the metropolitan church of Cyprus. He was celebrated, not only for the virtues he manifested and miraculous deeds during his life, but also for the honor that was rendered to him by God after his death; for it was said that demons were expelled, and diseases healed at his tomb. Many wonderful actions wrought while he lived are attributed to him.

(trans. C. D. Hartranft)

8. *Historia Ecclesiastica* 8.14.2–3 [ΑΚΕΠ I 135.10α; ΣΒΠΚΙ 7.5.2]

Epiphanius had long regarded the writings of Origen with peculiar aversion, and was therefore easily led to attach credit to the epistle of Theophilus. He soon after assembled the bishops of Cyprus together and prohibited the examination of the books of Origen. He also wrote to the other bishops, and, among others, to the bishop of Constantinople, exhorting them to convene Synods, and to make the same decision.

(trans. C. D. Hartranft)

9. *Historia Ecclesiastica* 8.14.6 [ΑΚΕΠ I 135.11α; ΣΒΠΚΙ 7.5.2]

Epiphanius was the first to sail from Cyprus; he landed at Hebdomos, a suburb of Constantinople; and after having prayed in the church erected at that place, he proceeded to enter the city.

(trans. C. D. Hartranft)

10. *Historia Ecclesiastica* 8.15.5–7 [ΑΚΕΠ I 135.12; ΣΒΠΚΙ 7.5.2]

Soon after he [Epiphanius] embarked for Cyprus, either because he recognized the futility of his journey to Constantinople, or because, as there is reason to believe, God had revealed to him his approaching death; for he died while on his voyage back to Cyprus. It is reported that he said to the bishops who had accompanied him to the place of embarkation, "I leave you the city, the palace, and the stage, for I shall shortly depart." I have been informed by several persons that John [Chrysostom] predicted that Epiphanius would die at sea, and that this latter predicted the deposition of John . . . For it appears that when the dispute between them was at its height, Epiphanius said to John, "I hope you will not die a bishop," and that John replied, "I hope you will never return to your bishopric."

(trans. C. D. Hartranft)

23. CYRIL of Alexandria (378–444)

1. *Commentarius in Isaiam* 23.1 [ΑΚΕΠ I 35.14]

By Kittian islands some mean either Helladic or Macedonia. Some insist that this refers to Cyprus, from one of the cities so named in it. And they say that those from the land of Kittion boast about Tyre and glory in their commercial activity . . . Let Tyre lament, for they are no longer coming from the land of the Kittieians, for it is now held captive.

(trans. P.W.W.)

24. NONNOS of Panopolis (first half, 5th c.)

1. *Dionysiaca* 5.611–615 [ΑΚΕΠ II 107α; 151.1]

He [Zeus] gazed at the whole body of Persephoneia, uncovered in her bath. Not so wild his desire had been for the Cyprian, when craving but not attaining he scattered his seed on the ground, and shot out the hot foam of love self-sown, where in the fruitful land of horned Cyprus flourished the two coloured generation of wild creatures with horns.   (trans. W. H. D. Rouse)

2. *Dionysiaca* 13.432–463 [ΑΚΕΠ I 14.42; 20.12; 24.2; II 1.7; 59.4, 5; 75.2; 149.5β; 151.1; 155.6, nos. 9α, 12δ, 29]

The Cyprian companies were under command of proud Litros and finehair Lapethos. Many took up arms: those whose lot was in Spheceia, the round brinebeaten isle; others from Cypros, godwelcoming island of the finefeathered Loves [Erotes], which bears the name of Cypris the selfborn. Nereus had traced the boundaries of this Cypros with the deepsea prong, and shaped it like a dolphin. For when the fertile drops from Uranos, spilt with a mess of male gore, had given infant shape to the fertile foam and brought forth the Paphian, to the land of horned Cypros came a dolphin over the deep, which with intelligent mind carried Aphrodite perched on his mane.—Those also were there who held the land of Hylates, and the settlement of Sestos, Tamasos and Tembros, the town of Erythrai, and the woody precincts of Panacros in the mountains. From Soloi also came many men-at-arms, and from Lapethos; this place was named afterwards from the leader who assembled them, who fell in the thyrsus-war and was honourably buried and left his name for his citizens. There were those also who had the city Cinyreia, that rock-island which still bears the name of ancient Cinyras; and those from the place where Urania lies, named after the heavenly vault, because it was full of men brilliant as the stars; and those who held Carpaseia, a land surrounded by sea; and those of Paphos, garlanded harbour of the softhaired Loves [Erotes], landingplace of Aphrodite when she came up out of the waves, where is the bridebath of the seaborn goddess, lovely Setrachos; here Cypris often took a garment and draped the son of Myrrha [Adonis] after his bath. Last is the city of ancient Perseus, for whom Teucros, fleeing from Salamis before the wrath of Telamon, fortified the younger Salamis so renowned.   (trans. W. H. D. Rouse)

3. *Dionysiaca* 14.193–202 [ΑΚΕΠ II 107]

Another tribe of twiform Centaurs was ready, the Cyprian. Once when Cypris fled like the wind from the pursuit of her lascivious father, that she might not see an unhallowed bedfellow in her own begetter, Zeus the Father gave up the chase and left the union unattempted, because unwilling Aphrodite was too fast and he could not catch her: instead of the Cyprian's bed, he dropt on the ground the loveshower of seed from the generative plow. Earth received Cronion's fruitful dew, and shot up a strange-looking horned generation.   (trans. W. H. D. Rouse)

4. *Dionysiaca* 29.340–343 [ΑΚΕΠ II 6.5]

Awake! Go to the upland plain of the Thracian mountain, and see your Cythereia in her own familiar Lemnos. See how her swarm of attendant Loves [Erotes] have crowned with flowers the portals of Paphos and the buildings of Cyprus.   (trans. W. H. D. Rouse)

5. *Dionysiaca* 29.369–372 [ΑΚΕΠ II 6.6; 151.1]

Ares mounted the car, and Rout [Phobos] took the reins and drove his father's chariot. From Libanos [Lebanon] to Paphos he sped, and turned the hurrying car from Cythera to the land of horned Cyprus.
(trans. W .H. D. Rouse)

6. *Dionysiaca* 32.71–73 [ΑΚΕΠ II 107β]

Not so did I desire the Paphian, for whose sake I dropt seed in the furrow of the plowland and begat the Centaurs, as I now feel sweet desire for you!
(trans. W. H. D. Rouse)

7. *Dionysiaca* 32.199–220 [ΑΚΕΠ I 11.4; 144]

Proud Echelaos fell, and was left unburied, crushed by the manbreaking rock from gigantic Morrheus: he was a Cyprian, with the down fresh around his cheeks. He lay then like a palm spire with a head of leaves; but in the battle he rushed about shaking his torch, a tender lad with uncropt hair, until he was struck on the top of the hip, where nature had fitted the axle in the cup of the thigh to grow together with the flesh of his body. He died holding the mystic pine still alight, and in his convulsions burnt his head to ashes with his own torch, setting fire to the braided hair with the smoking brand. Then Morrheus triumphed over him and mocked him:
Boy, you must be a stranger to the land which is called your nurse—Echelaos lad, you have belied your birth as a Cyprian! You are not sprung from Pygmalion, to whom Cypris gave a long course of life and many years. Ares the bridegroom of your Paphian did not save you. Your Cythereia did not grant you infinite circles of revolving years and a car that stumbled not, that you might escape your fate on that fatefending waggon, as you ever drove a kneeheavy run of mules! Wrong! You do come from Cyprus. Fate caught you also quick when Ares vanquished you just like Myrrha's son [Adonis].
(trans. W. H. D. Rouse)

8. *Dionysiaca* 33.4–8 [ΑΚΕΠ II 65.2]

One of the swiftshoe Graces was gathering the shoots of the fragrant reeds in the Erythraian [Eastern] garden, in order to mix the flowing juice of Assyrian oil with Indian flowers in the steaming cauldrons of Paphos, and make ointment for her Lady.
(trans. W. H. D. Rouse)

9. *Dionysiaca* 33.136–139 [ΑΚΕΠ II 57.15]

The two luminaries I [Eros] will drag down from heaven to be drudges in Paphos, and give my mother for a servant Phaëthon with Clymene, Selene with Endymion, that all may know that I vanquish all things!
(trans. W. H. D. Rouse)

10. *Dionysiaca* 41.95–118 [ΑΚΕΠ II 1.8]

Beroë [Berytos] first shook away the cone of darkling mist, and threw off the gloomy veil of chaos. Before Cyprus and the Isthmian city of Corinth, she first received Cypris within her welcoming portal. newly born from the brine; when the water impregnated from the furrow of Uranos was delivered of deepsea Aphrodite; when without marriage, the seed plowed the flood with male fertility, and of itself shaped the foam into a daughter, and Nature was the midwife—coming up with the goddess there was that embroidered strap which ran round her loins like a belt, set about the queen's body in a girdle of itself. Then the goddess, moving through the water along the quiet shore, ran out, not to Paphos, not to Byblos, set no foot on land by the dry beach of Colias [Kolias, Attica], even passed by Cythera's city itself with quicker circuit: aye, she rubbed her skin with bunches of seaweed and made it purpler still; paddling with her hands she cleft the birthwaters of the waveless deep, and swam; resting her bosom upon the sea she struck up the silent brine, marking it with her feet, and kept her body afloat, and as she cut through the calm, pushed the water behind her with successive thrusts of her feet, and emerged at Beroë [Berytos]. Those footsteps of the goddess coming out from the sea are all lies of the people of Cyprus.

(trans. W. H. D. Rouse)

11. *Dionysiaca* 41.320–321, 328–331 [AKEΠ II 12.13]

Which of the cities has the organ of sovereign voice? Which has reserved for it the unshaken reins of troublesolving Law? . . . I wish to learn whether the gift is reserved for the land of Cyprus or Paphos or Corinth, or Sparta whence Lycurgos came, or the noblemen's country of my own daughter Beroë [i.e. Berytos].

(trans. W. H. D. Rouse)

25. ACTS OF ST. BARNABAS (apocryphal) (middle, 5th c.)

The Travels and Martyrdom of St. Barnabas the Apostle

1. 1–4 ed. Bonnet

1. I, John [called Mark], have observed and witnessed the ineffable, holy, and blameless mystery of those who have obtained this holy hope and have been sealed as Christians from the incarnation of our savior Jesus Christ, generous, benevolent, and strong, shepherd, teacher, and healer. Therefore I have served him eagerly and felt it necessary to explain the mysteries which I had heard and seen.
2. Thus I followed Barnabas and Paul the holy apostles [cf. Acts 12:25], previously having been a servant of Cyrillus the chief priest of Zeus, but now having received the grace of the Holy Spirit through Paul and Barnabas and Silas [cf. Acts 15:22] who were worthy of their calling and who also baptized me in Ikonion [?].
3. After I had been baptized I had a dream and saw a man dressed in a white robe standing by me, and he said to me, "John, have courage; for your name will be changed to Mark, and your glory will be proclaimed in all the world. And the darkness that was in you has left you, and you have been given understanding to know the mysteries of God."
4. When I had seen the dream I trembled all over, went to Barnabas, and at his feet reported to him the mysteries which I had seen and heard from that man. But Paul the Apostle was not present when I reported the mysteries. And Barnabas said to me, "Do not speak to anyone of the

power which you have seen. For this night the Lord stood by me, too, and said, 'Since you have given your soul for the sake of my name to the point of dying and being alienated from your people, thus you will die. Take with you also the servant who is with you; for he has certain mysteries.' Now, my child, keep for yourself the words which you have seen and heard. For the right moment to reveal them will come."

2. 5 ed. Bonnet [AKEΠ I 110.14]

When I [John called Mark] had been taught these things by him [Barnabas] we remained in Ikonion [?] for a few days. For there was a venerable and pious man there who received us and whose house the Apostle Paul had previously sanctified. From there we proceeded to Seleukeia [the harbor of Syrian Antioch; cf. Acts 13:4] and then, after three days, we sailed to Cyprus. And I served them as long as we stayed in Cyprus. And upon leaving Cyprus we landed at Perge in Pamphylia [cf. Acts: 13:13]. And there I remained for approximately two months, intending to sail to parts west, but the Spirit did not allow me. Returning I again sought the apostles and learned that they were in Antioch; so I traveled there.

3. 6 ed. Bonnet

I found Paul in Antioch, weary from his travels and resting on a bed. When he saw me he was very grieved because I had delayed in Pamphylia. And Barnabas came and encouraged Paul, and he tasted bread. And Barnabas took Paul for a little while. And they preached the word of the Lord and baptized many of the Jews and Greeks. But I only gave heed to them and was afraid to approach Paul, because I had spent some time in Pamphylia and because he was quite upset with me. On bent knees I offered my apologies to Paul, but he did not accept them. For three weeks, on bent knees, I kept begging and beseeching him but was unable to reconcile him with me. His main complaint against me was that I had had several parchments in Pamphylia [cf. 2 Timothy 4:13].

4. 7–8 ed. Bonnet [AKEΠ I 110.21α]

7. When they had finished teaching in Antioch, one Sabbath day they sat together and decided to travel to the places in Anatolia and after that to Cyprus and to visit all the churches in which they had preached the word of God. But Barnabas asked Paul first to go to Cyprus and to visit his people there in his own village, while Lucius [cf. Acts 13:1 and Romans 16:21] asked him to visit his city, Cyrene. But Paul had a vision in his sleep telling him that he should hasten to Jerusalem and be received by the brethren there. But Barnabas urged them to go to Cyprus, spend the winter there, and then go to Jerusalem at the time of the [Passover] festival.
8. And there was a great dispute between them [cf. Acts 15:36–39]. Barnabas asked me, too, to follow them, because I had been their servant from the beginning; and I had served them in all of Cyprus until we came to Perge in Pamphylia, and there I had remained for a few days. But Paul raised his voice against Barnabas and said, "It is impossible for him to go with us." And those who were with us urged me to follow them, because I had made a vow that I would follow them to the end. Consequently Paul said to Barnabas, "If you wish to take John, whose name was

changed to Mark, with you, go some other way, for he shall not go with us." But Barnabas, when he had calmed down, said, "The grace of God does not turn away this man who once has become a servant of the gospel and has traveled with us. If then it is your pleasure, Father Paul, I shall take him and be on my way." And he [Paul] said, "Go in the grace of God, and we in the power of the Spirit."

5. 9–10 ed. Bonnet

9. On their knees they prayed to God. And Paul moaned and wept, and Barnabas did likewise, and they spoke one to the other, "It would have been good to finish our task among men together just as we began. But since this is your decision, Father Paul, pray on my behalf that my labors in the end might meet with approval. You know how I have served you in the grace of Christ which was given to us. Now I am going to Cyprus and I shall soon die. For I know that I shall no longer see your face, Father Paul." And falling on the ground at Paul's feet he wept mightily. 10. And Paul said to him, "I too have had the Lord standing by me this night and saying, 'Do not prevent Barnabas from going to Cyprus. For there it has been given to him to baptize many. But you, in the grace that has been given to you, go to Jerusalem to worship in the holy place and there it will be shown to you where your martyrdom has been prepared.'"

6. 11 ed. Bonnet [ΑΚΕΠ I 110.23]

And when we had reached Laodikeia [Latakia in Syria] we asked for a way to get to Cyprus, and when we had found a ship sailing to Cyprus we boarded it. And as we were sailing a contrary wind arose. We came to Korasion and when we had gotten ashore where there was a spring we refreshed ourselves, but we did not reveal ourselves to anyone because no one knew that Barnabas and Paul had separated. Departing from Korasion we came to the coast of Isauria [between Cilicia and Pamphylia] and from there to an island called Pityousa, where we stayed for three days when a storm had arisen. A pious man named Euphemos received us and Barnabas taught him many things so that he and his entire household accepted the faith.

7. 12–13 ed. Bonnet

12. From there we sailed past the Akonesiai Islands and came to the city of Anemourion; having entered the city we found two Greeks. They came to us and asked us where we were from and who we were. And Barnabas said to them, "If you wish to know where we are from and who we are take off the coat which you have and I shall give you a coat which will never be stained, and there are no stains on it, but it is always white." And they were astonished at his words and asked us, "What is this coat which he is going to give us?" But Barnabas said to them, "If you will confess your sins and accept our Lord Jesus Christ you will receive that coat which will never perish."

13. Moved by the Holy Spirit they fell down at his feet and begged him, "We ask you, Father, give us that coat; for we believe in the living and true God whom you proclaim." And he led them to the spring and baptized them in the name of the Father and of the Son and of the Holy Ghost. And they understood that they had been cloaked in holy power and a holy coat. And

Barnabas took one coat from me and placed it on the one man, and the other man he dressed in his own coat. And they brought him money, but he right away distributed it to the beggars, and the sailors, too, profited handsomely.

8. 14 ed. Bonnet [ΑΚΕΠ I 110.23]

When we had reached the shore he announced to them the word of God. And when he had blessed them we bid them farewell and boarded the ship. But one of them, named Stephen, wanted to follow us, but Barnabas would not let him. Having made the crossing we landed in Cyprus at night, and we came to the place Krommyakite [Kormakite; Cape Krommyon] and found Timon and Ariston, the priests, and stayed with them.

9. 15 ed. Bonnet

But Timon was laid up with a high fever. We laid our hands upon him and right away made the fever disappear, and we called upon the name of the Lord Jesus. But Barnabas had received the lessons [Gospel] from Matthew, the book of the voice of God and a record of miracles and teachings. He made it a practice to place this book on the sick in the country that we were encountering, and right away he brought about a cure of their ailments.

10. 16–17 ed. Bonnet [ΑΚΕΠ I 110.15; 110.24; II 128]

16. When we were in Lapithos and when idolatrous madness was going on in the theatre the people of the town would not let us enter, but we refreshed ourselves for a little while at the gate. And Timon, having recovered from his illness, went with us. We left Lapithos and passed through the mountains. Then we came to the city of Lampadistos where Timon was. We also found Herakleion with him, and we stayed there, with him.
17. He [Herakleion] was from Tamasos and he had come to visit his relatives. Gazing at him intently, Barnabas recognized him because he had previously met him, together with Paul, at Kition. And the Holy Spirit was given to him as he was baptized, and Barnabas changed his name to Herakleides. And when they had ordained him as bishop of Cyprus and had strengthened the church in Tamasos they left him to edify the brethren who live there.

11. 18 ed. Bonnet [ΑΚΕΠ I 110.25]

When we had passed through the Chionodes [Troodos] Mountains we reached Palaipaphos and there we found a certain Rhodon, a pagan priest; and he was converted and followed us. And then we came upon a Jew by name of Bar-Jesus [or Elymas; cf. Acts 13: 6–12], from Paphos, and he recognized Barnabas as previously having been with Paul. And he would not let us enter Paphos; so we turned away and went to Kourion.

12. 19 ed. Bonnet [AKEΠ I 110.26; II 84.3α]

We found a certain indecent race going on in the road near the city, where a crowd of women and men was racing in the nude. And there was much seductive roaming-about going on in that place. And Barnabas turned and censured this place, and the west end of it collapsed, so that many were injured. Many of them even died, and the rest fled to the sanctuary of Apollo, which is located on the so-called Sacred Way. And when we came close to Kourion a large crowd of Jews, having been suborned by Bar-Jesus, stood outside the city and did not allow us to enter the city, but we spent the day under a tree near the city and there refreshed ourselves.

13. 20 ed. Bonnet [AKEΠ I 110.19; 110.27; II 102; 129; 139]

The next day we came to a certain village where Aristoklianos dwelt. He had been a leper but had been healed in Antioch, and Paul and Barnabas had ordained him as bishop and had sent him to his own village because many Greeks live there. We stayed in a cave near-by in the mountain and remained there for one day. From there we went to Amathous, and a large crowd of Greeks was in the sanctuary on the mountain, unholy women and men, pouring libations. But here, too, Bar-Jesus had come before us and had roused the Jewish people and did not allow us to enter the city, except for one widow who was eighty years old, whose home was outside the city, and who did not worship idols. She attended to us and received us in her house for one hour [day?]. Upon leaving we shook the dust off our feet [cf. Matthew 10:14] as we passed that sanctuary where the priests were pouring libations.

14. 21 ed. Bonnet [AKEΠ I 110.28]

Leaving there, we passed through the uninhabited area, and Timon followed us. And when we had come to Kition there was a lot of commotion in the hippodrome. When we found out we left the city and all shook the dust off our feet [cf. Matthew 10:14]. For no one had received us, except that for one hour we rested at the gate near the aqueduct.

15. 22–26 ed. Bonnet [AKEΠ I 110.29; II 101.1; 103; 156.1]

22. When we had sailed from Kition we come to Salamis and landed at the so-called Islands, where the place was full of idols. And there were festivals and libations. There also we found Herakleides and we taught him how to proclaim God's gospel and how to establish churches and appoint priests in them. And when we had entered Salamis we went into the synagogue which is near the so-called Biblia. And when we had entered, Barnabas opened the Gospel which he had received from Matthew, his fellow-worker, and began to teach the Jews.
23. But two days later, after we had taught quite a few Jews, Bar-Jesus arrived and boldly assembled all the Jews. And they seized Barnabas and sought to turn him over to Hypatos, the governor of Salamis. They bound him and were ready to take him to the governor when a pious Jebusite, a relative of Nero, came to Cyprus. When the Jews learned about this they took Barnabas by night, bound him with a rope around the neck, and dragged him from the synagogue towards the hippodrome. When they had gotten outside the gate they surrounded him and burned

him with fire so that even his bones turned into ashes. At once, during the same night, they took his ashes and put them in a cloth, sealed the cloth with lead, and intended to cast them into the sea.

24. But I [John Mark] found the right moment during the night and, together with Timon and Rhodon, was able to take him [i.e. the ashes of Barnabas] And we went to a certain place, found a cave, and put him there, where the Jebusites used to live. And when we had found a hidden place we placed him in it together with the teachings which he had received from Matthew. And it was the fourth hour of the second night of the week.

25. And when we had hidden ourselves in that place the Jews made quite an effort to find us, and as soon as they had found us they drove us all the way to the village of Ledra. And when we had found a cave not far from the village we took refuge in it and thus escaped their notice. And we hid in the cave for three days, and when the Jews had left we emerged and left that place at night. Then, having added Ariston and Rhodon to our company, we reached the village of Limnes.

26. When we had come to the seashore we found an Egyptian ship; we boarded it and landed in Alexandria. And there I remained, teaching the word of the Lord to the brethren who came, baptizing them, and teaching them the things which I had learned from the apostles of Christ; it is they who had baptized me in the name of the Father and the Son and the Holy Spirit and who changed my name to Mark in the waters of baptism. And in these waters I hope to bring many to the glory of God through his grace, because to him are due honor and glory forever. Amen.

26. COUNCIL OF CHALCEDON (Fourth Ecumenical Council) (451)

1. Πρᾶξις Πρώτη (Mansi VI, cols. 568 and 577; *ACO* II.1.1, pp. 56 and 64)

568. Bishop Epiphanios, on behalf of Olympios, bishop of Constantia, from Cyprus.

577. Soter of Theodosiana [?] on behalf of Heliodoros, bishop of Amathous, and Proechios, bishop of Arsinoe.

Epaphroditos, bishop of the town of Tamasos, on behalf of Didymos, bishop of the town of Lapithos.

Dionysios, deacon, on behalf of Photinos of Kythroi.

27. THEODORET of Cyrrhus (ca. 393–ca. 466)

1. *Interpretatio in Jeremiam* 2.10 [ΑΚΕΠ I 35.6; II 150.2]

By Chettieim he means Cyprus, the islands around it, and generally the western parts.

2. *Interpretatio in Ezechielem* 27.6 [ΑΚΕΠ I 35.8]

Kittion [Kition] is a city in Cyprus and known by that name to the present day. The aspiration [of the k], in the Hebrew language, shows the relationship to Chettieim. Cyprus was at that time ruling the islands; therefore he calls the Greek islands Chettieim.

3. *Historia Ecclesiastica* 4.3.8 [ΣΒΠΚΙ 11]

Be aware, o Emperor most dear to God, that this is the doctrine which has been proclaimed from eternity, on which the Fathers assembled at Nicaea agreed, and to which all the churches everywhere have agreed: those in Spain, Britain, and the provinces of Gaul, those of all of Italy, Dalmatia, Dacia, Mysia, Macedonia, and all of Greece, all those in Africa, Sardinia, Cyprus, and Crete, those in Pamphylia, Lycia, and Isauria, those in all of Egypt, Libya, Pontos, Cappadocia, and the adjacent regions, and those in Anatolia, except for a few men who adhere to the teachings of Arius. [Athanasios of Alexandria to the emperor Jovian, 363–364]

28. VITA OF ST. HERAKLEIDES (*or* Herakleidios) (2nd half, 5th c.)

1. 2 (p.141 ed. Halkin) [ΑΚΕΠ I 110.24γ]

It came to pass that the venerable Father Theodoros departed from earthly life. And the venerable Herakleidios and Mnason [cf. Acts 21:16], the teacher, together with the faithful brethren, went and tended to his venerable body there where Chrysippos, Mnason's father, was. And they were all in deep sorrow. And it happened on the ninth day that Father Herakleidios called for the venerable Prokliane and ordained her a deaconess of the holy church. And we were feasting on the teachings of the holy fathers.

2. 4 (p.144 ed. Halkin) [ΑΚΕΠ I 110.24δ]

When we were finishing the work of God with all the people and had sung some songs, there came from the place which is called Peraton [Pera] and is a suburb [of Tamasos] a certain man who was driven by a fierce spirit. And this man went into the church of God and tore Father Herakleidios' coat . . . And from that hour this man was healed. When all the Greeks heard what had happened they brought all their sick to be near Father Herakleides and Mnason. And in the name of Christ all were healed through the laying-on of hands; and the word of God was fulfilled through the venerable fathers.

3. 7 (pp. 147–48 ed. Halkin [ΑΚΕΠ I 110.25α; II 155.6, no. 30β]

When it had gotten late and evening was approaching there came a certain man named Nicholas with a letter for Father Herakleidios. When he had greeted all the people he delivered the letter, which was from Paul and Barnabas, the disciples of our Lord Jesus Christ. And Father Herakleidios handed the letter to Mnason, who unfolded it and explained it fully to Father

Herakleides . . . And the contents of the letter were as follows, "We know that you are strong in your knowledge of the Lord, and we are anxious, venerable Father, to write to you briefly. You know what has happened to us in Paphos . . . Be fearless in proclaiming [the gospel] to those who live in Paphos."

4. 7–8 (p. 149 ed. Halkin) [AKEΠ I 110.25β; II 155.6, no. 5]

7. The venerable Father Herakleidios said to them [the peope of Tamasos], "I have hidden nothing from you, beloved children. For I must go to Paphos and accomplish what has been enjoined upon me." And all who heard him were saddened and begged him, saying, "Do not leave us, Father." But he said to them, "I shall return to you, God willing." Then we entered the holy church while the service was going on, and he ordained Father Gregory a presbyter and instructed him to teach the people and to perform the whole liturgy. Then he took Mnason and me, Rhodon, and we went to Paphos.
8. We were in the district of Anogyra, and the next day we came to the city of Paphos.

5. 8 (pp. 150–51 ed. Halkin) [AKEΠ I 110.24α]

As we were resting at night Father Herakleidios spoke to the teacher Mnason, "Father Mnason, I wish you to know all things that happened to me. As we were making sacrifice to the non-gods the servants of [the true] God, Barnabas and Mark, came. When Hierokles, my father, saw them he invited them to come with us. But they said to him, 'Far be it from us to let anything mean or unclean touch our lips. But show us the way to the Troodos Mountains.' Then my father Hierokles told me to show them the way, and I went with them. And Barnabas said to me, 'Son, what were you doing?' And I said to him, 'We were making sacrifice to the gods.' And Barnabas said to me, 'Son, listen to us and save your soul. For the gods who have not made the heavens and the earth shall perish [cf. Jeremiah 10:11]. What sort of god is one who cannot help himself? But listen to me, son, and save your soul.' And when I heard these words I was pricked in my soul and I was not able to turn back. But they taught me even more . . . And I was their follower. And when we came to the river of Soloi [the Karkotes, Kargotis, or Karyotis] they baptized me in the name of the Father, of the Son, and of the Holy Spirit. When God had mercy on me I listened to the disciples of the Lord and followed them into all the districts and received the word of God. And we came to a place called Kormiakite. And from there we came to the city of Tamasos, and when the townspeople had received us we stayed in a cave, when you yourself joined us. And I know, Brother Mnason, that a great trial is upon us." And Mnason said to him, "we must fulfill all things which have been enjoined upon us, Father."

6. 9 (p. 152 ed. Halkin) [AKEΠ I 110.25γ; II 84.3]

When the citizens [of Paphos] heard what had happened they came out in a multitude and drove us from this place. And we came to the town of Kourion. And when we had entered there were dishevelled women and a large multitude running about. Then the venerable Father Herakleidios took us and we left that place. And when we had gone the distance of about one milestone we found a spring and there we refreshed ourselves. And they [Herakleides and Mnason] broke bread and gave me to eat, but they themselves rested. And when the sun was setting Father Herakleidios said, "Children, let us go to our own city [Tamasos]. For these people are not receiving the teachings of the Lord." So we rose and said Amen.

7. 10 (p. 153 ed. Halkin) [АКЕП II 155.6, no. 24]

We were happily walking along our way when the sun set in the district of Lithou Kolone.

8. 11 (p. 153 ed. Halkin) [АКЕП II 155.6, no. 27]

We arose and went on our way. And when we reached the district of Melene the son of the presbyter Gregory met us and reported to us that Herakleidiane, the sister of Father Herakleides, had left earthly life. And we were much saddened.

9. 12 (p. 154 ed. Halkin) [АКЕП II 155.6, no. 20]

After ten days there came a man from the town of Lampadistos.

10. 14 (pp. 156–57 ed. Halkin) [АКЕП II 155.6, no. 32]

The servants of God who dwell in Peraton [Pera], the suburb [of Tamasos], and had come to be baptized were unable to cross the spring-flooding, and the deacon Klesippos reported this to Father Herakleides, who, taking us with him, went out . . . And when he had thus prayed he struck the water here and there with a rod, making the sign of the venerable cross of Christ. And at that very hour the water receded.

11. 16 (pp. 160–62 ed. Halkin) [АКЕП II 15; 25.1]

After three days it happened that the son of a man named Philotheos passed away. Now this man was a Greek [pagan] and he begged all the pagan priests to bring him [the images of] their gods, so that they might resurrect his son. And the priests of Peraton [Pera] brought Apollo, Gorgias [?], and Artemis, and the priests of Tamasos brought Asklepios, Dionysos, and Aphrodite. And they were all shouting, each to his own god, "Resurrect Hiereios, the son of Philotheos." But there was no voice and no response [cf. 1 Kings 18:26]. But when the crowd stood around the bier the corpse stirred, and then they all congratulated Philotheos, because his son was about to be resurrected by the gods. But his wife came running, touched her son, and said, "What are you imagining? Look, he is dead. Take your gods, each of you, and let each [image] return to its shrine. Let him stand aside who has separated you from the hope of Jesus Christ. Come, my husband, let us go to the servants of the [true] God and ask them to come and resurrect our son, and we shall see our son alive." And Nympha took her husband Philotheos, leaving all others in her house with the dead, and thus they came to us . . . And Father Herakleidios put his face to the face of the corpse and wept. Then he prayed, "I call upon you, life-giving Jesus Christ, you who have resurrected Lazarus from the dead and raised the widow's son from the dead. Among those who call upon you [cf. Psalms 99:6] and need assistance, you have given power to us to call upon you. Raise up the son of Philotheos, so that they [his parents] and the witnesses might become your, God's, temple and you might dwell in them." And he placed a seal [made the sign of the cross] upon the corpse three times and kissed him. At that the dead rose up, as if he had been asleep, and all shouted, "Great is the One God, the God of Herakleides and Mnason, the God who accomplishes these signs through them."

12. 18 (p. 167 ed. Halkin) [ΑΚΕΠ I 110.31]

With these words the venerable Father Herakleidios placed his maniple on Mnason's throat, granted peace to all, and told Klesippos to say a prayer. Then he lifted his eyes up to heaven and said, "I thank you, Jesus Christ, and I thank you, Father in heaven. Send your Holy Spirit from on high. Dwell with Mnason the priest so that he may offer your body and your blood with blameless hands. Become an undestructable wall for him; become his guide to the people; for to you glory is due forever."

13. 20 (p. 169 ed. Halkin) [ΑΚΕΠ I 110.31α; II 138]

And when Father Herakleidios said these things to the venerable Father Mnason, a large crowd gathered. And Father Herakleidios put his mouth on Father Mnason's throat and kissed him, and he did similarly to Gregory the protopresbyter. But me he took by the hand and and spoke, "My son, Rhodon, emulate the master and follow in his footsteps, so that you might become a shepherd of the sheep." Then he greeted all and gave up the ghost. And we all made a loud lament upon his death.

But the priest Mnason told me to go into the church of God and to bring white linens. And when they had bound up the venerable body they buried it in the cave in which he used to hold service with the disciples of our Lord Jesus Christ.

And our venerable Father Herakleidios had lived ten years after the death of his sister [Herakleidiane]. And he died peacefully on September 17, glorifying the Father, the Son, and the Holy Spirit now and forever. Amen.

29. HESYCHIOS of Alexandria (5th/6th c.)

Lexicon

1. s.v. ἀγήτωρ [ΑΚΕΠ II 56]

The priest in Cyprus who oversees the offerings to Aphrodite.

2. s.v. ἀερία [ΑΚΕΠ II 149.6]

Mist among the Aitolians. So they call the island of Thasos, Egypt, Libya, Crete, Sicily, Ethiopia, and Cyprus.

3. s.v. ἀκάμαντα [ΑΚΕΠ I 23.4; II 160, #1]

Also a mountain in Cyprus so-called. It took its name from Akamas, the brother of Demophon and son of Theseus.

4. s.v. ἀρὰς ἐπισπεῖραι (to sow seeds) [ΑΚΕΠ II 124]

It is the practice of the Cypriots, when they sow barley seeds, to curse some of them with salt.

5. s.v. Aphroditos [ΑΚΕΠ II 30]

Theophrastus [*Characters* 16.10] calls him Hermaphroditos, but Paion, who wrote about Amathous [terminus ante quem: Plutarch], says that the goddess took the form of a man in Cyprus.

6. s.v. ἀχαιομάντεις [ΑΚΕΠ II 111]

Those who hold the priesthood of the gods in Cyprus.

7. s.v. βομβοία [ΑΚΕΠ II 163γ]

The swimming (pickled) olive, as the Cypriots say.

8. s.v. βοῦς Κύπριος (Cypriot ox) [ΑΚΕΠ II 164.7β]

Dung-eating, useless, unclean; means uncouthness to the Cypriots. And Eudoxos [of Knidos, 4th c. B.C.] tells that they eat dung.

9. s.v. Κύπριος βοῦς (Cypriot ox) [ΑΚΕΠ II 164.7β]

. . . since Cypriot oxen eat dung.

10. s.v. βύβλιοι [ΑΚΕΠ II 125]

The guards of tombs, as the Cypriots say.

11. s.v. Bokaros [ΑΚΕΠ II 162, #3]

A river in Salamis flowing from Mt. Akamas.

12. s.v. γένεσις Κύπρου (birth of Cyprus) [ΑΚΕΠ II 126]

    The libation, among the Cypriots.

13. s.v. γῆς ὀμφαλός (navel of the earth) [ΑΚΕΠ II 12.14]

    Paphos and Delphi.

14. s.v. δημίην Κύπριν [ΑΚΕΠ II 33]

    A prostitute.

15. s.v. δίπτυον [ΑΚΕΠ II 167.1]

    The Cypriots: a measure; others: the *hemimedimnon*.

16. s.v. Encheios [ΑΚΕΠ II 34]

    Aphrodite (Cypriots).

17. s.v. Eileti [ΑΚΕΠ II 93.1]

    Zeus, in Cyprus.

18. s.v. Elaious [ΑΚΕΠ II 93.2]

    Zeus, in Cyprus.

19. s.v. Elaious [ΑΚΕΠ II 93.9]

    The sanctuary of Zeus in Cyprus.

20. s.v. Eleemon [ΑΚΕΠ II 35]

    Aphrodite in Cyprus and Karchedonia [Carthage].

21. s.v. ἐλεία or ἔλα [ΑΚΕΠ II 94]

    The rays of the sun; also Hera in Cyprus and Artemis in Messene.

22. s.v. Endeïdes [ΑΚΕΠ II 105]

    The nymphs in Cyprus.

23. s.v. Epikoinios [ΑΚΕΠ II 93.6]

Zeus in Salamis.

24. s.v. Euelides [ΑΚΕΠ II 93.3]

Impudent. And, in Cyprus, Zeus.

25. s.v. ἐῴα [ΑΚΕΠ II 116]

The East. And sheepskin. And, in Cyprus, sacrifice.

26. s.v. Zeter [ΑΚΕΠ II 93.4]

Zeus in Cyprus.

27. s.v. ἡμιπέλεκκον [ΑΚΕΠ II 167.2]

The three-mina, four-mina, or five-mina; for the ten-mina is called *pelekys* by the Paphians.

28. s.v. κάρπωσις [ΑΚΕΠ II 48.1]

Sacrifice to Aphrodite in Amathous.

29. s.v. Kerastias [ΑΚΕΠ II 149.4γ]

At one time, Cyprus.

30. s.v. Kinyradai [ΑΚΕΠ I 14.38; II 56.1α]

Priests of Aphrodite.

31. s.v. κίτταρις [ΑΚΕΠ II 168.1]

The headband which the Cypriots wear; and those who wear the headbands are called *kittaroi.*

32. s.v. κιχητός [ΑΚΕΠ II 48α]

(A vessel) in which incense is dipped, in Cyprus.

33. s.v. Kleides [ΑΚΕΠ II 161, # 2α]

A promontory of Cyprus.

34. s.v. Κυπρία πάλη (Cypriot wrestling) [ΑΚΕΠ II 169]

Some call this *pammachon*, and others rustic and not sportmanlike, because the Cypriots wrestle without rules.

35. s.v. Kypris [ΑΚΕΠ II 20.140]

A prostitute.

36. s.v. Malika [ΑΚΕΠ II 108]

Herakles (Amathousians).

37. s.v. Miones [ΑΚΕΠ I 9]

Cyprians.

38. s.v. μνάσιον [ΑΚΕΠ II 167]

A measure equal to two medimnoi.

39. s.v. μοττοφαγία [ΑΚΕΠ II 114]

A certain sacrifice made at Salamis in Cyprus.

40. s.v. Myrikai [ΑΚΕΠ II 54]

A sacred place of Aphrodite in Cyprus.

41. s.v. μυρίκη [ΑΚΕΠ II 54α]

A kind of tree, so-called from the idea that the daughter of Kinyras was shedding tears when she had been transformed into such a tree.

42. s.v. ὀρτός [ΑΚΕΠ II 123]

An altar (Cypriots).

43. s.v. Peirethoi [ΑΚΕΠ II 106]

Nymphs in Cyprus.

44. s.v. περιόρια [ΑΚΕΠ II 127]

A festival in Cyprus.

45. s.v. Pygmaion [ΑΚΕΠ II 73]

Adonis among the Cypriots.

46. s.v. Ῥοίκου (Ῥύκου) κριθοπομπία (Rhoikos sending barley) [ΑΚΕΠ I 59.6]

Eratosthenes says in the ninth book of his *Amathousians* that Rhoikos, having been taken prisoner and then returned to his own home, sent barley to the city of the Athenians.

47. s.v. σάπιθος [ΑΚΕΠ II 48.2; 115]

Sacrifice (Paphians).

48. s.v. Σολοιτύπος [ΑΚΕΠ II 173.8)

Hammering iron. And a kind of bronze on Cyprus.

49. s.v. Tamiradai [ΑΚΕΠ II 56.2]

Some priests in Cyprus.   (nos. 1–3, 5–36, 38–40, 43–45, 47, and 49 trans. P.W.W.)

30. ZOSIMOS (5th/6th c.)

1. *Historia Nova* 2.22.1–2 [ΑΚΕΠ I 126; ΣΒΠΚΙ 10.1]

When Licinius [308–324] heard of Constantine's preparations, he sent messengers throughout his realm bidding them to make ready war-ships, infantry and cavalry. The Egyptians immediately sent eighty triremes, the Phoenicians as many more, the Ionians and Dorians in Asia sixty, the Cyprians thirty, the Carians twenty, the Bithynians thirty, and the Africans fifty. [A.D. 324]   (trans. R. T. Ridley)

2. *Historia Nova* 2.33.1 [ΑΚΕΠ I 127; ΣΒΠΚΙ 10.2]

Constantine [I, 306–337] upset this sound organisation and divided the one office into four. He assigned to one prefect all Egypt, in addition to the Pentapolis in Africa, the east as far as Mesopotamia; Cilicia, Cappadocia and Armenia; the whole coast from Pamphylia to Trapezus and on to the forts near Phasis; Thrace and the neighbouring provices of Moesia . . . and Rhodope; . . . Cyprus; and the Cyclades save Lemnos, Imbros and Samothrace.   (trans. R. T. Ridley)

3. *Historia Nova* 5.18.1–3 [ΣΒΠΚΙ 10.3]

As soon as the emperor Arcadius heard this, he sent for Eutropius and stripped him of his honours, but the eunuch ran into a Christian church, to which he himself had granted right of sanctuary. When, however, Gainas was insistent that Tribigildus would not give up unless Eutropius was put out of the way, he was arrested contrary to the law of church asylum and sent to Cyprus under strong guard. And when Gainas persisted in urging Arcadius to do away with him, the officials evaded the oath they had given Eutropius when he was dragged from the church, had him fetched from Cyprus, and then, as if they had sworn not to kill him only as long as he was at Constantinople, sent him to Chalcedon, where they murdered him. So Fate dealt unexpectedly with Eutropius on both counts, in raising him to heights previously unattained by a eunuch and then in bringing about his death through the hatred of the enemies of the state. [A.D. 399]

(trans. R. T. Ridley)

31. THEODORE LECTOR or ANAGNOSTES (d. after 527)

1. *Historia Ecclesiastica, Epitome* [ΣΒΠΚΙ 13.1]

The church of Antioch was again in a state of confusion, with some supporting Paulinus and others Flavianus. The Egyptians, Arabs, and Cypriots sided with Paulinus as the injured party, but the Syrians, Palestinians, Phoenicians, Armenians, Cappadocians, Galatians, and most of those in Pontos favored Flavianus.

2. *Historia Ecclesiastica, Epitome* [ΣΒΠΚΙ 13.2]

Among the Scythians all the cities have their own bishop. Among the Cypriots and Arabs there are bishops even in the villages, similarly among the Novatians and Montanists in Phrygia.

3. *Historia Ecclesiastica, Epitome* 273 [ΣΒΠΚΙ 13.3.1]

Epiphanios of Cyprus was an excellent bishop and distinguished himself by his miracles. Even after his death God granted him again to perform many miracles.

4. *Historia Ecclesiastica, Epitome* 288 [ΣΒΠΚΙ 13.3.2]

When Epiphanios of Cyprus had come to Hebdomon [a suburb of Constantinople], he performed ordinations and held services without authorization of John [Chrysostom]. And when John was willing to come to an agreement with him and invited him to stay with him in the episopal residence, Epiphanios chose not to do this; for he had been won over by the plots of Theophilos [of Alexandria].

5. *Historia Ecclesiastica, Epitome* 291 [ΣΒΠΚΙ 13.3.3]

Epiphanios departed for Cyprus when God, so it seems, had foretold him of his death. It is said that he himself revealed death in exile for John, and that John revealed death on board ship for Epiphanios. It is said also that Epiphanios, when he was about to depart, said to those who accompanied him, "I am in a hurry, yes, in a hurry; I leave to you the palace, the city, and the theater."

6. *Historia Ecclesiastica, Epitome* 436 [ΑΚΕΠ I 110.34δ; II 163.6. ΣΒΠΚΙ 13.3.4]

The remains of the apostle Barnabas were found in Cyprus [at the time of Zeno I, 474–491] under a carob tree, with the Gospel of Matthew, by Barnabas' own hand, on his chest. On these grounds the Cypriots form an autocephalous metropolis of their own and are not subject to Antioch. But Zeno deposited said Gospel in his palace, in [the Chapel of] St. Stephen [478].

32. PROKOPIOS of Gaza (ca. 465–ca. 528)

1. *Declamatio* 5 (p. 94 ed. Garzya-Loenertz) [ΣΒΠΚΙ 12]

We shall not sail past Cyprus and her Aphrodite. I shall debark from the ship, I shall see the island of Adonis, and I shall tell of Aphrodite, the picture of her suffering, and the memory of her love.

33. STEPHEN of Byzantium (floruit ca. 528–535)

Ethnica

1. s.v. Aipeia [ΑΚΕΠ II 155.2]

A city in Laconia . . . there is another in Cyprus . . . the ethnic term is Αἰπεάτης.

2. s.v. Akra [ΑΚΕΠ II 155.2]

A city in Iapygia [Calabria] . . . the seventh one in Cyprus . . . the ethnic term is Ἀκραῖος.

3. s.v. Ἀκράγαντες πόλεις πέντε (five cities named Akragas) [ΑΚΕΠ II 155.2]

There are [cities by this name] in Thrace, Euboea, Cyprus, and Aitolia . . . the ethnic term is Ἀκραγαντῖνος.

4. s.v. Ἀλεξάνδρειαι πόλεις ὀκτωκαίδεκα (eighteen cities named Alexandria) [ΑΚΕΠ II 155.2]

  The ninth one in Cyprus . . . the ethnic term is Ἀλεξανδρεύς .

5. s.v. Amathous [ΑΚΕΠ I 14.8; II 81.2; 155.2]

  A very ancient city of Cyprus. There Adonis Osiris, whom the Cypriots and Phoenicians identify as Egyptian, was honored. Named from Amathous, son of Herakles, or from Amathousa, mother of Kinyras.

6. s.v. Amamassos [ΑΚΕΠ II 86; 155.2]

  A city of Cyprus, where Apollo Hylates is worshipped. The ethnic terms are Ἀμαμάσσιος and Ἀμαμασσεύς.

7. s.v. Arsinoe [ΑΚΕΠ II 155.2]

  A city in Libya . . . the seventh, which previously was called Marion, in Cyprus . . . the ethnic terms are Ἀρσινοΐτης and Ἀρσινοεύς.

8. s.v. Asine [ΑΚΕΠ II 155.2]

  A city in Laconia, named after Asine, the daughter of Lakedaimon . . . the third one on Cyprus . . . the ethnic terms are Ἀσιναῖος and Ἀσινεύς.

9. s.v. Asphax [ΑΚΕΠ I 8.1]

  A race which settled in Cyprus.

10. s.v. Aphrodisias [ΑΚΕΠ II 155.2]

  A city on Cilicia . . . the tenth one in Cyprus . . . the ethnic term is Ἀφροδισιεύς.

11. s.v. Golgoi [ΑΚΕΠ I 28; II 25; 155.2]

  A city in Cyprus, from Golgos, who was the leader of the settlers from Sikyon. It is also called Golgion, in the neuter, whence Aphrodite is called Golgia. The ethnic terms are Γόλγιος, Γολγία, and Γολγηίς.

12. s.v. Dionia [AKEΠ II 155.2]

A city which Theopompus [of Chios] counts among the cities of Cyprus in the fifteenth book of his *Philippica* [*FHG* I 299, fr. 127; *FGrH* IIB 115, fr.115] The ethnic term is Διωνιᾶται, as in Κυδωνιᾶται.

13. s.v. Erythrai [AKEΠ II 155.2]

A city in Ionia . . . there are others [by that name] in Boeotia and in Cyprus; the latter is now called Paphos. The citizen is called Ἐρυθραῖος.

14. s.v. Erystheia [AKEΠ II 87; 155.2]

A city in Cyprus where Apollo Hylates is worshipped. Dionysios [Periegetes] writes in the third book of his *Bassarika*, "And they held the abode of the god Apollo Hylates, Tembros, Erystheia, and Amamassos by the sea."

15. s.v. Idalion [AKEΠ I 27; II 155.2]

A city of Cyprus. An oracle was given . . . to build a city where he saw the sun rising. Chalkenor, then, traveled about, and one of those with him said, "O King, I saw the sun (εἶδον ἅλιον)," whereby the city is named. The ethnic term is Ἰδαλιεύς.

16. s.v. Karpasia [AKEΠ I 11.5; II 155.2]

A city of Cyprus, which Pygmalion founded, according to Hellanicus [of Lesbos, ca. 480–395 B.C.] in his *Kypriaka* [*FHG* I 65, fr. 147; *FGrH* IA 4, fr. 57]. But Dionysios [Periegetes], in Book 3 of his *Bassarika,* spells it with a diphthong: "and all those who . . . Κινύρεια and lofty Κραπάσεια." And Xenagoras [Περὶ νήσων; *FHG* IV 527, fr.11; *FGrH* IIB 240, fr.34] calls it Κάρπαθος. But Demetrios of Salamis [*Kypriaka*; *FHG* IV 382; *FGrH* IIIC 756, fr.1] calls it Καρβασία, because he thinks that it is located in (the way of) the wind called κάρβα. The citizen is called Καρπασεώτης, as in Μαρσεώτης, and the possessive forms are Καρπασεωτικός and Καρπασεωτική. But Theopompus in the tenth book [of his *Philippica*; *FHG* I 293, fr. 93; *FGrH* IIB 115, fr. 19] calls them Καρπασεῖς, perhaps from Κάρπασος . . . and Καρπάσεια from that.

17. s.v. Koroneia [AKEΠ II 155.2]

A city in Boeotia . . . the fourth one in Cyprus . . . the fifth city is Korone of the Salaminians. The citizen is called Κορώνιος and Κορωνεύς. But at Κορώνεια they say Κορωνιεύς and at Κορώνη (they say) Κορωναεύς.

18. Korone [ΑΚΕΠ II 155.2]

A city in Messene . . . there is also Κορώνη, a section of Salamis in Cyprus.

19. s.v. Kourion [ΑΚΕΠ I 14.19; II 155.2]

A city of Cyprus, from Koureous, the son of Kinyras. Herodotus, Book 5 [*Histories* 5.113]. The ethnic term is Κουριεύς. And Aristokles was a Κουριεύς. The feminine form is Κουριάς, and so is the country. There is also a city [by this name] in Aitolia.

20. s.v. Kresion [ΑΚΕΠ II 155.2]

A city in Cyprus. Theopompus [of Chios] (mentions it) in the 15th book of his *Philippica* [*FHG* I 299, fr. 128; *FGrH* IIB 115, fr. 116]. The ethnic term is Κρησιεύς, as in Σουνιεύς.

21. s.v. Cyprus [ΑΚΕΠ II 149.4]

A large and very renowned island located in the Gulf of Pamphylia. Thus says the geographer Dionysios [Periegetes; Οἰκουμένης Περιήγησις or *Orbis Descriptio* 508–509]: "Cyprus [lies] in the east of the Gulf of Pamphylia." It was so named from Kypros, the daughter of Kinyras, or of Byblos and Aphrodite, as Philostephanos [of Cyrene, 3rd c. B.C.] has reported in his *On Islands* [*FHG* III 30, fr.11] and Istros ["the Callimachean," 3rd c. B.C.] in *On The Settlements of the Egyptians* [*FHG* I 423, fr. 39; *FGrH* IIIB 334, fr.45] or from the flower *kypros*, which grows [there]. But Astynomos [*FHG* IV 343] says that it was called Kryptos, because it is often hidden by the sea, and [only] later Cyprus. It was also called Kerastis on account of its having many heights, and Kerastias, Amathousia, Meionis, Sphekeia, and Akamantis. The ethnic terms are *Kyprios, Kypria, Kyprion, Kypriakos, Kyprieus and Kyprites.*

22. s.v. Constantia [ΑΚΕΠ II 155.2]

In Cyprus, now Salamis. The name derives from the family name Constans [actually the emperor Constantius II], . . . The ethnic term is Κωσταντειάτης. Also found with a ν [i.e. Κωνστάντεια].

23. s.v. Lakedaimon [ΑΚΕΠ II 155.2]

Most famous among the cities of the Peloponnese, formerly Sparta . . . there is another Lakedaimon in the central district of Cyprus. The citizen is called Λακεδαιμόνιος, and the possessive is Λακεδαιμονικός.

24. s.v. Lapethos [ΑΚΕΠ I 24.3; II 100; 155.2]

A city of Cyprus with anchorage and dockyards. Alexander of Ephesus [1st c. B.C. epic poet]: "Baal's Kition and lovely Lapethos." The ethnic terms are Λαπήθιος and Λαπηθεύς.

25. s.v. Marion [ΑΚΕΠ II 155.2]

A city in Cyprus, which had its name changed to Arsinoe; (the former name is derived) from Marieus. The citizen is called Μαριεύς. Hence also the proper name ὁ Κινύρου Μαριεύς (Marieus, son of Kinyras).

26. s.v. Panakra [ΑΚΕΠ II 155.2]

A mountain on Crete . . . there is also Panakron, a city in Cyprus. The ethnic term is Πανακραῖος or Πανάκριος.

27. s.v. Paphos [ΑΚΕΠ II 155.2]

A city in Cyprus. The citizens are called Πάφιοι.

28. s.v. Pegai [ΑΚΕΠ II 155.2]

A settlement of Megara. The inhabitants are called Πηγαῖοι. There is also a city by that name in Keryneia in Cyprus.

29. s.v. Sphekeia [ΑΚΕΠ I 8.1; II 149.4α]

A city of Euboea . . . So also Cyprus is called. The ethnic term is Σφήκης. Cyprus is called both Sphekeia and Kerasteia.

30. s.v. Tamasos [ΑΚΕΠ I 18.4; II 155.2]

A city in the center of Cyprus, which has a different kind of bronze . . . Hence some write, "to Tamasin for bronze," but this is unlikely.

31. s.v. Tegessos [ΑΚΕΠ II 155.2]

A city in Cyprus. Dionysios [Periegetes] (mentions it) in the third book of his *Bassarika*. The ethnic terms are Τεγήσσιος and Τεγησσεύς.

32. s.v. Tembros [ΑΚΕΠ II 88; 155.2]

A city of Cyprus in which Apollo Hylates is honored. The ethnic term is Τέμβριος.

33. s.v. Tremithous [ΑΚΕΠ II 19.1; 155.2]

A village of Cyprus. The inhabitants are called Τρεμιθούσιοι and Τρεμιθοπολῖται. They say that when Aphrodite came to this place it was shaken by a τρόμος (tremor) because of the presence of the goddess and that for this reason it has been called Tremithous. But to me it seems that it derives its name from the terebinth trees which grow around the place and which the Cypriots call τρεμίθους.

34. s.v. Hyle [ΑΚΕΠ II 85; 155.2]

A city of Cyprus in which Apollo Hylates is honored. Lycophron [*Alexandra* 447–48] (writes), "they came to Setrarchon and to the land of Hylates."

35. s.v. Chytroi [ΑΚΕΠ I 26; II 155.2]

A city of Cyprus which Xenagoras [Περὶ νήσων; *FHG* IV 527, fr. 10; *FGrH* IIB 240, fr. 27b] says was named from Chytros, son of Alexander son of Akamas. The citizen is called Χύτριος. Alexander [Polyhistor, 1st c. B.C.], writes in his book *On Cyprus* [*FHG* III 236, fr.94], "they gave Gordia [?] to the people of Chytroi," and again, "the king of the people of Chytroi married Eurynoe [?]." The ethnic term relates to the singular Χύτρος, as does Κύπριος to Κύπρος.

36. Otieis [*for* Κιττιεῖς] [ΑΚΕΠ II 155.2]

A district of Cyprus. Ephoros [of Kyme, 4th c. B.C.] writes in book 19 [of his *History*; *FHG* I 271, fr. 134; *FGrH* IIA 70, fr. 76], "the Amathousians and the Solians and the Otieis are still at war one with another."

34. HIEROKLES (first half, 6th c.)

1. *Synekdemos* 706–707 ed. Honigman [ΑΚΕΠ II 155.3. ΣΒΠΚΙ 14]

Cyprus: Constantia, Tamassos, Kition, Amathous, Kourion, Paphos, Arsinoe, Soloi, Lapethos, Keramaia, Chytroi, Karpasia, Keryneia, [Tremithous, Leukosia].

35. PROKOPIOS of Caesarea (first half, 6th c.)

1. *De Aedificiis* 5.9.34–36 [ΑΚΕΠ I 114.1; ΣΒΠΚΙ 17]

At the city of Curicum [Kourikos in Mesopotamia], he [the emperor Justinian, 527–565] restored a bath and a poor-house, the poor-house of St. Conon. He renewed the aqueduct of the same in Cyprus.
(trans. H. B. Dewing with G. Downey)

36. KOSMAS INDIKOPLEUSTES (floruit first half, 6th c.)

1. *Topographia Christiana* 2.27 [ΑΚΕΠ I 35.4]

The inhabitants of Cyprus he [Moses] calls Ketioi, and those of Rhodes, Rhodians.
(trans. J. W. McCrindle, p. 36)

2. *Topographia Christiana* 2.58

Inscription on the Tablet.

The great king, Ptolemy [III Euergetes, 246–221 B.C.] . . . having received from his father the Kingdom of Egypt and Libya and Syria and Phoenicia and Cyprus and Lycia and Caria and the Islands of the Cyclades, made an expedition into Asia.   (trans. J. W. McCrindle, p. 57)

3. *Topographia Christiana* 10.42

But, taking our leave of this author [Severianus], let us pass on to his fellow-servant, Epiphanius the Bishop—the fifth in order, to show that he also testifies to our words and is in agreement with them.

From the Work of Epiphanius, Bishop of Cyprus, *On Measures and Weights.*
                    (trans. J. W. McCrindle, p. 344)

4. *Topographia Christiana* 10.56

It is Philon then the bishop of Carpathus [better, Karpasia], who gives us the same testimony as the other six.

From the Commentary on Canticles [Song of Solomon], by Philon Bishop of Carpathus on the passage; "The King brought me into his inner chamber" [1:4].
                    (trans. J. W. McCrindle, pp. 349–50)

37. ALEXANDER THE MONK (middle, 6th c.)

1. *Laudatio in Apostolum Barnabam* 2.29 (lines 533–49 ed. van Deun) [ΑΚΕΠ I 110.29γ]

Then Barnabas entered the synagogue [in Salamis] and taught the Jews, persuading them of the Lord Jesus, that he is the Christ, the son of the living God. Filled with wrath the Jews from Syria rose up and laid hands on him and put him in a dark room of the synagogue until late evening. The lawless ones then brought him out, tortured him severely, and stoned him; and lighting a great fire they threw the body on it so that nothing of him would remain. By the providence of God the body of the apostle remained whole and the fire caused it no harm. Mark, as he was commanded, in the evening went out of the city with some of the brothers and in secret carried away the remains of Saint Barnabas. They buried them in a cave about five stadia fom the city and went away, making great lamentation for him.   (trans. P.W.W.)

2. *Laudatio in Apostolum Barnabam* 4.40–41 (lines 739–68 ed. van Deun) [ΑΚΕΠ I 110.34ε; II 163.6α]

The bishop [Anthemios of Constantia, in a dream] answered, opening his mouth, "Who are you, my Lord, who are telling me these things?" He said, "I am Barnabas, the disciple of our Lord Jesus Christ, who was separated by the Holy Spirit for the apostleship of the gentiles, with

Paul the apostle, the chosen vessel. Let this be to you a sign: Go, he said, out of the city five stadia to the west, to a place called Hygieia, for God works miracles through me in that place. Dig near the carob-tree, and you will find a cave, and a chest in it. There lies my whole body and a gospel written in my hand, which I received from Matthew the holy apostle and evangelist. And when the unrighteous charge you, claiming up and down that the apostolic throne belongs to Antioch, counter them by saying that my throne, too, is apostolic and that I have an apostle in my own country." Having said this he departed.

The bishop rose, worshipped the Lord, assembled all his holy clergy and the Christ-loving people, and went out to the place which had been shown to him, under the sign of the cross and with great preparation. Then he said a prayer and ordered that the place be dug up. When they had dug a little they found a cave closed with stones. Rolling these away they found the coffin; uncovering it they found the sacred remains of the holy and glorious apostle Barnabas, giving forth the fragrance of spiritual grace. They found also the gospel lying on his breast.

(trans. P.W.W.)

3. *Laudatio in Apostolum Barnabam* 4.44–45 (lines 818–41 ed. van Deun) [ΑΚΕΠ II 142]

The emperor [Zeno, 474–491] greatly honored Bishop [Anthemios] and sent him to Cyprus with much money and with instructions, commanding him to raise up a church to St. Barnabas the Apostle in the place where his precious body had been found. Many of the nobles also gave him money for the construction of the church.

When he had reached Cyprus and gathered a large number of craftsmen and workmen he energetically carried the construction forward. He built an exceedingly large church to the apostle, splendid in workmanship, even more splendid in the variety of its decoration, and girt round-about on the outside with buttresses. On the west wing of the church he built a large court with three stoas and from one side to the other of the court he built apartments. He ordered the monks who perform the divine services in the church to live in these apartments. He also built an aqueduct, which carried water from a far distance, and made the water come up abundantly in the middle of the court; also a beautiful cistern so that those living in the place and any visitors might have unlimited enjoyment of running water. He also built many other accommodations in the place for the refreshment of visiting strangers. One could see this place equaling in beauty a small and very pleasant city.

4. *Laudatio in Apostolum Barnabam* 4.46 (lines 844–53 ed. van Deun) [ΑΚΕΠ II 166.4]

The day of the glorious remembrance of the thrice-blessed apostle and noble martyr Barnabas they deemed to be observed every year, according to the Romans three days before the Ides of June [June 11], according to the Cypriot Constantians on the 11th of the month Mesoros (the tenth month), according to the Asianoi (the Paphians) on the 19th of Helethypaton (the ninth month), when they gather together and celebrate the spiritual services, to the glory of the Father, and of the Son, and of the Holy Spirit, because his is the glory forever and ever. Amen.

(trans. P.W.W.)

5. *De Inventione Sanctae Crucis* (Migne, *PG* 87.3, col. 4029) [ΑΚΕΠ II 166.3γ]

Our Lord Jesus Christ was born in Bethlehem of Judea, in fulfillment of the prophecy, in the 33rd year of the reign of Herod, the son of Antipater [37–4 B.C.], eight days before the Calends of January [December 25]. But Epiphanios, the great and holy bishop of the Cypriots, contradicts emphatically, saying that the true birth of our Lord Jesus Christ by Mary, the holy Mother of God and forever Virgin, took place eight days before the Ides of January [January 6]. But all the other teachers of the holy, catholic, and apostolic church, wise in the things of God, as if with one voice, affirm that Christ's birthday is eight days before the Calends of January.

38. JUSTINIAN I (527–565)

1. *Novellae* 8 (pp. 80 and 82 ed. Schoell and Kroll) [ΣΒΠΚΙ 16.1]

A record of the amounts due to be paid by each of the subordinate provinces, by reason of long tradition; and let no one of those who govern these provinces presume either to take or to give more than has been prescribed . . .

13. From the province of Cyprus thus:
    to the honorable *chartularii* of the sacred chamber: 9 *solidi.*
    to the chief of the renowned *tribuni notarii* : 24 *solidi.*
    to his assistant: 3 *solidi.*
    to the office of the illustrious praetorian prefects: 40 *solidi.*

2. *Novellae* 41 (pp. 262–63 ed. Schoell and Kroll) [ΣΒΠΚΙ 16.2]

An order to Bonus, quaestor of the army, directing to whom legal appeals from the five provinces of Caria, Cyprus, the Cycladic Islands, Mysia, and Scythia are to be addressed.

The same emperor Justinian to the excellent Bonus, quaestor of the army.

Preamble: We note that we have recently issued an executive order by which we have placed under the control of your excellence these five provinces: Caria, Cyprus, the Cycladic Islands, Mysia, and Scythia, i.e. they shall be subject to your excellence. Furthermore we have ordered that legal appeals, too, in the provinces enumerated no longer be directed to our distinguished governors but to your excellence. Many from Caria, Rhodes, and Cyprus have approached us and complained of often being forced to travel, even during the winter, to Scythia and Mysia, where you reside, and there to file their appeals, perhaps not even involving large amounts, and to take the risk of crossing large seas and entering regions troubled by the barbarians. Therefore we have decided to issue the following directive to your excellence: suits from the neighboring provinces of Scythia and Mysia are to be heard by your excellence itself; but those from Caria, the islands mentioned, and Cyprus (i.e. those which previously were administered by our distinguished prefects and upon our sacred order passed on to the provincial governor) are also to be addressed to you when you are staying in the capital and to be heard by you together with the quaestor of our sacred palace in the sacred *auditorium,* as the law passed concerning appeals provides, but when you yourself are in Scythia and Mysia appeals are to be addressed to whoever is taking your place in this blessed city.

39. JOHN LYDOS (490–ca. 565?)

1. *De Mensibus* 4.47 [ΑΚΕΠ II 113]

In Cyprus I found a book of this Hebrew Sibyl [Sambethe], which contains many prophecies also concerning Greek affairs. Even concerning Homer, that God will raise up a wise man who will record the war of the heroes and sing the noblest of them. She prophesies also concerning Christ and the things that happened after his coming. And indeed about the things which will happen at the end of the world. Among other things she prophesies some disasters concerning Cyprus and Antioch, that the one will fall in war and never rise again and that the other will become a submerged island. For she says:

> Unhappy Antioch, people will never call you a city
> when you fall by your follies under the spears.

And as follows:

> Alas, poor Cyprus, a huge wave will overpower you
> with wintry storms and a stirred-up sea.

This Sibyl antedates the coming of Christ by 2000 years, and yet hers is this word predicting the holy cross: O blessed wood on which God was spread out.

2. *De Mensibus* 4.64 [ΑΚΕΠ II 4.2]

Euripides [*Troades* 989–90] asserts that she is named Aphrodite because she deprives lovers of their senses. But Chrysippus [*SVF* II 1098] maintains that she is named not Dione but Didone, because she gives [διδόναι] the pleasures of procreation, and Cypris because she grants conception, and similarly Cythereia because she gives conception not only to men but also to the beasts. Therefore Hermes [Trismegistos] says in his *Creation of the World* that those parts of Aphrodite's body which are above the waist are male, but those which are below the waist are female. Therefore the Pamphylians say that Aphrodite once had a beard. They assert that she was begotten from the loins of Kronos, that is from time, but the nature of these things is timeless and imperishable. To have sexual intercourse is called *venizai* by the people. But Plato [*Symposium* 180d] holds that there are two Aphrodites, a heavenly one and a popular one, and that the one belongs to the gods, the other to men. Other poets hold that there are four: one born from Ouranos [Sky] and Hemera [Day], the second one from foam (Eros was born by her and Hermes), the third one from Zeus and Dione (by her and Ares, it is said, Anteros was born), and the fourth one who hails from Syria and Cyprus and is called Astarte.

3. *De Mensibus* 4.65 [ΑΚΕΠ II 48.3]

In Cyprus people covered with fleeces used to make a common sacrifice to Aphrodite of a sheep—this kind of sacrifice came to Cyprus from Corinth—and then they used to sacrifice to her wild boars because of the treacherous attack on Adonis; this [used to take place] four days before the Nones of April, that is on the second day of April.

4. *De Magistratibus Populi Romani* 2.29 [ΑΚΕΠ II 149.5. ΣΒΠΚΙ 15]

He (Justinian) instituted, therefore, as I have just said, a prefect as overseer of the Scythian forces, having set aside for him three provinces, which were almost the most prosperous of all: Kerastis (it is called now Cyprus, having had its name changed in consequence of Cypris, who, according to legend, had been honored there), all of Caria, and the Ionian islands.

(trans. A. C. Bandy)

40. MALALAS, JOHN (ca. 490–570s)

1. *Chronographia* 1 (pp. 14–15 ed. Dindorf)

The regions allotted to Sem are the following . . . and also the islands of Sardinia, Crete, and Cyprus.

2. *Chronographia* 5 (p.102 ed. Dindorf) [ΑΚΕΠ I 15]

They [the Hellenes] . . . appointed others in his [Achilles'] place—Teukros, the brother of Aias Telamonios, and Idomeneus. These captured Cyprus, Isauria and Lykia, and plundered and destroyed them.

(trans. E. Jeffreys, M. Jeffreys, and R. Scott)

3. *Chronographia* 5 (p.122 ed. Dindorf) [ΑΚΕΠ I 20.7]

Teukros, the brother of Aias Telamonios, arrived soon after, coming from Salamis, a city in Cyprus, to help his brother. He found Pyrrhos and learnt from him what had happened.

(trans. E. Jeffreys, M. Jeffreys, and R. Scott)

4. *Chronographia* 5 (p. 132 ed. Dindorf) [ΑΚΕΠ I 20.7]

Standing up, Teukros embraced Pyrrhos and asked him if he might take with him the sons of Aias, his brother, that is Aiantides, his child by Glauke, Aias' first wife, and Eurysakes, his child by Tekmessa, and Tekmessa herself. Pyrrhos granted them to him. Teukros took them and set sail for Salamis.

(trans. E. Jeffreys, M. Jeffreys, and R. Scott)

5. *Chronographia* 8 (pp. 201–202 ed. Dindorf) [ΑΚΕΠ I 7.1]

He [Seleucus I Nicator, 358–281 B.C.] also brought down from the acropolis the Cretans whom Kasos, the son of Inachos, had left to live up there. They had migrated to Antioch with the Cypriots, since the emperor Kasos married Amyke, also known as Kitia, daughter of Salaminos, emperor of Cyprus. Cypriots came with her and made their homes on the acropolis.

(trans. E. Jeffreys, M. Jeffreys, and R. Scott)

6. *Chronographia* 12 (p. 313 ed. Dindorf) [ΑΚΕΠ I 129.7; ΣΒΠΚΙ 18]

In his [Constantius'] reign [337–361] the city of Salamias in Cyprus suffered from the wrath of God, and the greater part of the city was plunged into the sea by an earthquake. The remainder was levelled to the ground [342]. Constantius restored it and gave many extremely generous gifts, undertook buildings and remitted taxes from the surviving citizens for four years. As he provided a variety of buildings for what was previously known as Salamias, it had its name changed from that time to Constantia. It is now the metropolis of Cyprus.

(trans. E. Jeffreys, M. Jeffreys, and R. Scott)

41. VITA OF ST. TYCHON by St. John the Almoner (ca. 610)

1. 1 (p. 229 ed. Delehaye) [ΑΚΕΠ I 133]

Tychon, our holy father and miracle worker, was born of pious Christian parents, who consecrated him to God, trained him in the scriptures, and destined him to recite the holy readings in church. Earnestly striving to do good deeds, he became an admirable servant of God and was ordained a priest by the holy bishop Epiphanios. Now his father was a baker, who sent him out when he was a boy to sell loaves of bread . . . When his father had died and he was left with his mother he sold all his assets and distributed [the proceeds] to the poor; then, having rid himself of the cares of the world, he took upon himself the yoke of Christ.

2. 2 (pp. 229–30 ed. Delehaye) [ΑΚΕΠ I 132; 133.2; II 97.1]

Mnemonios, the holy bishop of Amathous, gladly received him in his church, ordained him a deacon, and told him to administer the affairs of the church. He refuted the godless and foolish beliefs of the pagans and the Jews. Teaching them, admonishing them, and conversing with them, he brought most of them to the bishop and made them worthy to receive holy baptism. And when Bishop Mnemonios died the people chose St. Tychon as the bishop of Amathous. And he enlightened the church by the word of God and caused those who believe in Christ to emulate him. He turned most of the pagans from the worship of idols to the worship of Christ. But when some remained in error and were making sacrifices on the altars at the temple of the idols the saint went and by the power of God overthrew their abominations. Taking a scourge in his hands, he forcefully drove out the priestess of Artemis, whose name was Miaranathousa and who had offended him. And she understood the power of Christ which was upon the saint, marveled at it, and accepted God and our master, the Lord Jesus Christ. Then Tychon baptized her and changed her name to Euetheia.

3. 3 (p. 230 ed. Delehaye) [ΑΚΕΠ I 133.2; II 12.15α; 14.1; 146]

Some pagans, both men and women, carrying an image of Cypris [Aphrodite], torches, and vessels of incense, were passing close by the holy church, reveling and dancing. When St.

Tychon became aware of them he went out with his clergy, smashed the image, and explained their error. Then he taught them by the word of God and persuaded them to abandon their impious ways and to come to Christ. And he baptized them and counted them among the flock of Christ. And a great many who were possessed by daemons he healed and those who were making plots against him he pacified. But Kalykios and Cleopatra, who were practicing paganism, wrote up an unjust complaint against the saint and submitted it to the governor. They complained that he had destroyed their supposedly sacred image, had insulted their other gods, and had destroyed their sanctuaries; furthermore that he had anointed with oil and baptized with water pagan men and women and had, supposedly, treated them disrespectfully; and there were numerous other complaints as well. Making such claims, the pagans brought the saint before the governor. But he took courage in the faith of Christ and courageously explained to them the meaning of the holy gospel, pointing out the filth of the images and telling them that the Aphodrite of Paphos on Cyprus had been buried. And then he brought many others to God through the power of his teaching.

4. 7 (p. 232 ed. Delehaye)

The vita of this venerable man has been written by John the Almsgiver, holy archbishop of Alexandria [610–619], who is himself a Cypriot. Through the intercession of St. Tychon, o Christ our God, grant us your abundant mercy, because you are blessed forever and ever.

42. SERGIOS, archbishop of Cyprus (643)

1. Letter to Pope Theodore I (642–649) (Mansi X, col. 913)

To the lord Theodore, most holy, blessed, and beloved of God, Father of Fathers, archbishop and universal patriarch, Sergios humbly sends greetings in the Lord.
[Note: The letter rejects monotheletism and affirms the dual nature of Christ.]

43. SIMOKATTES, THEOPHYLAKTOS (first half, 7th c.)

1. *Historiae* 3.15. 15 [ΣΒΠΚΙ 21]

When they had taken 100,000 Persians prisoner, the men of the army gave one third of these to the Roman general Maurice [to become emperor in 582] and thus made the wages of war not incurable [578]. The general reported the presence of the prisoners to the Caesar [Tiberios, to become emperor later in 578], but the Caesar distributed the booty in Cyprus.

44. VITA OF ST. AUXIBIOS (first half, 7th c.)

1. 3–6 [ΑΚΕΠ Ι 111]

3. Auxibios came from the great city of Rome. His parents were wealthy and of the pagan religion . . . His father educated him in all the wisdom of the world.

4. When he had reached his majority his parents wanted him to get married. But he, having an inspired mind, perfect reasoning, and a virtuous life, objected. For he had heard of Christ and had a desire to become a Christian.

5. . . . And when he had strengthened his resolve, without having told anyone, when a few days had passed, he secretly left his parents, went down to the harbor, and found a ship which was about to sail to parts east . . .

6. Having set sail from Rome they reached Rhodes in a few days. From there they crossed the sea of Pamphylia, came to Cyprus, and landed at a village called Limne [Limnetes], about four milestones from the city of Soloi; providence had guided the blessed man [Auxibios] to the end that many souls might be saved. And when he had left the ship he spent some time in Limne to recuperate from the voyage.

2. 7 [ΑΚΕΠ I 110. 29α]

It came to pass that Barnabas, the apostle of Christ, came to Cyprus on his second journey; this was after he and Paul had parted company [Acts 15:36–39], in person, but not in heart. He took Mark with him, and they landed at Lapithos. Traversing the entire island, they came to Salamis, now Constantia, as Mark reports. There they found Herakleides, the archbishop of the island, and when they had recognized him they taught him how he must proclaim the gospel of Christ, establish churches, and appoint priests for them. Then they bid him farewell and dismissed him in peace. When Barnabas had completed his course and fought the good fight of faith [cf. 2 Timothy 4:7] and had obtained the crown of martyrdom in Constantia the lawless Jews sought to destroy Mark. He fled from them and they pursued him as far as Ledra [Leukosia]. There he found a cave, entered it, hid for three days, and then left that place. When he had crossed the mountains he came to Limnetes. Timon and Rhodon were with him.

3. 8–9 [ΑΚΕΠ I 110.30; II 93.12]

8. When they [Mark, Timon, and Rhodon] had reached the village [Limnetes], they found there the blessed Auxibios, who had recently arrived from Rome, and they met by chance. Mark asked Auxibios, "From what city do you come?" And he answered, "From the great city of Rome, and I have come here to become a Christian." And the apostle, seeing that Auxibios had the desire to come unto Christ and was a faithful and learned man, instructed him sufficiently and taught him the word of God concerning the truth; then, when he came upon a spring, he baptized him in the name of the Father and of the Son and of the Holy Ghost. And after Auxibios had been baptized Mark put his hands upon him and bestowed the Holy Ghost upon him. Then he ordained him a bishop, taught him how he must proclaim the gospel of Christ , and sent him to the city of Soloi . . . But Mark found an Egyptian ship, boarded it, and came to Alexandria; there he continued to preach the gospel and to teach concerning the kingdom of God.

9. . . . But the blessed Auxibios left Limnetes and went on his way. When he had inquired he came to Soloi. There, near the gates of the city, towards the west, was a temple of Zeus, whom the people falsely believed to be a god, and the priest lived in it.

4. 13–14 [ΑΚΕΠ I 110.33; II 133; 93.12α]

13. When Paul had learned that Barnabas had departed this life and that there was none of the apostles in Cyprus to teach and proclaim Christ he immediately sent Epaphras and Tychikos and some others to Cyprus to Herakleides, the archbishop of the island, writing to him that he should install Epaphras as bishop in Paphos and Tychikos in Neapolis. He wrote, "In each city install others. Go also to the city of Soloi and seek out in it a Roman by name of Auxibios. Appoint him in Soloi, but take care not to place your hands on him to ordain him, because he has already been found worthy of the priesthood and been ordained by Mark."
14. When the blessed Herakleides had received and had read the letter sent to him by the apostles he at once without hesitation did what had been commanded him. And when he had come to to the city of Soloi and was seeking out the blessed Auxibios the place where he dwelt was pointed out to him. When he had passed outside the city and had come to the so-called place of Zeus he found him there . . . Then St. Herakleides, taking the venerable father Auxibios with him, went into the city, said a prayer, and marked the plan of the church on the ground in an outline, a large church by the grace of Christ. And when he had taught the whole canon of the church, just as it had been taught to him by the apostles, he entrusted him [Auxibios] to the Lord, bade him farewell, and returned to his own city.

5. 17 [ΑΚΕΠ I 111.2]

There was a certain man, named Auxibios, from the village which is called Salapotamias. He, having heard about the blessed Auxibios, his teaching, and his virtue, came to him, cast himself at his feet, and begged him, "Father, give me the seal [of baptism] in Christ." And he [St. Auxibios] took him [Auxibios of Salapotamias], taught him from the divine scriptures all the things about the Father, the Son, and the Holy Spirit, and baptized him in the name of the consubstantial Trinity. And Auxibios of Salapotamias remained with the venerable Father Auxibios all the time of his life, being taught by him.

6. 21 [ΑΚΕΠ I 111.1; II 143]

When the grace of God was upon the city of Soloi and almost all its inhabitants were believing in our Lord Jesus Christ through the teaching of our holy Father [Auxibios] with the help of the Holy Spirit, he recognized that the church was too small to accommodate all comers and considered building a larger one in the name of God; so, kneeling in prayer, he asked that God might assist him. He rose, said a prayer, drew up the plan of the holy church, and, with God's approval and help, raised up this large and admirable temple, the holy catholic church, having adorned it with all manner of embellishment, as a gift to Christ, our God.

7. 24 [ΑΚΕΠ I 111.2]

Having put all things in good order, having become a herald of the truth, having honored his priesthood for fifty years, more or less, and having baptized many in the faith in Christ, he at last reached the end of his life . . . When he had said these things and many more he took the holy Auxibios, his disciple, bade him farewell, and said, "God has chosen you to be a priest. You will be the shepherd over the flock of Christ, which he has acquired through his blood."

45. LEONTIOS of Neapolis (Cyprus) (first half, 7th c.)

Life of St. John the Almoner (Eleemon), after 641 (with parts by Sophronios and John Moschos)

1. 2 (pp. 321–22 trans. Festugière; p.199 trans. Dawes and Baynes)

This renowned light of the Church [St. John the Almoner, patriarch of Alexandria 611–619) and great father among saints was the noble offspring and precious nursling of the island of the Cyprians, and was descended not from ignoble or ordinary ancestors, but from those of an illustrious family and of brilliant renown.

For John's father, Epiphanius by name, did so many conspicuous and remarkable things in his life in accordance, we may say, with his name that he was chosen by the rulers of that time to be entrusted with the reins of government in the island of the Cyprians. And we may, I think, reasonably suppose that his wife, I mean the mother of our wonderful John, had like her husband her share of good fortune and distinction.

(trans. E. Dawes and N. H. Baynes)

2. 13 (p. 328 trans. Festugière; pp. 205–206 trans. Dawes and Baynes)

On hearing of the wholesale devastation of the Roman realm by the Persians John decided to go to the Emperor [Herakleios, 610–641] and open negotiations for peace. But, although he had drawn up his farewell speech and read it to all, the people of the city would not allow him to leave. After the Persian armies had utterly laid waste the whole of Syria, Phoenicia and Arabia and various cities besides, these sinners threatened to take even Alexandria itself. And then the holy man, having found out by God's help, that a murderous plot was being hatched against him, sailed away to his native country, Cyprus.

Now a general, one Aspagurius by name, had been sent to Constantia in Cyprus but had not been admitted by the town; so he prepared himself for war against its citizens and they on their side were arming themselves against him. And they were just on the point of engaging in this slaughter of each other when the all-admirable John, the disciple of the God of Peace, intervened and induced both parties to seek reconciliation and succeeded in bringing them to terms.

(trans. E. Dawes and N. H. Baynes)

3. 15 (pp. 328–29 trans. Festugière; p. 206 trans. Dawes and Baynes)

Isaac who was general at that time betrayed the city of the Alexandrians (to the Persians) and then fled for refuge to Cyprus [619]. There he found the most holy Patriarch (Papas) and formed a murderous intrigue against him, intending to kill him on the Monday before Palm Sunday. The divine man was informed of this and therefore stayed at home and received nobody, and thus by God's providence he was miraculously saved from this deadly attack. But the author of this plot, the miserable Isaac, by the just judgment of the unsleeping providence of God was savagely set upon by some men and murdered on the very day on which he had planned death against the righteous Patriarch.

John, the all-holy Patriarch (Papas), when he had arrived at Constantia paid reverent worship to the relics of the saints there, namely, Barnabas, the all-praiseworthy apostle, and Epiphanius, the great miracle-worker, and afterwards went on to Amathus and it was from there that he departed to be with his beloved Lord [November 11, 619].

(trans. E. Dawes and N. H. Baynes)

4. Supplement 8 (p. 15 ed. Gelzer; p. 351 ed. Festugière; p. 450 trans. Festugière; p. 215 trans. Dawes and Baynes) [ΣΒΠΚΙ 20.1.1]

When I [John] was in Cyprus and was but a stripling of about fifteen years old, I saw one day in my sleep a certain maiden whose countenance outshone the sun and who was adorned beyond all human imagining, and she came and stood by my bed and touched me on the side.

(trans. E. Dawes and N. H. Baynes)

5. Supplement 22 (p. 40 ed. Gelzer; p. 368 ed. Festugière) [ΣΒΠΚΙ 20.1.2]

They had, he says, a certain servant in Cyprus at my disposal, quite faithful and unmarried until his end.

6. Supplement 25 (pp. 52–53 ed. Gelzer; p. 375–76 ed. Festugière; pp. 480–81 trans. Festugière; p. 235 trans. Dawes and Baynes)

He [John] told the following story: 'A short time ago,' he said, 'a man was captured by the Persians, and when taken to Persia was confined in the dungeon called Lethe. Some other prisoners who escaped and reached Cyprus were asked by his parents whether they had seen him by any chance; to which they replied: "We buried him with our own hands." But that was not really the man about about whom they were questioned, but another exactly like him. They also told the parents the month and the day of his death, and so the latter had prayers said three times a year for him whom they presumed to be dead.

'Four years later he escaped from the Persians and returned to Cyprus. Then his relatives said, "We heard for certain, brother, that you were dead and therefore we held memorial services for you three times a year."' (trans. E. Dawes and N. H. Baynes)

7. Supplement 44B (pp. 90–92 ed. Gelzer; p. 402–403 ed. Festugière; pp. 515–16 trans. Festugière; p. 255 trans. Dawes and Baynes) [ΣΒΠΚΙ 20.2.1 and 20.2.2]

When by God's permission, or rather because of our sins, Alexandria was on the point of being betrayed to the impious Persians [619] the shepherd, recalling our Lord's words: 'When they drive you out of this city, flee into the next' [Matthew 10:23], was going to flee to his native country, Cyprus, where was the city in which he was born.   So the patrician, Nicetas, seizing upon this favourable opportunity said to the holy man: 'I beseech you, if I have found grace in your sight, deign to take the trouble of travelling to the Queen of Cities [Constantinople] and grant to our most pious sovereigns your acceptable prayers.'   The Patriarch, yielding to his friend's great faith, agreed to his suggestion, for God wished to show His purpose and the great honour in which He held the blessed Patriarch . . .

When continuing their course they had reached Rhodes, the Saint whom God had called saw with his waking eyes a eunuch in gleaming apparel, a golden sceptre in his right hand, standing by him and saying: "Come, I beg you, the King of Kings is asking for you!'   Without delay he forthwith sent for the patrician, Nicetas, and said to him with many tears: 'You, my master, called me to go to our earthly king, but the heavenly King has anticipated you and has summoned to Himself my humbleness.'   He then related to him the vision which he had just seen of the eunuch, or rather of the angel.

The most glorious patrician heard his words with mixed sorrow and joy, but did not attempt to hinder the holy man, but, after richly receiving of his holy prayers, and having treasured them up for the Emperors, with great respect he encouraged him to return to Cyprus.

(trans. E. Dawes and N. H. Baynes)

8. Supplement 45 (pp. 92–94 ed. Gelzer; p. 404–405 ed. Festugière; pp. 517–19 trans. Festugière; pp. 256–57 trans. Dawes and Baynes) [ΣΒΠΚΙ 20.3]

As soon as he reached his own city, Amathus by name, he bade those who ministered to him to draw up his will with all speed . . .

After he had yielded up and commended his soul to the hand of the Lord . . . his revered body was to be laid to rest reverently and with fitting ecclesiastical rites in the oratory of the miracle-worker St. Tychon.

(trans. E. Dawes and N. H. Baynes)

9. Supplement 46 (pp. 100–102 ed. Gelzer; pp. 408–409 ed. Festugière; p. 523 trans. Festugière; pp. 260–61 trans. Dawes and Baynes)

And when some folk arrived from Cyprus, those living in Alexandria asked about the Saint's translation and found that the vision was true, as it had come at the very hour in which the blessed man had died . . .

Some considerable time after the holy man's falling asleep the yearly service of the song was being held in the church of St. Tychon (of whom I have previously spoken) where the revered body of the most blessed Patriarch John was laid to rest; it was the solemn all-night service of psalm-singing held yearly in remembrance of the miracle-working St. Tychon . . .

And let not anyone of you, my Christ-loving readers, refuse to believe this great miracle, for to the present day in this Christ-loving island of the Cyprians this wonderful grace of God can be seen at work in the bodies of various saints.

(trans. E. Dawes and N. H. Baynes)

46. GEORGE of Alexandria (first half, 7th c.)

1. Life of St. John Chrysostom (*Auct.* 873bd) 40–41 (pp. 190–91) ed. Halkin

40. . . . Theophilos [of Alexandria] sent letters to the bishops in every city, hiding his true purpose and pretending only to criticize the books of Origen, the very books which before him Athanasios had often cited in his writings against the Arians as witnesses of the true faith. He professed friendship for Epiphanios, the blessed bishop of Constantia on the island of Cyprus, a saintly man, who had guided his church for thirty-six years, but denounced him to Damasus [pope 366–384] and the blessed Siricius [pope 384–399] as a heretic and a deceiver and quarreled with him in the past for not paying attention to the books of Origen but discarding them. For Theophilos, because of his hostility towards the others, denied in public what he thought. Then he befriended Epiphanios, expressing regrets and pretending to be reconciled to him, and prevailed upon him to convene a council of the bishops of Cyprus for the purpose of condemning the books of Origen. And Epiphanios, because of his excessive piety, was quickly convinced by Theophilos' letter. He convened a council of the bishops on the island and forbade them to read such books. He also sent a letter to John advising him to refrain from reading the books of Origen, to convene a council of the bishops serving under him, and to agree to this. Then Theophilos, having won over Epiphanios, a man renowned for his piety, and knowing that his cause was advancing, became bold, assembled many bishops, and, along with Epiphanios, maligned the books of Origen, who had died about two-hundred years ago [actually in 254]. But this was not his chief purpose; rather he was anxious to revenge himself against the followers of Dioskoros [bishop of Hermopolis].

41. But John paid no attention to the things communicated to him by Epiphanios and by Theophilos himself and focused on teaching the churches, and in this he was very successful. But of the mischief done to him he made no mention. [cf. Socrates, *Historia Ecclesiastica* 6.10]

2. Life of St. John Chrysostom (*Auct.* 873bd) 43–44 (pp. 198–202) ed. Halkin

43. This chapter has been taken verbatim from Socrates, *Historia Ecclesiastica* 6.12 and 14, q.v.

44. When the empress [Eudoxia] learned of the trouble between Epiphanios and John she summoned Epiphanios and said to him, "Father Epiphanios, as you are well aware, the whole Roman empire is in my hand. Look, I will give you this day the priesthood over the churches in the empire, if you will listen to my words and heal the pain which I suffer in my soul." And the great Epiphanios replied, "Speak, my daughter, and I shall do all in my power for the edification and salvation of your soul." Then, when she believed that he would play along and dance to her tune, she said, "Since this John has become unworthy of the priesthood, is acting disrespectfully towards the emperors, is denying to me the honor that is due me, and reportedly adheres for a long time to some heresy contrary to our doctrine, my thinking has been for some time to hold a council, to declare him unworthy of the priesthood, and to place on the throne in his stead another man, one capable of holding the priesthood, so that the empire may be at peace everywhere from now on." When the empress spoke these things to Epiphanios she became very emotional about it. Then she spoke to him again, "Since your holiness is here with the help of God, there is no need then to trouble the other fathers and to bring them here. Thus, appoint as bishop whomever God reveals to you. But cast John out of the church, and I shall see to it that all will obey you." Epiphanios responded, "My daughter, listen patiently to your father." And she said, "Tell me, Father, what you desire, and I shall in every way tend to my father." Then the great Epiphanios said to her, "If John is guilty of the heresy of which you speak and does not acknowledge his

error and repent, he is unworthy of the priesthood, and we shall do what you order. But if you seek to oust John from the church because he has offended you, then Epiphanios does not approve of it. Especially so, my daughter, because it is given to kings to be offended and to forgive, since you, too, have a king in heaven, against whom you sin habitually and who forgives you, as is written in the holy gospels. Be merciful, as your father in heaven is merciful" [Luke 6:36]. But the empress replied to Epiphanios, "If you will stand in the way of John being exiled I shall open the temples of the idols and make them be worshipped by the people. And the last will become worse than the first" [Matthew 12:45]. And as she bitterly spoke these things she poured forth tears from her eyes. But Epiphanios said, "I have no part of this judgement." And with these words he departed from the palace.

And a rumor circulated through the entire city to the effect that the great Epiphanios, priest and bishop of the island of Cyprus, had gone to the empress and had brought about the banishment of John. And John took a tablet and wrote to Epiphanios, "Wise Epiphanios, have you agreed to my exile? You will no longer sit on your throne." Similarly Epiphanios wrote back to John, "Athlete, be beaten and win. You will not reach the place to which you have been exiled." But let no one attach blame to Epiphanios in this matter. For a man who had done so many good deeds would not descend to such depths of evil and without cause deprive the world of such a light. Nevertheless both men came to this end. For Epiphanios did not reach Cyprus alive, as he died on his way on board his ship. And John was driven from his throne a little later and did not reach the place of his second exile, as the next chapter will show.

47. THEODORE of Paphos (12 December 655)

Panegyric of St. Spyridon

1. Prologue (pp. 6–7 ed. van den Ven) [AKEΠ I 121.5]

His (Spyridon's) life truly shone forth through the grace of the Holy Spirit which dwelt in him and walked with him, and he became known to all the inhabitants of the island of Cyprus, because of his virtuous life, as was already mentioned, and also to all the world, as will shortly be pointed out.

2. Prologue (pp. 7–8 ed. van den Ven) [AKEΠ I 121.2]

He (Spyridon) acquired such a virtuous life and attained such a height of perfect self-control, through the grace and the power of the Holy Spirit that, rightly through the righteous will of God, he was the first to be found worthy to be entrusted with the helm of the holy church of the city of Tremithous. And he proved himself to be an excellent shepherd of the spiritual flock of Christ and a worthy bishop, offering a bloodless sacrifice to God for the misdeeds of the people. This was at the time of Constantine the Great, who was a man of great faith and the first emperor of the Christians, pious, and a lover of Christ.

3. 1 (p. 10 ed. van den Ven) [ΑΚΕΠ I 129]

After our holy and reverend Father Spyridon had been ordained bishop of the holy church of God at Tremithous, there occurred a great drought and consequently a great famine was expected in the country of the Cypriots.

4. 2 (p. 11 ed. van den Ven) [ΑΚΕΠ I 129α]

When there was a famine on the island, the dealers and distributors of grain created hardships for the people.

5. 6 (pp. 27–28 ed. van den Ven) [ΑΚΕΠ I 121.6]

In the days of Constantine I . . . the holy Council of Nicaea was held, in the consulship of Paulinus and Julian [325], on the twentieth of May of the fourteenth indiction . . . 318 fathers were gathered with the pious emperor Constantine in the city of Nicaea. . . . Among them was also Spyridon, with whom this account is concerned, the servant of God and miracle-worker.

6. 6 (p. 30 ed. van den Ven)

He (Spyridon) did not hold back, stepped up to the man, and said to him, "In the name of Jesus Christ, philosopher, hear the teachings of the truth." And the philosopher replied, "If you would speak, I am ready to listen." And Spyridon said, "There is one God, who has fashioned heaven and earth and who has made man from earth. He has made all things, visible and invisible, subject to his Word and to the Spirit. And this Word we know to be the Son of God, whom we worship. And we believe that he was borne by a virgin for our salvation and that through the cross and his death he has freed us from eternal condemnation, and that through his resurrection he has given us eternal life. And we hope that he will come again to judge all of our deeds. Do you believe this?" [At the Council of Nicaea, 325].

7. 8 (pp. 37–43 ed. van den Ven) [ΑΚΕΠ I 121.10]

After the death of Constantine [I, 306–337], who had reigned piously, his son Constantius [II, 337–361] ruled the East and lived in the great city of Antioch and fell ill with a bodily ailment . . . And as he was earnestly praying, an angel of the Lord showed him in a nightly vision an assembly of many holy bishops . . . And he beheld among them standing two bishops, and the angel told the emperor, that they were the healers of his ailment . . . And he ordered the holy bishops from everywhere in the Roman empire to come to him. And the holy man (Spyridon) came with Triphyllios, as has been mentioned, and with his deacon, whose name was Artemidoros, and he went to the palace of the emperor . . . The emperor sat on a lofty throne and saw St. Spyridon—who was worthy of ruling with Christ—standing . . . Then he joyfully rose from his throne, paid homage to Spyridon, the servant of God, and reverently rested his head upon him. Spyridon, the miracle-worker, touched the emperor's head and at once, by the knowledge and will of God, cured the illness.

8. 11 (p. 56 ed. van den Ven) [ΑΚΕΠ II 144]

There is a certain village called Erythra, which belongs to the metropolis of Constantia, and is about thirty milestones distant from the pious, shiny metropolis. When the servant of God (Spyridon) happened to be there for some reason he entered the church to pray.

9. 14 (p. 63 ed. van den Ven) [ΑΚΕΠ I 125.2; II 160, no. 6]

Among the cities of the island of Cyprus there is one which is called Kyrenia. When our holy father Spyridon wanted to go there, for some reason, from his own city of Tremithous, he happened to pass through the city of Kythrea and to make his way through the mountain which is called Pentadaktylos. His traveling companion was Triphyllios, his own student, who already had been appointed to the bishopric of the city of Kallinikesiai, i.e. of the church of Leukosia [Nicosia]. When they were traveling and had come to the place which is called Parymne, Triphyllios the bishop was pleased by the place and because of its loveliness desired to acquire it . . . Then the holy man knew by divine inspiration the things that Triphyllios cared about and said to him, "Why do you seek in your heart to acquire fields and vineyards and why do you desire things of the earth and things that lie on the ground? We have our property in heaven, we have a home not made by hands and enduring for ever, and we have in the heavens many good things, which neither eye has seen nor ear has heard and which have not reached the heart of man. These God has prepared for those who love him. Think about these, care about these, desire these; abide in these, so that . . . you will be shown to have a share in the things which are eternal and never perish."

10. 17 (p. 77 ed. van den Ven) [ΑΚΕΠ I 125.1]

These things I have found in the book which is composed in iambic verse and is said to have been written by our holy father Triphyllios, his (Spyridon's) student, who was the bishop of the holy church of the city of Kallinikesiai or Leukosia [Nicosia].

48. ANASTASIOS SINAITES (floruit between 640 and 700)

1. Ἐρωτήσεις καὶ ἀποκρίσεις (*Quaestiones et Responsiones*) 96 (Migne, *PG* 89, col. 745) [ΣΒΠΚΙ 22]

A short time ago I was at the Dead Sea, in the area of Zoeri and Tetrapyria, where the climate is pernicious, hot, and causing things to rot, just as it is in Cyprus. And I found all the prisoners on the state farms to be Cypriots. When I was astonished and inquired as to the reason, the men in charge gave me this answer: the climate here does not accept other bodies, only from Cyprus. And often, they say, prisoners sent here from other countries have fallen ill and died within a short period of time.

49. THIRD COUNCIL OF CONSTANTINOPLE (Sixth Ecumenical Council)
(680)

1. Πρᾶξις ΙΔ´ (Mansi XI, col. 597)

The distinguished judges and the holy synod have spoken: The God-pleasing bishops of the island of Cyprus have declared that they have in their hands a book of St. Athanasios. Let those who record the proceedings of this holy synod accept this book, [which is titled] νῦν ἡ ψυχή μου τετάρακται [*Nunc anima mea turbata est*; Now my soul is perturbed], and read, so that we all might hear, the sermon contained in it.

2. Subscriptions (Mansi XI, cols. 639, 669, 673, and 688)

639. I, Theodore, by God's grace bishop of the town of Tremithous on the island of Cyprus, on behalf of the holy archbishop Epiphanios, having properly determined, subscribe. [After the representatives of Pope Agatho and the bishops of Constantinople, Alexandria, Antioch, Jerusalem, and Thessalonike]
669. I, Theodore, by God's grace bishop of the city of Tremithous on the island of Cyprus, also representing the holy archbishop Epiphanios, have likewise subscribed. [In the same order]
673. I, Stratonikos, bishop of Soloi on the island of Cyprus, have likewise subscribed. I, Tychon, bishop of Kition on the island of Cyprus, have likewise subscribed.
688. I, Theodore, by God's grace bishop of the city of Tremithous on the island of Cyprus, have signed, also on behalf of Epiphanios, my holy archbishop, of the same island of Cyprus.

50. THEODORE of Tremithous (ca. 680)

1. Life of St. John Chrysostom (*BHG* 872b) 24 [ΑΚΕΠ I 135.11δ and 12δ]

In those days the great Epiphanios, bishop of Constantia in Cyprus, was also present in Constantinople. [The empress] Eudoxia summoned him and said to him, "Reverend Father, John [Chrysostom, bishop of Constantinople 398–404] is a heretic, and all have subscribed to his exile. Now you, too, subscribe." But he replied, "If John is a heretic he deserves to be exiled. But if he is not and you mean to exile him because of some slight, there is need to forgive him, as we, too, are sinning against our king in heaven." But she responded, "If you will not obey me and will not subscribe, as all the rest [of the bishops] have done, I shall close the churches and open the shrines of the idols, so that all will worship there." At that he said, "If you know what is good for your soul, do it. Even if all have subscribed, Epiphanios will not."

It was [falsely] reported to John that Epiphanios had subscribed. And John sent this message to Epiphanios, "Epiphanios, you, too, have subscribed to my exile. I tell you that you will not sit on your throne." He, in turn, sent this message, "John, athlete of Christ, be beaten and win; for you will never reach the place which has been designated for your exile." And as the two of them spoke, so it happened.

51. COUNCIL IN TRULLO (Trullan Synod or Quinisext Synod) 691–692)

1. Canon 39 (Mansi XI, col. 961; Joannou I.1, pp. 173–74) [ΣΒΠΚΙ 24]

Our brother and fellow-minister John, bishop of the island of Cyprus, together with his people, because of the attacks of the barbarians, to be freed from enslavement to non-believers, and to be entirely subject to the scepter of a Christian power, has removed from the afore-mentioned island to the province of the Hellespont by the foresight of our compassionate God and the care of our Christ-loving and pious emperor. Therefore we decree: the privileges which the holy fathers previously assembled at Ephesus [431] have bestowed upon the throne of the afore-mentioned bishop shall be preserved intact; New Justinianopolis shall have the rights of Constantinople [*better* the city of the Constantinians]; and the reverend bishop serving there shall preside over all the bishops of the province of the Hellespont and shall be ordained by his own bishops according to ancient practice. For our holy fathers have also decreed that the customs in each church shall be preserved; thus the bishop of the city of Kyzikos shall be subject to the bishop of the afore-mentioned Justinianopolis, to be an example to all the other bishops under the afore-mentioned most reverend bishop John, who, when the need arises, shall also ordain the bishop of the city of Kyzikos itself.

2. Subscriptions (Mansi XI , col. 989)

I, John, the unworthy bishop of New Justinianopolis, have examined and subscribed. [After the patriarchs of Constantinople, Alexandria, Jerusalem, and Antioch]

52. VITA OF ST. SPYRIDON, anonymous, "Laurentianus" (7th c.)

1. Prologue (p. 104 ed. van den Ven) [ΑΚΕΠ I 121]

St. Spyridon was a farmer by background, so to speak; he had been born in the village called Askia, in the province of Cyprus.

2. 2 (p. 106 ed. van den Ven) [ΑΚΕΠ I 129]

When a famine, resulting from a drought, held the island of Cyprus in its grip, the Saint (Spyridon) asked God, as one friend would another, to grant the gift of rain, so that the famine might depart and all might live. And immediately the friend, being God and Lord, granted the request of his friend and servant.

3. 8 (pp. 112–114 ed. van den Ven)

Once the needs of the emperor required the Saint (Spyridon) to visit the city of Antioch. This was at the time of the emperor Constantine [I, 306–337]. The emperor's ailment called for this physician, through whom God wanted to grant the emperor release from his suffering. For God showed the emperor in a dream a boundless number of bishops, and in their midst two beautiful lights which possessed the skill to heal the ailment. And the emperor's interpreter said to him that the undefiled priests of God were by far the best healers of his illness. But he revealed neither their city nor their country nor their names . . . And the great healer (Spyridon) came to the city of Antioch . . . And when the emperor saw the holy man he at once recognized him . . . And when he rested his head [on Spyridon's shoulder] he at once received help; for it was not any other power which came to bring salvation, nor [the physician's] skill through human medications, but at once heavenly grace came, offering salvation and healing from his illness.

4. 14 (p. 122 ed. van den Ven) [ΑΚΕΠ I 125.2α; II 155.6, no. 17]

Another time the Saint (Spyridon) desired to see the city which is named after Kyrinos [Kyreneia] and climbed up, on foot, from Kythria. He had with him young Triphyllios, his disciple and a lover of divine things, who occupied the see of the church of Leukosia. And when he came with him to the height of the mountain and beheld the fruitful countryside of the region which is called Parymne, the blessed Triphyllios conceived in his heart a desire for the place.

53. GEORGE of Cyprus (7th c.)

1. *Descriptio Orbis Romani* 1095–1110 ed. Gelzer [ΑΚΕΠ II 155.4; ΣΒΠΚΙ 19]

Thus also the eparchy of Cyprus has continued, having sovereignty for itself, because here the holy apostle Barnabas was found, having the Gospel of Mark [the Gospel of Matthew according to other accounts] on his chest. But the cities in Cyprus are the following: Constantia the metropolis, Kition, Amathous, Kourion, Paphos, Arsinoe, Soloi, Lapithos, the birthplace of George of Cyprus who wrote the book from which these things have been excerpted; Kyreneia, Tamasos, Kytroi, Trimithous, Karpasis.

54. VITA OF ST. SPYRIDON, anonymous, abbreviated (7th c. or later)

1. Prologue (p. 173 ed. van den Ven) [ΑΚΕΠ I 121.1]

Our father Spyridon, blessed among the Saints and a worker of miracles, was the blessed bishop of the city of Tremithous on Cyprus. He flourished at the time of the emperor Constantine the Great and of his son Constantius [II, 337–361].

55. FRAGMENT Of A LOST LIFE OF ST. JOHN CHRYSOSTOM (*BHG* 873e) (7th c. or later)

1. 10 (p. 294) ed. Halkin

What then did this dreadful and wily Theomises do? [Theomises, "hater of God," for Theophilos, "lover of God"; Theophilos, bishop of Alexandria] When he had learned of these things he stirred up even more trouble against the chief shepherd and his flock, who reported his unspeakable deeds to the emperor. And having forged the decree against Origen he won over the great Epiphanios of Cyprus and professed friendship for him, all for the purpose of securing the condemnation of the books of Origen by a synod. Epiphanios was led astray by these arguments and cooperated with Theophilos, whose only purpose, eagerly pursued, was to condemn the holy man and the ascetics previously mentioned [reculcitrant monks from Nitria]. And what did he do after this? He persuaded Epiphanios to write a letter to John, [advising him] to stay away from the books of Origen and in no way to agree with them. But when Chrysostom, truly a great man, had received this message, in the purity of his mind he paid no attention to the things coming upon him and his only concern throughout was the salvation of everyone.

2. 13–14 (pp.297–98) ed. Halkin

13. Not much time passed between these events, and Epiphanios of Cyprus arrived. Theophilos had won him over by his subtle devices and by the other allurements of his character and persuaded him to do those things which brought grief to the holy man [John] and showed Epiphanios himself to be disdainful of church law. What were these things? The assemblies before [the gates of] the city, the ordinations, the unilateral condemnation of the books of Origen, and all the other acts of arrogance and rashness. And what were the responses of the chief priest to these acts? Let them be made known, too: The patience, the brotherly love, the introduction of the pertinent church laws, and all the other deeds which were better than the judgement and will of Epiphanios or according to human understanding. Warned by these, Epiphanios yielded a little and changed his position, but he gave much grief to those who were forcing him [?], and they, as quickly as they could, reported these things to the empress [Eudoxia].
14. She quickly engaged Epiphanios in her own designs and revealed the things which filled her unrighteous desire and ruined the holy man; she added what should not have been said—oh for the daring of mortals and the forbearance of God—namely that the chief priest and servant of God was a heretic. Let us find out what the response of the wise Epiphanios was. He said, "My Empress, if you have a reason to suspect heresy let John appear, give an account of himself, and repent. But if you are bringing these charges against him for the sake of some slight, Epiphanios does not approve of these things." This response aroused her anger and she burst out in foul talk such as this: "Epiphanios, if you will stand in the way of John's exile I shall open the temples of the idols and see to it that they are worshipped." Then Epiphanios could no longer endure to have his ears assaulted by the flood of her filthy and hateful speech, wept bitterly, declared that he had no guilt in such things, and finally consented to the exile. I do not know how these things were broadcast to those on the outside by enmity, especially that he who was called Epiphanios

had consented to the condemnation of John. When John heard these things he wrote to him, "Wise Epiphanios, did you agree to my exile? You will not be seen after this sitting on your throne." And Epiphanios replied, "Athlete John, be beaten and win. You will not reach the place to which you have been exiled." And as they wrote, so it happened. For Epiphanios died aboard his ship and John died without reaching the place of his second exile, as we shall forthwith relate.

56. COUNCIL OF HIEREIA (754)

1. Mansi XII, col. 577

Constantine [II, patriarch of Constantinople 754–766] of Pamphylia . . . was publicly executed in a place of worship. He was followed in office by Niketas [I, 766–780], and he in turn by Paul [IV, 780–784] of Salamis in Cyprus.

57. JOHN OF DAMASCUS (ca. 675–ca. 753/754)

1. *Oratio Tertia de Imaginibus 92* (Migne, *PG* 94, col. 1393; p.185 ed. Kotter)

From the Life of St. Symeon the miracle worker, an account by Arkadios, archbishop of Cyprus . . .
[St. Symeon the Younger, Syrian stylite, 521–592; Arkadios, archbishop of Constantia, 6th c.; the attribution rejected by Paul van den Ven, *La vie ancienne de s. Syméon Stylite le Jeune* (Brussels 1962–1970) I 101–108.]

58. SECOND COUNCIL OF NICAEA (Seventh Ecumenical Council) (787)

1. Πρᾶξις Πρώτη (Mansi XII, cols. 994 and 995)

Constantine, bishop of Constantia on the island of Cyprus . . .
Spyridon, bishop of Kythroi, Eustathios, bishop of Soloi, Theodore, bishop of Kition, George, bishop of Tremithous, Alexander, bishop of Amathous.

2. Πρᾶξις Τετάρτη (Mansi XIII, cols. 133 and 144)

I, Constantine, bishop of Constantia in Cyprus . . . have subscribed by my own hand [endorsing the veneration of icons].
Spyridon, bishop of Palaia of Kythroi, likewise; Eustathios, bishop of Soloi, likewise; Theodore, bishop of Kition, likewise; George, bishop of Tremithous, likewise; Alexander, bishop of Amathous, likewise.

3. Πρᾶξις Ἑβδόμη (Mansi XIII, cols. 365 and 368)

Giving the same names as 2 above.

4. Πρᾶξις Ἑβδόμη (Mansi XIII, cols. 379 and 388)

I, Constantine, by God's grace bishop of Constantia on the island of Cyprus, following the teachings of the Fathers and the tradition of the Catholic Church, have examined and signed . . .

Eustathios, unworthy bishop of Soloi, likewise; Spyridon, unworthy bishop of Kythroi, likewise; Theodore, unworthy bishop of Kition, likewise; George, unworthy bishop of Tremithous, likewise; Alexander, unworthy bishop of Amathous.

59. VITA OF ST. STEPHEN THE YOUNGER, by Stephen, deacon of Hagia Sophia (808)

1. Migne, *PG* 100, col. 1117 [ΣΒΠΚΙ 30]

Since there are three areas which are on our [the iconodules'] side and do not participate in this foul heresy, I advise you to go there . . . and to the island of Cyprus.

[Stephen the Younger, iconodule, martyred at Constantinople under Constantine V Kopronymos in 765]

2. Migne, *PG* 100, col. 1120

Then it could be seen that the monastic order and the monastic habit had been banished from Byzantium. Some [of the monks] sailed away to the Black Sea, others headed for Cyprus, and yet others considered moving to Rome. And thus, driven from their own monasteries, they became known as aliens and refugees.

60. GEORGE THE SYNKELLOS (d. after 810)

1. *Ecloga Chronographica* 91–92 [ΑΚΕΠ I 35.16]

The sons of Javan . . . the fourteenth were the Kitioi, from whom came the Latins, that is the Romans . . . There are also Cypriots from the Kitiaioi and others in the north of the same race of the same Kitiaioi, or Romans; and also the nations of the Greeks.   (trans. P.W.W.)

2. *Ecloga Chronographica* 299 [ΑΚΕΠ I 21.4]

Melos, Thasos, and Alkisthe (?) were founded, also Paphos.

3. *Ecloga Chronographica* 380 [AKEΠ I 35.3α; II 150.4]

Aphrikanos [Julius Africanus, historian, 2nd/3rd c. A.D.] says that Tharsis is Rhodes and also Cyprus.

4. *Ecloga Chronographica* 491 [AKEΠ I 66.42]

The Gauls and the Celts seized Rome except the Capitol [387 B.C.].
Evagoras [411–374/373 B.C.] lost control of the kings of Cyprus.
. . .
Dionysios, tyrant of Sicily, died, having reigned 18 years.
[Note: Dionysios I 405–367; Dionysios II 367–343/342 B.C.]

5. *Ecloga Chronographica* 522 [AKEΠ I 80.3α]

The Romans established colonies.
Ptolemy [I Soter] ruled Cyprus.
The Lamian War broke out [322 B.C.].

6. *Ecloga Chronographica* 538 [AKEΠ I 97.5α]

Again they [Ptolemy VI Philometor and Ptolemy VIII Euergetes Physcon] quarreled, and from the 18th year [163 B.C.] the rule of Egypt fell to Philometor alone, since he had given to his brother the rule of Libya and Cyrene after the battle in Cyprus.   (trans. P.W.W.)

7. *Ecloga Chronographica* 550 [AKEΠ I 98.2]

He [Ptolemy IX Lathyrus *or* Soter] was the older son of Ptolemy [VIII] Euergetes and Cleopatra [III]. His mother drove him out in the tenth year of his reign [107 B.C.], and he became king of Cyprus. She made her younger son and Lathyrus' brother [Ptolemy X] Alexander king with her, and he ruled in Alexandria fifteen years. When he was driven out by the army he went with his wife and daughter to the city of Myra in Lycia, and from there to Cyprus (with his child?). Going to war he was killed by the admiral Chaereas.   (trans. P.W.W.)

8. *Ecloga Chronographica* 593 [AKEΠ I 109.9]

Augustus granted a tax-exemption to the Samians.
The Cantabrians [in Spain] revolted and were destroyed.
An earthquake destroyed many places in Cyprus [15 B.C.].

9. *Ecloga Chronographica* 647 [AKEΠ I 115.2]

On Rhodes the bronze Colossus, 127 feet high, was erected.

Rome was struck by a great plague, so that thousands died daily for many days. On Cyprus three cities were destroyed by earthquake.

10. *Ecloga Chronographica* 657 [ΑΚΕΠ Ι 116.2]

The Jews killed the Greeks of Salamis in Cyprus and destroyed the city.
The senate declared Trajan a god.
Trajan died of illness [A.D. 116].

61. THEOPHANES THE CONFESSOR (ca. 760–817)

Note: In the conversion of Theophanes' *annus mundi* dates into A.D. dates I have followed C. Mango and R. Scott throughout, even when quoting the translation of H. Turtledove. The actual dates of events or persons have been supplied in the text wherever possible.

1. *Chronographia* annus mundi 5816 [A.D. 323/324] [ΑΚΕΠ Ι 121.6β]

In this year [325] the 20th year of the reign of the Augustus Constantine was observed. And the first holy and ecumenical council of the 318 fathers was held. Among them there were many who had worked miracles and were equal to the angels, bearing on their bodies the stigmata of Christ, the result of earlier persecutions. Among them were Paphnoutios [of Egypt], Spyridon [of Cyprus], Makarios [of Jerusalem], and Jacob of Nisibis, men who had worked miracles, raised the dead, and accomplished marvelous things.

2. *Chronographia* annus mundi 5824 [A.D. 331/332] [ΑΚΕΠ Ι 129.1]

In this year, as the seventh indiction [actually the fifth] was about to take place, there occurred a famine of extraordinary severity in the East, so that [entire] villages in the region of Antioch and in Cyprus [ΑΚΕΠ Κύπρου; Mss. Κύρου] gathered in a large crowd in the same place, turned one upon another, and plundered.

3. *Chronographia* annus mundi 5824 [A.D. 331/332] [ΑΚΕΠ Ι 129.4; ΣΒΠΚΙ 28.1]

In the same year [332] a terrible earthquake occurred in Cyprus and the city of Salamis fell in ruins, killing a considerable number [of people]. (trans. P.W.W.)

4. *Chronographia* annus mundi 5825 [A.D. 332/333] [ΑΚΕΠ Ι 128; ΣΒΠΚΙ 28.2]

In this year [335] Dalmatius was proclaimed Caesar. Kalokairos was ruling in the island of Cyprus, and he could not withstand the Roman attack. He was defeated along with his accomplices and executed in Tarsos of Cilicia, being burned alive by the Caesar Dalmatius [actually by the Caesar's father, the censor Dalmatius]. (trans. P.W.W.)

5. *Chronographia* annus mundi 5834 [A.D. 341/342 [ΑΚΕΠ I 129.6; ΣΒΠΚΙ 28.3]

In this year [344] Constantius [II, 337–361] celebrated a triumph after defeating the Assyrians [Persians] . . . A great earthquake happened in Cyprus and most of the city of Salamis was destroyed.
(trans. P.W.W.)

6. *Chronographia* annus mundi 5896 [A.D. 403/404] [ΑΚΕΠ I 135.11β; ΣΒΠΚΙ 28.4.1]

In this year . . . a letter was sent by Theophilos [bishop of Alexandria] to Epiphanios. By this letter a plot was hatched against John [Chrysostom, bishop of Constantinople]. And Epiphanios of Cyprus came to Hebdomon [a suburb of Constantinople], where he performed ordinations and held services without John's authorization. John, in godly love, overlooked this and invited Epiphanios to stay with him in the episcopal residence; but Epiphanios declined, having been won over by the plots of Theophilos against the blessed John.
(trans. P.W.W.)

7. *Chronographia* annus mundi 5898 [A.D. 405/406] [ΑΚΕΠ I 135.12β; ΣΒΠΚΙ 28.4.2]

Epiphanios set sail for Cyprus, for God, so it seemed, had foretold his death. They say that Epiphanios declared that John's end would be in exile, and that John [Chrysostom] declared that Epiphanios' death would be at sea. Epiphanios said to those who sent him off, "I am in a hurry, and I leave to you the books, the city, and the theater." [403]
(trans. P.W.W.)

8. *Chronographia* annus mundi 6140 [A.D. 647/648] [ΣΒΠΚΙ 28.5]

In this year [649] Muawiyah [governor of Syria, to become the first caliph of the Umayyad dynasty in 661] attacked Cyprus with 1,700 ships. He took and devastated Constantia and the whole island. When he heard the *cubicularius* [chamberlain] Kakorizos was moving against him with a large Roman force, he sailed across to Arados [a coastal city of Phoenicia].
(trans. H. Turtledove)

9. *Chronographia* annus mundi 6178 [A.D. 685/686] [ΣΒΠΚΙ 28.6]

In this year [688] Abd al-Malik [*also* Abimelech; of the Umayyad dynasty, 685–705] sent envoys to Justinian [II, 685–695 and 705–711] to secure peace. It was arranged on these terms . . . Both sides would share equally the tribute from Cyprus, Armenia, and Iberia [in the Caucasus].
(trans. H. Turtledove)

10. *Chronographia* annus mundi 6183 [A.D. 690/691] [ΣΒΠΚΙ 28.7]

In this year [691], thanks to a lack of good sense, Justinian [II, 685–695 and 705–711] broke peace with Abd al-Malik [Abimelech]. He was foolishly anxious to resettle the island of Cyprus . . . A number of Cypriots who made the effort drowned or died of sickness; the rest did return to Cyprus.
(trans. H. Turtledove)

11. *Chronographia* annus mundi 6234 [A.D. 741/742] [ΣΒΠΚΙ 28.8]

In the same year [742/743] Walid [II, 743–744, of the Umayyad dynasty, 661–744] re-settled the Cypriots in Syria.

(trans. H. Turtledove)

12. *Chronographia* annus mundi 6238 [A.D. 745/746] [ΣΒΠΚΙ 28.9]

In this year [747] . . . An Agarene [Arab] expedition presently came to Cyprus from Al-exandria while a Roman fleet was there. The general of the Kibyrhaiot theme suddenly attacked the Arabs in the harbor and captured the mouth of the harbor. They say that, although there were 1,000 warships, only three got away.

(trans. H. Turtledove)

13. *Chronographia* annus mundi 6245 [A.D. 752/753] [ΣΒΠΚΙ 28.10]

On the twenty-seventh of the same month [August, 754] the Emperor [Constantine V Kopronymos, 741–775] went to the Forum with his unholy president [patriarch] Constantine [II, 754–766] and the rest of his bishops. In the presence of all the people they declared their evil-doctrined heresy, anathematizing the holy Germanos [I, patriarch of Constantinople 715–730], George of Cyprus, and John Chrysorrhoas [of the Golden Stream] of Damascus, the son of Man-sour, who were holy men and venerable teachers.

(trans. H. Turtledove)

14. *Chronographia* annus mundi 6262 [A.D. 769/770] [ΣΒΠΚΙ 28.11]

In the same year [Michael] Lakhanodrakon [general of Constantine V], imitating his teacher, collected at Ephesus every monk and nun under the jurisdiction of the Thrakesian theme. Bringing them to the plain known as Tzoukanisterin, he told them, "Let he who wishes to obey the Emperor and us put on white clothing and take a wife at this hour; those who do not want to do so shall be blinded and exiled to Cyprus." His speech and action were simultaneous, and on that day many martyrs were revealed and many who abandoned their vocations were lost: to these Drakon was friendly.

(trans. H. Turtledove)

15. *Chronographia* annus mundi 6264 [A.D. 771/772] [ΣΒΠΚΙ 28.12]

In this year . . . Sergios Kourikos was captured outside Syke [15 km. east of Anemourion, on the coast of Cilicia], as was Sergios Lakhebaphos in Cyprus—he was legate for that area.

(trans. H. Turtledove)

16. *Chronographia* annus mundi 6272 [A.D. 779/780] [ΣΒΠΚΙ 28.13]

On February 6 (the Sunday of cheese-eating) of the third indiction died the Slavic eunuch Niketas [I, 766–780], the patriarch of Constantinople. Although he tried to beg off, on the sec-ond Sunday of Lent the honored Paul was chosen patriarch of Constantinople [Paul IV, 780–784]; he was under strong duress because of the dominant heresy. A Cypriot in origin, he was a reader brilliant in speech and action.

(trans. H. Turtledove)

17. *Chronographia* annus mundi 6282 [A.D. 789/790] [ΣΒΠΚΙ 28.14]

    In this year [790] . . . An Arab fleet had gone to Cyprus; as the Empress [Irene] had fore-
knowledge of this, she assembled all the Roman naval forces and sent them against the Arabs.
When they reached Myra, both Roman admirals doubled the cape of Khelidonion and entered the
bay of Attaleia. The Arabs moved out from Cyprus and, since they had fair weather, turned
about on the sea. When they reappeared, the Roman admirals saw them from land; mustering
their forces, they made ready to attack. But Theophilos, the general of the Kibyrhaiotai . . . went
out to engage them ahead of anyone else. They defeated him . . .   (trans. H. Turtledove)

18. *Chronographia* annus mundi 6298 [A.D. 805/806] [ΣΒΠΚΙ 28.15]

    In this year [806] . . . He [Harun al-Rashid, of the Abbasid dynasty, 786–809] also sent a
fleet to Cyprus, tore down its churches, and resettled the Cypriots. He broke the peace and did a
great deal of damage.   (trans. H. Turtledove)

19. *Chronographia* annus mundi 6305 [A.D. 812/813] [ΣΒΠΚΙ 28.16)

    In the same year many Christian monks from Palestine and all Syria reached Cyprus,
fleeing the boundless evil of the Arabs . . . Some men became martyrs; others got to Cyprus, and
from it to Byzantium. The Emperor Michael [I Rhangabe, 811–813] and the holy patriarch Nikephoros [I, 806–815] kindly entertained them. Michael helped them in every way. He gave the
men who entered the city a famous monastery, and sent a talent of gold to the monks and laymen
still on Cyprus.   (trans. H. Turtledove)

62. CHOIROBOSKOS, GEORGE (floruit early 9th c.)

1. *Orthographia*, s.v. κῖρις (ed. Cramer, *Anecd. Gr. Oxon.* II, p. 228) [ΑΚΕΠ II 72]

    Kiris: this is a kind of falcon. But among the Cypriots Adonis is called *Kiris*.

63. NIKEPHOROS, patriarch of Constantinople (806–815, d. 828)

1. *Historia Syntomos, Breviarium,* or *Short History* 56 [ΣΒΠΚΙ 29.1]

    After this a son was born to the emperor [Leo III, 717–741]. And the emperor named
him Constantine [the future Constantine V Kopronymos]. On the fifteenth day of the following
month, that being August, all the cavalry and all the naval forces of the Saracens withdrew from
the capital. And they lost most of their ships when they got caught in a storm and in fierce
winds; many were scattered on the islands as far as Cyprus, while others were lost to the depths
of the sea together with their crews. [718]

2. *Historia Syntomos, Breviarium,* or *Short History* 68 [ΣΒΠΚΙ 29.2]

At this time he [Constantine V Kopronymos, 741–775] sent a force against the territory of the Saracens; it was under the command of the man who at that time was the general of the so-called army of the Kibyrhaiots. And the fleet put in at the island of Cyprus. There at once a Saracen fleet from Alexandria came down upon it. But the [Byzantine] general, having prior knowledge of this, suddenly attacked it [the Saracen fleet], burned the ships with fire, and captured all the equipment. Then, having overwhelmingly defeated the enemy, he returned to Constantine. [747]

3. *Historia Syntomos, Breviarium,* or *Short History* 72

Together with these [the holy icons] they [priests appointed by Constantine V Kopronymos, 741–775], like children, anathematized in public Germanos, who had been archpriest of Byzantium [715–730], George, who was a native of Cyprus, and John of Damascus in Syria, whose surname was Mansour. [754]

64. VITA OF THE BLESSED PETROS OF ATROA (d. 837)

1. 14 (p. 101 ed. Laurent [ΣΒΠΚΙ 31]

After this he again set out for Cyprus. There he wandered about for ten months, venerated the sacred objects there, as he desired, and healed many people of their illnesses. Then he returned to Mt. Olympus [in Mysia].

2. 51 (p. 169 ed. Laurent)

When the blessed man learned that the lady was there he took his servants Philotheos and Barnabas with him. He also asked a certain bishop, a Cypriot named John, who had humbly offered his service to the blessed father, to meet with them in the chapel of the most holy Theotokos.

65. *Taktikon Uspenskij* (842–843)

1. p. 57.10–15 ed. Oikonomides [ΣΒΠΚΙ 34]

the *droungarios* of the Aegean
the governors of Dyrrachion
the governor of Dalmatia
the governors of Cherson
the duke of Calabria
the governor of Cyprus.

66. THE SYNODIKON OF ORTHODOXY with revisions and additions to 920 (844)

On the Church of Cyprus, ed. Gouillard 111–12

1. Encomium of the metropolitans

Recension A

Sergios, Dometios, Porphyrios, Ploutarchos, Barnabas, Theodoros, Basileios, Arkadios, Anthimos, Damianos, Sabinos, Akakios, Gelasios, Theophanes, Ioannes, Epiphanios, Gregorios, Euthymios, Ioannes, Alexios, Epiphanios, Gregorios, Basileios, Nikolaos, Theodoretos, Ioannes, Barnabas, Esaias, Hilarion, Neilos, and Germanos, venerable archbishops of Cyprus, to be remembered forever.

Recension B

Sergios, Dometios, Porphyrios, and Ploutarchos, blessed archbishops of Cyprus etc.
Barnabas, Theodoros, Basileios, Arkadios, and Anthimos, blessed archbishops etc.
Gelasios, Sabinos, Ioannes, Theophanes, Epiphanios, Gregorios, Euthymios, and Ioannes, blessed archbishops etc.
Alexios, Epiphanios, Basileios, Nikolaos, Theodoretos, Ioannes, and Barnabas, holy and blessed archbishops etc.
Sophronios, holy and blessed archbishop of Cyprus etc.
Isaac, holy and blessed archbishop of Cyprus etc.
Hilarion, holy and blessed archbishop of Cyprus etc.

2. Encomium of some important saints of the island

Recension A

Herakleidios, Mnason, Rhodon, Demetrianos, Makedonios, Lazaros, Tychon, Zeno, Philagrios, Arkadios, Nikon, Auxibios, Eulalios, Theodotos, Demetrianos, Pappos, Athanasios, Eustathios, Niketas, Spyridon, Philon, Synesios, Sosikrates, Triphyllios, Tychikos, and Zeno, who piously held office in the holy bishoprics of Cyprus and were remarkable for their miracles, to be remembered forever.

Recension B

Triphyllios, the outstanding bishop of Leukosia, to be remembered forever.
Herakleides, Mnason, Rhodon, Demetrianos, and Makedonikos, the holy bishops of Tamaseia, to be remembered forever.

Lazaros, the holy bishop of Kytaioi [?], to be remembered forever.

Tychon, the miracle worker and bishop of Amathous, to be remembered forever.

Zeno, the holy bishop of Kourion, to be remembered forever.

Philagrios, the miracle worker and bishop of Paphos, to be remembered forever.

Arkadios and Nikon, the holy bishops of Arsinoë, to be remembered forever.

Auxibios, the miracle worker and bishop of Soloi, to be remembered forever.

Eulalios, the blessed bishop of Kerinia, to be remembered forever.

Demetrianos, Pappos, Athanasios, Eustathios, and Niketas, blessed bishops of Kytheria, to be remembered forever.

Spyridon, the miracle worker and bishop of Tremithous, to be remembered forever.

Philon, Synesios, and Sosikrates, the apostles and bishops of Karpasion, to be remembered forever.

Tychikos and Zeno, the holy bishops of Neapolis Nemesos [?], to be remembered forever.

3. The Church of Kyrenia

Theodotos, the wise, holy, and God-fearing martyr and bishop of Kyrenia, to be remembered forever.

Ioannes, Epiphanios, Meletios, Theodosios, Ephraim, Gregory, and Athanasios, the holy and God-fearing bishops of Kyrenia, to be remembered forever.

Athanasios, the holy and blessed bishop of Kyrenia, to be remembered forever. Ignatios, etc.

67. PHOTIOS, patriarch of Constantinople 858–867 and 877–886 (ca. 810–after 893)

1. *Bibliotheca* 72 (35b, 44a, and 44b) [ΑΚΕΠ I 66.15]

Read a work of Ctesias of Cnidos, the *Persica* in twenty-three books . . . In Books 21, 22, and 23 (the last in the work) the contents are as follows . . .

Ctesias expounds the reasons why king Artoxerxes [Artaxerxes II, 404–359 B.C.] quarrelled with king Euagoras of Salamis [411–374/373 B.C.]. Messengers were sent from Euagoras to Ctesias in order to receive letters from Abuletos, and Ctesias wrote a letter promoting reconciliation between him and king Anaxagoras of Cyprus. Messengers came from Euagoras to Cyprus, Ctesias' letters were delivered to Euagoras, Conon discussed with Euagoras a visit to the king of Persia. Euagoras wrote a letter about the honors accorded him by the king. Conon wrote to Ctesias; Euagoras sent tribute to the king; letters were consigned to Ctesias. Ctesias spoke to the king about Conon and sent him a letter. Gifts from Euagoras were passed to Satibarzanes. Messengers arrived in Cyprus. Conon wrote to the king and Ctesias. [398 B.C.]

(trans. N. G. Wilson)

2. *Bibliotheca* 82 (64a–b) and 92 (71b) [AKEΠ I 78.1ε]

Read the *After Alexander* [the *Diadochi*] of Dexippus [Publius Herennius D., 3rd c. A.D.], in four books . . . It begins with the king's death itself . . . and then describes the division of Alexander's empire . . . Sibourtios governed Arachosia and Gedrosia, and Stasanor of Soloi ruled the Areii and Draggae . . . Antipater [Macedonian regent, 397–319 B.C.], as before, was chosen to hold (supreme) power. He made his own division of Asia, overruling the previous division and making new arrangements as circumstances demanded . . . And he appointed Stasander as ruler of the land of the Areii and Draggeni, but Stasanor as ruler of Bactria and Sogdiana. [322 B.C.]

3. *Bibliotheca* 176 (120a–b) [AKEΠ I 14.7; 66.41; 66.43ε]

Read Theopompus' *History* . . . [*Philippica*; *FHG* I 295–96, fr. 111; *FGrH* IIB 115, fr.103].

Book 12 contains the story of the Egyptian king Akoris [*or* Achoris, 393–380 B.C.]: how he made a treaty with the inhabitants of Barke and sided with Euagoras of Cyprus against Persia; how Euagoras unexpectedly came to power in Cyprus [411 B.C.], capturing Abdymon of Citium the governor; how the Greeks under Agamemnon took Cyprus, driving out the subjects of Kinnyras, the remnants of whom are the population of Amathus; how the king of Persia [Artaxerxes II, 404–359 B.C.] was persuaded to declare war on Euagoras, employing Antophradates the satrap of Lydia as his general and Hekatomnos as his admiral; about the peace which the king of Persia himself arranged for the Greeks; how he intensified his campaign against Euagoras, and about the sea-battle off Cyprus; how the city of Athens tried to honour its treaty with Persia, whereas the Spartans arrogantly broke the agreement; how the peace of Antalkidas was made [386 B.C.]; how Tiribazos [satrap of Armenia] campaigned and plotted against Euagoras, but the latter criticised him to the king and with the help of Orontes [*or* Aroandas, the king's son-in-law] had him arrested; how when Nektenibis [II, *or* Nektabenos, 360–341 B.C.] succeeded to the throne in Egypt Euagoras sent a delegation to Sparta; how the war in Cyprus was terminated; about Nikokreon's plot and how it was unexpectedly unmasked and he escaped; how Euagoras and his son Pnytagoras without realising it both slept with Nikokreon's surviving daughter, thanks to the eunuch Thrasydaios of Elis, who helped each of them in turn to satisfy their lust; this was their undoing, since Thrasydaios assassinated both of them [374/373 B.C.].

(trans. N. G. Wilson)

4. *Bibliotheca* 190 (153a) [AKEΠ II 79.3; 89]

After the death of Adonis, so it is reported, Aphrodite wandered about looking for him, found him in Argos, a city of Cyprus, in the temple of Apollo Erithios, and took him up (to bury him), revealing her love for Adonis to Apollo.

5. *Bibliotheca* 229 (264b) [AKEΠ I 122]

Both Proklos of Constantinople and Kyriakos [*or* Cyril], bishop of Paphos, who was one of the 318 holy fathers [who attended the Council of Nicaea], say the same thing [concerning the union of the natures in Christ]. The former says so in his *Poulcherianai,* after Christmas, the latter in his treatise on theophany. The same author says the same thing in his *On the Incarnation.*

6. *Bibliotheca* 243 (353a and 372b) [AKEΠ II 1.10; 10.12]

Read several of the declamations of the sophist Himerios . . . From his treatise on the arrival of the Cypriots:
The proem: The poets grant Cyprus to Aphrodite among the gods, as they do Delos to Apollo. For Cyprus is a large city; her people are unquestionably Greek, judging by their language.

7. *Bibliotheca* 246 (400b) and 248 (425b) [AKEΠ I 61.10]

Read the *Panathenaicus* of [Aelius] Aristides . . .
From the discourses concerning Cimon . . . he died while besieging Kition on Cyprus.

8. *Bibliotheca* 256 (471a–b) [AKEΠ I 121.8]

But the venerable Spyridon was also present [at the Council of Nicaea]. Of the countless stories about him I shall relate two briefly. Once he was guarding his sheep, although he held the office of bishop. Some thieves came upon his flock and were bound with invisible bonds. And when he found them bound, whom he himself had bound by his prayers, he loosed them of their bonds by equal wisdom, and he gave them a ram, saying that he wanted it to be compensation for their night-time troubles. He had an unwed daughter who lived with him. She took a deposit from some man and later passed away. And the man who had deposited the money (he had been sent into exile) returned and sought his money. Spyridon searched but could not find it. Therefore he approached his daughter's grave and said, "My daughter Irene," (for that was the young woman's name) "where is the deposit?" And she answered from the grave and told him the place and how to find the deposit. And when he had easily found the deposit he returned it to the depositor. By these things we wish to describe him, as a lion by his claws.

9. *Bibliotheca* 260 (486b and 487b) [AKEΠ I 68.8α]

Read various speeches by Isocrates . . .
He was fairly well to do, not only making money from his acquaintances, but also receiving twenty talents from Nikokles the king of Cyprus—he was the son of Euagoras—for the deliberative speech written for him.
(trans. N. G. Wilson)

10. *Epistulae* 247 (ed. Laourdas and Westerink)

Just as the renowned Barnabas, a vessel of mildness and kindness, was by ancestry a Jew but by nationality a Cypriot . . . so also St. Paul . . .

11. *Epistulae* 278 (ed. Laourdas and Westerink) [ΣΒΠΚΙ 35]

   To Staurakios, *spantharocandidatos* and governor of Cyprus . . .

12. *Lexikon*, s.v. μοτοφαγία [ΑΚΕΠ ΙΙ 114]

   See Suidas M 1283.

13. *Lexikon*, s.v. νησαίη λίθος [ΑΚΕΠ ΙΙ 174.1]

   Some say that it is sardonyx from the island. Others say that it is smaragd; for it is mined in Cyprus.

14. *Lexikon*, s.v. πάρνοπες [ΑΚΕΠ ΙΙ 164.3γ]

   But others call Cypriot locusts by that name.

15. *Lexikon*, s.v. Σόλοι [ΑΚΕΠ ΙΙ 155.6, no.35]

   A city of Sicily [Cilicia] and Cyprus. Hence the word "solecism," since they speak in their own barbaric tongue. Some call it a city of Cyprus, others a city of Cilicia.

16. *Lexikon*, s.v. τιάρα [ΑΚΕΠ ΙΙ 168.1α]

   A headdress which among the Persians only the kings wore upright, but the generals bent-over. It is said to be the same as the *kitaris*. But Theophrastus in his *On Kingship* [fr. 589.11 ed. Fortenbaugh] says that the *kitaris* of the Cypriots is different.

68. PHILOTHEOS, protospatharios (899)

1. *Kletorologion,* p. 179 ed. Bury, p. 235 ed. Oikonomides [ΣΒΠΚΙ 38]

   After these I have listed the cities and bishoprics which belong to each eparchy and metropolis, taking my material not only from my own *kletorologion* but for the most part from the account of the divine Epiphanios, archbishop of Cyprus [pseudo-Epiphanios].

69. *ETYMOLOGIUM GENUINUM* (late 9th c.)

1. s.v. Ἀῶς (*FGrH* IIIC, fr. 758.7) [ΑΚΕΠ Ι 2; 14.25; ΙΙ 69; 160, no. 2]

   A river in Cyprus. For Adonis was called Aoos, and from him stem the kings of Cyprus. But Zoilos ὁ Κεδρασεύς [?] says that he is named after his mother. For, he says, the daughter of

Theia [a Titaness] was called not Smyrna, but Aoa. But Phileas [of Athens, 5th c. B.C.?] says that Aoos was the first king and was the son of Eos and Kephalos. After him also a mountain in Cyprus is called Aoon, and from this mountain spring two rivers, Seraches and Plieus. Parthenios [of Nicaea, 1st c. B.C.] has called one of these rivers Aoos.

70. VITA OF ST. JOHN THE ALMONER (9th c.) [ΣBΠKI 36]

This 9th c. anonymous paraphrase differs only by a few minor verbal variations from the 7th c. vita by Leontios of Neapolis; see **45**.1–9.

71. *NOTITIAE EPISCOPATUUM ECCLESIAE CONSTANTINOPOLITANAE* (9th c.)

1. *Notitia* 3.1–9 (p. 230 ed. Darrouzès) [ΣBΠKI 27.1]

The order of precedence of the most holy patriarchs, metropolitans, and autocephalous bishops:
1. the [bishop] of Rome
2. the [patriarch] of Constantinople
3. the [patriarch] of Alexandria
4. the [patriarch] of Antioch
5. the [patriarch] of Jerusalem.

The metropolitans under the patriarch of Constantinople:
1. the eparchy of Cappadocia: the [bishop] of Caesarea
2. the eparchy of Asia: the [bishop] of Ephesus
3. the eparchy of Cyprus: the [bishop] of Constantia
4. the eparchy of Europe: the [bishop] of Herakleia in Thrace.

2. *Notitia* 3.143–59 (p. 234 ed. Darrouzès) [ΣBΠKI 27.2]

The island of Cyprus has 15 cities:
the metropolis of Kyrine or Constantia
   1. the [bishop] of Paphos
   2. the [bishop] of Tamasos
   3. the [bishop] of Arsinoe
   4. the [bishop] of Soloi
   5. the [bishop] of Lapethos
   6. the [bishop] of Kyrenia
   7. the [bishop] of Karpasos
   8. the [bishop] of Kythroi
   9. the [bishop] of Leukosia
  10. the [bishop] of Kition

11. the [bishop] of Amathous
12. the [bishop] of Neapolis
13. the [bishop] of Kourion
14. the [bishop] of Trimithous.

72. Ὑποτύπωσις γεωγραφίας ἐν ἐπιτομῇ (*A Concise Outline of Geography*) (9th c)

1. 8.27 [ΑΚΕΠ II 157.2]

Among the largest islands in the world Salike [Taprobane, Ceylon, Sri Lanka] occupies the first place, Albion the second, and Hibernia the third. Among the other islands which are large but smaller than those just mentioned Sicily is first, Sardinia second, Cyprus third, Crete fourth, and Euboea fifth. Of the remaining islands, in the third rank, according to size, the first is Corsica, also known as Cyrnus, the second Lesbos, and the third Rhodes.

73. *CHRESTOMATHIAE* (Epitome of Strabo) (9th c.)

1. 2.24 [ΑΚΕΠ II 159]

According to Strabo . . . longitude is measured along the parallel which runs through the Pillars [of Herakles], Sicily, the Peloponnese, Rhodes, Cyprus, the Gulf of Issos, Armenia, central Media, and on to the east, behind the mountains, as far as the Indian Ocean.

74. GEORGE HAMARTOLOS *or* GEORGE THE MONK (9th c.)

1. *Chronicon* 1.20 (p. 41 ed. de Boor) [ΑΚΕΠ I 35.15]

Macedonians were once called Kitians.

2. *Chronicon* 9.14 (p. 619 ed. de Boor) [ΣΒΠΚΙ 32]

Repeating Theodore Lector no. 4 (*Historia Ecclesiastica, Epitome* 436), q.v.

3. *Chronicon,* Migne, *PG* 110, col. 761 [ΣΒΠΚΙ 33]

An inferior edition of the *Chronicon,* based on a heavily interpolated text, was published be Édouard de Muralt in St. Petersburg in 1859; it was reprinted in Migne, *PG*, in 1863. The passage corresponding to no. 2 above reads as follows:

During the reign of Zeno [474–475 and 476–491] the relics of the apostle Barnabas were found by revelation in Cyprus (in the city of Constantia) under a carob tree. The apostle had the

Gospel of Matthew, written by his [Barnabas'] own hand, on his chest. On the grounds of this discovery and deposition of the apostle the Cypriots prevailed over Peter the Fuller [patriarch of Antioch], who was contending that the churches of Cyprus are subject to Antioch and that the metropolis of Cyprus is [not] autocephalous. The Gospel which had been found Zeno deposited in his palace in the Chapel of St. Stephen.

75. VITA OF ST. SPYRIDON, anonymous, metaphrasis (9th c.?)

1. 1 (p. 133 ed. van den Ven) [ΑΚΕΠ I 129α]

There was at that time on the island of Cyprus a drought which lasted for a long time, and famine was expected to descend upon that entire country.

2. 2 (p. 134 ed. van den Ven) [ΑΚΕΠ I 129α]

When a severe famine for some time gripped the whole island of Cyprus, the dealers of grain . . .

3. 7 (p.145 ed. van den Ven)

In the time of Constantine the Great, the first divinely chosen emperor of the Christians, the Council of Nicaea in the province of Bithynia was held, in the consulship of Paulinus and Julian [325], in the fourteenth indiction, beginning on the 20th of May. From the various provinces and cities 318 chosen holy fathers were assembled in council with the pious emperor Constantine. With all the other fathers there was also Spyridon, the great miracle-worker, with whom our account is concerned.

4. 15 (pp. 161–62 ed. van den Ven) [ΑΚΕΠ II 155.6, no. 17]

At one time for some reason the divine man (Spyridon) was traveling from his own city of Tremithous to the city which is called Kyrenia, one of the noteworthy cities on Cyprus, and he had need to pass through the town of Kythrea and through the mountain which is called Pentadaktylos. His traveling companion was Triphyllios, who has already been mentioned, his disciple, who had been appointed bishop of the city of Kallinikesiai or Leukosia [Nicosia]. And as they were traveling and came to a well-situated and lovely place called Parymne, Triphyllios was pleased by the loveliness of the place and conceived a desire to acquire it . . . Then this inspired man (Spyridon) knew through some divine inspiration what was on the mind of Triphyllios the bishop and said to him . . . And when Triphyllios the bishop heard these things from his good teacher he was astounded and wondered that such a gift of foreknowledge had been given to him by God.

76. VITA OF ST. CONSTANTINE THE JEW (9th/10th c.)

1. 26 (*AASS* Nov. IV, p. 635) [ΣΒΠΚΙ 37.1]

He [St. Spyridon] then seemed to speak through his icon to the blesssed man [St. Constantine] according to his prayer: "There is oil available to you from the desert. Therefore, light a lamp for me there, leave the monastery, and come to Cyprus. I, in turn, will meet you there and stretch out my hand to you." Thus spoke the voice of the icon of the great Spyridon . . . Thus, encouraged even more by this voice and having been found worthy almost of the grace of Paul, that heavenly man, in his callings, he departed on the journey set out for him with much eagerness, anxious to reach Cyprus.

2. 28 (*AASS* Nov. IV, p. 635) [ΣΒΠΚΙ 37.2]

When he [St. Constantine] had reached the city of Attaleia [in Pamphylia], from which most travellers bound for Cyprus are wont to make their departure, he encountered a man who put too much stock [reading ἀναθέμενος for ἀναθέμενον] in the virtue of quietude. This man gave to the blessed saint words of his own counsel, dampened his enthusiasm, and persuaded him to stay with him and to give up the journey to Cyprus . . .

For a lion was not sent against this man, most holy and indeed admirable for his virtue, but in a dream the great Spyridon, expecting to make him head [reading πρόεδρον ποιῆσαι for προοδοποιῆσαι] of the monastery, stood by him, frightened him by some angelic power, reproached him for his cowardice, chided him for his lack of faith, and urged him to start on the journey to Cyprus and to think that he [Spyridon], having commanded the journey, would be with him and swiftly undertake the journey with him.

3. 29 (*AASS* Nov. IV, p. 636) [ΣΒΠΚΙ 37.3]

And this divine dream deemed the blessed man worthy of such voice. And he delayed no further but condemned his own cowardice and the delay up to this point. So he boarded one of the ships which usually ply this route and made the journey to Cyprus in the hope of attaining the salvation that was promised [?] . . . With the help of a favorable wind blowing gently he accomplished the voyage, reached Cyprus, and left the ship.

4. 30 (*AASS* Nov. IV, p. 636) [ΣΒΠΚΙ 37.4]

When he left the ship he met some of the local men and, as it was the blessed man's habit always to inquire about things of the spirit rather than about other aspects of life, he learned from them something of value. This was that in some place in the area, hard to reach and precipitous, there were the holy relics of saints (these were called the Shiny Ones) and there the sound of holy singing was heard. And so great was the fear of the inhabitants that they thought of that precipice as dangerous and held their assemblies close to the saints. Only the bishop dared to approach that tomb, to lower a fire from above the steep grotto, and spread the sweet smell of spices. But the blessed man, upon hearing this, without delay went to that holy tomb, taking no account of the danger.

5. 33 (*AASS* Nov. IV, p. 637) [ΣΒΠΚΙ 37.5]

At this point he again heard a divine voice: a certain man by name of Palamon was calling him to himself. This man was outstanding among the ascetics and the martyrs, and the history that was written about him has recorded his valiant fights for Christ's sake . . . Giving heed to these words he went in all haste to the shrine of the divine Palamon.

6. 35 (*AASS* Nov. IV, p. 637) [ΣΒΠΚΙ 37.6]

Thus, having indeed obtained this venerable and precious treasure [the right hand of St. Palamon] and having been commanded to deposit it in a specified holy place, he left Cyprus and made his way to the monastery which is named after St. Hyakinthos [in Nicaea].

7. 38–39 (*AASS* Nov. IV, p. 638–39) [ΣΒΠΚΙ 37.7]

When the blessed man had not yet left Cyprus, but was, with the gift of the arm [of St. Palamon] in his possession, making the rounds of other holy places in holy desire and for the purpose of prayer, there happened to him a miracle, which was not ignoble but showed the wealth of the grace within him. For, as he was performing prayer in one of the oratories on the island (it happened to be the holy precinct of the Prodromos [St. John the Baptist], the Ishmaelite Saracens came upon the sanctuary. For they [the Saracens] had a part in the government of Cyprus [by the treaty of 686] . . . This prompted the blessed man quickly to leave Cyprus and to move to the opposite mainland.

77. LEO VI, emperor 886–912 (ca. 905)

1. *Taktika* 212 (Migne, *PG* 107, col. 1072) [ΣΒΠΚΙ 39]

General, when you are at war against people who are being collected from many places, you must not wait until they have been assembled in one place. But attack them while they are still [reading ἔτι for ἔστι] being prepared in their own respective countries or in other places, before they have come together. So it is with the barbarians who are now being collected from Egypt, Syria, and Cilicia to make war on the Romans. The naval commanders must seize Cyprus with their naval forces, before the barbarians' ships have been assembled, and send a sufficient naval force against them to engage them while they are still [reading ἔτι for ἔστι] divided or to burn their ships before they set sail from their own country.

78. NICHOLAS I MYSTIKOS, patriarch of Constantinople 901–907 and 912–925

1. *Ep.* 1. [To the Caliph Al-Muqtadir] (Aug. 913/ Feb. 914) [ΣΒΠΚΙ 43]

Summary

Inasmuch as all power comes from God, those united by this common gift should communicate through letters and envoys. This is especially true of the two supreme powers, Romans and Saracens (3–22). Such contact is all the more necessary in view of the present events, in which the issue is justice, the virtue most essential to the ruler (23–43).

Since the time when the Cypriotes became tributary to you, their right to protection was always respected by your successive rulers; now all the oaths and treaties are suddenly void, and they are slaughtered by those who should be their protectors (44–46). A nation which has served you loyally for nearly three centuries has fallen victim to the frenzy of a renegade. Even if they had undertaken anything against you (as they have not), they should not be treated as enemies without having been heard and warned (67–92).

Will not your fame, present and future, suffer from this? What must your forefathers, who concluded the treaties, think of it? Should this impious wretch Damianus be allowed to exterminate a nation (93–115)?

The alleged reason, the killing of Saracens in the island by Himerius, would be valid only if the Cypriotes had cooperated with him. As it is, they were powerless to interfere with the operations of the Roman army. Why not punish those who are responsible? It would be equally absurd to use Himerius' invasion of Syria as an excuse for action against Cyprus. Traditionally, Cyprus has always been recognized as a common sphere of interest between the Romans and you. The hostilities on the island have nothing to do with this, no more than the Syrian Christians ought to be victimized because of your war with the Christian Empire (116–57).

You must be aware of the way in which the divine wrath overtook Damianus: not only his death, but also his illness from the time of the atrocities in Cyprus, and the destruction of your fleet in the very island he intended to lay waste (158–69). Act in accordance with your wisdom and restore the old conditions (170–81).

Addressee: Jenkins has argued convincingly that the letter is not to the Emir of Crete, but to the Caliph (head of the Muslims, ruler of Syria), to whom St. Demetrianus about this time appealed on behalf of the Cypriotes.

Date: After Damianus' death (Aug. 913/July 914) and during Nicholas' regency (no emperor mentioned).

This summary from: Nicholas I Patriarch of Constantinople, *Letters*, edd. R. J. H. Jenkins and L. G. Westerink (*CFHB* 6; Washington, D.C., 1973), pp. 525–526. Quoted by permission of Dumbarton Oaks Research Library and Collection, Washington, D.C. The complete text and translation are found ibid., pp. 2–13.

79. ARETHAS, archbishop of Caesarea (ca. 860–after 932)

1. *Scripta Minora* 58 (vol. II, pp. 7–8 ed. Westerink) [ΣΒΠΚΙ 41.1]

Speech for the venerable relics of Lazarus,
which Leo [VI the Wise, 886–912], the Christ-loving emperor,
transferred from Cyprus.

. . .

This man was once called from Cyprus and now dwells among us by decree of the emperor. We must in no way fall short of such holiness. [901/902]

2. *Scripta Minora* 59 (vol. II, pp. 11–12 ed. Westerink) [ΣΒΠΚΙ 41.2]

Description by the same author of the holy procession which Leo [VI the Wise, 886–912], the pious emperor conducted for the venerable relics of Lazarus, the friend of Christ, when he first transferred them from Cyprus . . .

Lazarus the friend of Christ, having sounded the trumpet loud and clear for his own appearance, again gathers and leads the people who love God and holiness . . . so that, having come from Cyprus by decree of the emperor, he might himself walk in procession.

80. KAMINIATES, JOHN (authenticity suspect) (first half, 10th c.)

1. *The Capture of Thessalonike* 77 (p. 66 ed. Böhlig) [ΣΒΠΚΙ 40]

On the fifth day of our voyage we already reached the island of Cyprus and docked in the harbor of Paphos. There we stayed briefly, while the barbarians left the ship and bathed in the nearby waters. Then we set sail again and after another day's voyage reached Tripolis on the very day of the Exaltation of the Cross [September 14, 904].

81. CONSTANTINE (VII) PORPHYROGENNETOS (905–959)

1. *De Thematibus* 1.15 [ΑΚΕΠ I 14.20; 66.46α; 77.6δ; 109.8β; II 152.1β; 155.5; ΣΒΠΚΙ 44]

Theme 15, called the eparchy of Cyprus.

The eparchy of the island of Cyprus is administered by a *consularis*, i.e. a member of the senate. It contains 15 cities: Constantia (the capital), Kition, Amathous, Kyreneia, Paphos, Arsinoe, Soloi, Lapithos, Kermia or Leukosia, Kytherea, Tamasos, Kourion, Nemesos, Trimythos (the city of St. Spyridon), and Karpasion.

Cyprus is a large and very renowned island located in the Gulf of Pamphylia, as Dionysios Periegetes [Οἰκουμένης Περιήγησις or *Orbis Descriptio* 508–509] says.

Cyprus lies to the east, in the sea of Pamphylia.

Cyprus was named from Kypros the daughter of Kinyras, or that of Byblos, and from Aphrodite, as Philostephanos [of Cyrene, 3rd c. B.C.] says in his *On Islands* [*FHG* III 30, fr. 11] and Istros ["the Callimachean," 3rd c. B.C.] in his *On the Settlements of the Egyptians* [*FHG* I 423, fr. 39; *FGrH* IIIB 334, fr. 45.]

They were previously governed by many and various kings. But the kingdom of Cyprus was dissolved by the Macedonians, i.e. the Ptolemies. Until the time of Alexander king of Macedon it was ruled by kings or tyrants; the philosopher Anaxarchos was put to death by these tyrants after Alexander's death.

And Isocrates the orator made several speeches to Demonikos [son of Evagoras], who was the king (of Cyprus).

When the Romans were in power Cyprus was an eparchy and, as already mentioned, was divided into 15 cities. In due time, when Roman power declined through neglect, the Saracens seized it; this was during the reign of Herakleios [610–641]. The first to cross over to it and to seize it was Abubacharos [Abu-Bakr, father-in-law of the Prophet Muhammad]; and his daughter's tomb is shown there, too [an erroneous reference to the Hale Sultan Tekke?]. But the blessed and renowned emperor Basil [I, 867–886], my grandfather, made it again one of the themes. He posted there the general Alexios, a renowned man, an Armenian by nationality, who governed it for seven years. Then it was seized again by the Saracens, and they imposed tribute on it, as they had done before.

2. *De Ceremoniis Aulae Byzantinae* 2.44 (Migne, *PG* 112, cols. 1117–20) [ΣΒΠΚΙ 45]

Leo, the *protospatharios* [member of the imperial hierarchy] and governor of Cyprus, who was from Symbatike [?], undertook to send reliable scouts to the Gulf of Tarsos and the district of Stomia [?] and also to Tripolis and Laodikeia, so that they might send him information from both regions on the Saracens' plans.

3. *De Administrando Imperio* 20 [ΣΒΠΚΙ 46.1]

The fourth chief of the Arabs, Outhman: He [Othman, caliph 644–656] took Africa by war, and arranged imposts with the Africans and returned. His general was Mauias [Muawiyah], who pulled down the colossus of Rhodes and took the island of Cyprus and all its cities. He took the island of Arados [off the coast of northern Lebanon] also and burnt its city and made the island desolate to this day. [649]

(trans. R. J. H. Jenkins)

4. *De Administrando Imperio* 22 [ΣΒΠΚΙ 46.2]

Quotation from Theophanes the Confessor, *Chronographia*, annus mundi 6178; *see* **61**.9.

5. *De Administrando Imperio* 47 [ΣΒΠΚΙ 46.3]

Of the migration of the Cypriots the story is as follows: When the island was captured by the Saracens and remained uninhabited seven years, and the archbishop John came with his folk to the imperial city [691], a dispensation was made by the emperor Justinian [II, 685–695 and

705–711] in the holy sixth synod [actually the Council in Trullo or Quinisext Council of 691] that he, with his bishops and the folk of the island, should take over Cyzicus and should make his appointments whenever a bishopric should fall vacant, to the end that the authority and rights of Cyprus might not be interrupted (for the emperor Justinian himself also was a Cypriot, as from the Cypriots of olden days the tale has persisted unto this day); and so it was ordained in the holy sixth synod that the archbishop of Cyprus should appoint the president of Cyzicus, as it is recorded in the 39th chapter of the same holy sixth synod.

But after seven years, by God's will the emperor was moved to populate Cyprus again, and he sent to the commander of the faithful of Baghdad three of the illustrious Cypriots, natives of the same island, called Phangoumeis, together with an imperial agent both intelligent and illustrious, and wrote to the commander of the faithful [the caliph] asking him to dismiss the folk of the island of Cyprus that were in Syria to their own place. The commander of the faithful obeyed the emperor's epistle, and sent illustrious Saracens to all the parts of Syria and gathered together all the Cypriots and carried them over to their own place. And the emperor, for his part, sent an imperial agent and carried over those who had settled in Romania, that is, at Cyzicus and in the Kibyrrhaiote and Thrakesian provinces, and the island was populated.

(trans. R. J. H. Jenkins)

6. *De Administrando Imperio* 48 [ΣΒΠΚΙ 46.4]

Chapter 39 of the holy sixth synod, held in the Domed Hall of the Great Palace [Council in Trullo, or Quinisext Council, 691]: Whereas our brother and fellow-minister John, president of the isle of the Cypriots, because of the barbarian assaults and to the end that they might be free from slavery to the infidel and be subject unfeignedly to the sceptre of his most Christian majesty, hath with his own folk migrated from the said isle to the province of Hellespont, by the providence and mercy of God and by the labour of our Christ-loving and pious emperor; we do resolve: that the privileges accorded unto the throne of the aforesaid by the fathers inspired of God at their sometimes meeting in Ephesus [431] shall be preserved unaltered; that the new Justinianoupolis shall have the right of the city of the Constantinians; and that the most pious bishop who is over it shall preside over all the bishops of the province of Hellespont, and shall be appointed by his own bishops, according to the ancient custom (for our fathers inspired of God have resolved that the practices in each church are to be preserved), the bishops of the city of the Cyzicenes being subject to the president of the said Justinianoupolis in like manner as are all the rest of the bishops under the said most pious president John, by whom as need shall arise the bishop also of the same city of the Cyzicenes shall be appointed. (trans. R. J. H. Jenkins)

82. SYMEON MAGISTROS, logothete, or LEO GRAMMATIKOS (floruit mid 10th c.)

1. *Chronographia,* p. 117 ed. Becker [ΣΒΠΚΙ 50.1]

Zeno [474–475 and 476–491] spent his time in unseemly pleasures and unseemly activities. It was in his days that the body of the apostle Barnabas was found in Cyprus under a carob tree, having on its chest the Gospel of Matthew, written by Barnabas' own hand. On these grounds [Cyprus] became a metropolis and is subject not to Antioch but to Constantinople. Zeno placed this gospel in his palace, in the Chapel of St. Stephen.

2. *Chronographia*, p. 191 ed. Becker [ΣΒΠΚΙ 50.2]

When the Arabs had left, the emperor [Leo IV, 775–780] sent out the army and gained a great victory . . . And when the patriarch Niketas [I, 766–780], the Slavic eunuch, had died, Paul [IV, 780–784] was ordained patriarch; he was a Cypriot and a honorable man, highly regarded for his words and deeds.

83. *Taktikon Escurial* or *Escoriale* (971–975)

1. p. 265.25–29 ed. Oikonomides [ΣΒΠΚΙ I 48]

the [general] of the Kibyrrhaiotai
the [general] of Cyprus
the [general] of Crete
the [general] of Greece
the [general] of Sicily.

84. MENOLOGION OF BASIL II (ca. 979–986)

1. November 12 (Migne, *PG* 117, col. 157) (*PG* erroneously October 12) [ΣΒΠΚΙ 56.4]

Commemoration of our holy father John the Almoner, patriarch of Alexandria.
He was a Cypriot by birth, son of Epiphanios, who was the governor of the island at that time.

2. December 3 (Migne, *PG* 117, col. 192) [ΣΒΠΚΙ 56.5]

Commemoration of the holy Theodoulos.
The holy Theodoulos was a native of the island of Cyprus. Already in his youth he abandoned the world, loved Christ with all his heart, and became a monk . . . When he had lived in this manner and saved many, both by his example and by his teaching, he died in peace. His remains were laid to rest in Cyprus, where they brought about many healings.

3. December 9 (Migne, *PG* 117, col. 197–200) [ΣΒΠΚΙ 56.6]

Commemoration of our holy father Sophronios, bishop of Constantia in Cyprus.
Our holy father Sophronios was a native of the great island of Cyprus and the son of pious Christian parents . . . He was so virtuous and pious that he was found worthy of great gifts and performed many miracles. Therefore, after the death of Damianos, the holy archbishop of Cyprus, he was made archbishop of the holy church of Cyprus by all the people and the bishops.

4. December 12 (Migne, *PG* 117, cols. 201–204) [ΣΒΠΚΙ 56.1]

Commemoration of our holy father Spyridon, bishop of Tremithous in Cyprus.

Our holy father Spyridon lived at the time of the emperor Constantine; he was simple in manner and lowly in heart. He was a shepherd. He took a wife and begot a daughter. When his wife died he became a bishop; he also became a miracle-worker. At a time of drought he caused it to rain, and he turned famine into prosperity . . . And he attended the Council of Nicaea [325] and put the heretics to shame . . . And when he had done many other things he died peacefully.

5. January 19 (Migne, *PG* 117, cols. 265–68) [ΣΒΠΚΙ 56.2]

Martyrdom of the holy martyr Theodotos, bishop of Kyrenia in Cyprus.

He lived at the time of Licinius the emperor [308–324] and Sabinus [the praetorian prefect of Maximinus Daia 311–312?] the governor of the island of Cyprus. Because he confessed Christ he was seized, taken before the governor Sabinus, and severely beaten with dry whips. Then he was hung up on a rack and had his flesh scraped; after that he was stretched out on a fiery iron bed, but miraculously, through the grace of Christ, he was rescued from the fire. Then iron sandals with sharp nails were put on him and he was forced to run. Finally he was cast into prison. When . . . the persecution was ended by decree of Constantine the Great, who was then ruling the Roman empire, he was released from confinement. He carried on in his own church, fearlessly teaching the word of our Lord Jesus Christ. He lived for another two years and turned many to piety before passing on to the Lord. He was honorably buried by his devoted disciples.

6. February 17 (Migne, *PG* 117, cols. 317–20)

Commemoration of our holy father Auxibios, bishop of the city of Cyprus [sic].

He came from the ancient city of Rome, but was a Greek. He followed the holy apostle and evangelist Mark, was taught the word of truth by him, baptized, and ordained first a deacon, then a presbyter, and after that bishop of the city of Soloi in Cyprus . . . He called upon God night and day to have mercy on his people and to stop the persecution of the Christians by the tyrants, so that all might come to know true worship and reject impiety. Doing this, having turned many towards the living God, and having been found worthy of many miracles, he peacefully passed on to God, rejoicing forever in the company of the other saints.

7. March 8 (Migne, *PG* 117, col. 344) [ΣΒΠΚΙ 56.3]

Commemoration of the holy Arkadios of Cyprus and martyrdom of Euboulos and Iulianus.

The holy Arkadios was a native of the island of Cyprus, became a monk in his youth, and pleased God by his service. He suffered martyrdom during the reign of Constantine the Great and not only through his virtuous life, but also by his teaching and his exhortation benefited many; among them were Euboulos and Iulianus.

8. May 12 (Migne, *PG* 117, col. 452) [ΑΚΕΠ I 135.12γ; 135.14α; ΣΒΠΚΙ 56.7 erroneously December 12]

Commemoration of our holy father Epiphanios, archbishop of Constantia in Cyprus.

Our holy father Epiphanios was a native of Phoenicia and the son of Jewish parents. They adhered to the observance of the Law, but he himself turned to Christ, was baptized, and became a monk. Then he was ordained bishop of Cyprus. And he so served God that he was deemed worthy of performing miracles. He fought valiantly for the orthodox faith and suffered many trials at the hands of the heretics. And when he had strengthened the truth by his words and had driven the heretics from the church he traveled to Constantinople. There [the empress] Eudoxia pressured him to subscribe to the exile of [John] Chrysostom, but he would not consent to do it. But when she threatened to open the pagan temples unless he did subscribe he was persuaded and subscribed. When Chrysostom found out he wrote to Epiphanios, "Since you have agreed to my exile, Epiphanios, you will not sit on your throne." And Epiphanius responded, "Athlete John, be beaten and win." Then, on his way to Cyprus he died on board his ship [403].

9. May 25 (Migne, *PG* 117, col. 473) [ΣΒΠΚΙ 56.8]

Martyrdom of the holy martyr Therapon.

We are unable to say whence Therapon, the holy martyr of Christ, came, who his parents were, or when he lived, since all records of him, it seems, have been lost. This only [we can say] that he was a monk and a bishop of Cyprus . . . These things happened earlier. But at a later time, when the Saracens were about to descend upon Cyprus, [the spirit of] the holy man appeared to his caretaker and spoke to him: "Rise quickly, take my relics, and bring them to Constantinople; for the enemies of the Cross of Christ are about to descend upon this island and to devastate these places." Thus the relics were translated to Constantinople, where they brought about many healings.

10. June 11 (Migne, *PG* 117, cols. 493–96)

Martyrdom of the holy apostles Bartholomew and Barnabas.

Of these Bartholomew was one of the twelve disciples . . . But Barnabas, who is also called Joseph in the Acts of the Apostles [4:36], was one of the Seventy and accompanied Paul on his travels. His name means "Son of Consolation." He was of the tribe of Levi and had been born and raised on the island of Cyprus. He was the first to preach the gospel of Christ in Jerusalem, Rome, and Alexandria, but when he came to Cyprus he was stoned and burned by the Jews and Greeks. Mark, the apostle and evangelist, obtained his body and placed it in a cave; then he sailed to Ephesus and reported the death of Barnabas to Paul. And Mark wept for Barnabas for a long time. It is reported that he was buried together with the Gospel of Matthew, which he had copied and which was later found together with the apostle's body. From this circumstance the faithful [of Cyprus] derive the privilege whereby their island shall not be subject to any foreign bishop but shall be administered by its own bishop.

11. June 16 (Migne, *PG* 117, col. 500) [ΣΒΠΚΙ 56.9]

    Commemoration of our holy father and miracle worker Tychon.
    Tychon was born of pious parents and consecrated by them to the service of God. And when he had learned the holy scriptures he was ordained a deacon by the bishop of Tremithous. When the latter had died he was elevated to the bishop's throne by the great Epiphanios. And when he had led many from error to the Lord and had performed many miracles he was called home to the Lord.

12. June 23 (Migne, *PG* 117, col. 508) (Col. 506 erroneously gives June 13.)

    Martyrdom of the holy martyr Aristokles and his companions.
    St. Aristokles was from Cyprus, a presbyter of the church of God. During the reign of Maximian [Galerius, 293–311], fearing persecution, he retired to a mountain and hid in a cave. There, while he was praying, he heard a voice from heaven commanding him to go into the metropolis and there to suffer martyrdom. And when he had come to the house of the holy apostle Barnabas he found there the deacon Demetrianos and the reader Athanasios, who received him and to whom he related all that he had been told in his vision. Taking them as his companions he went to the governor. When he had confessed Christ he was cast into prison together with his companions. After that he himself was beheaded, but Demetrianos and Athanasios were consigned to fire; when they emerged unharmed from the fire they, too, were beheaded.

13. August 14 (Migne, *PG* 117, col. 584) [ΣΒΠΚΙ 56.10]

    Commemoration of the holy martyr Marcellus, bishop of Apameia.
    This man lived at the time of the emperor Theodosios [I, 379–395] and was a native of the island of Cyprus. He was engaged in secular government and was charged with the administration of the island; he amazed all by the piety and honesty with which he administered affairs. Then he changed to the ranks of the clergy, became bishop of Apameia in Syria, and in all regards served in righteousness and holiness.

85. SYNAXARION OF CONSTANTINOPLE (10th c.)

1. September 17, no. 5 (col. 54 ed. Delehaye) [ΑΚΕΠ I 110.31γ]

    The martyrdom of the holy martyrs Herakleides and Myron, bishops of Tamassos in Cyprus.

2. October 17, no. 3 (col. 146 ed. Delehaye) [ΣΒΠΚΙ 58.1]

    On the same day commemoration of the translation of the relics of the holy and righteous Lazarus. This translation was undertaken by the faithful emperor Leo [VI the Wise, 886–912]. He was moved by divine zeal, as if by some inspiration, first to build a beautiful church and then to send [agents] to the island of Cyprus. There he found the holy relics in the city of Kition lying under the ground in a marble chest, almost a thousand years having passed. An inscription in the chest, in a foreign tongue, read: "Lazarus, who was raised from the dead on the fourth day and was a friend of Christ." Forthwith they took the precious treasure, put it in a silver casket, and brought it to Constantinople.

3. December 8, no. 3 (cols. 289–90 ed. Delehaye) [ΑΚΕΠ I 110.33γ]

On the same day the commemoration of the Holy Apostles, of the Seventy . . . Epaphro-ditos, whom the same Apostle [Paul] mentions [Philippians 2:25–30 and 4:18], was bishop of Adrake [?] . . . All these served well, were shepherds in holiness, and governed the churches as-signed to them and the people. When they had endured many trials and tests for the sake of Christ they were put to death by the idolaters; they committed their souls to the Lord, for whose sake they willingly suffered death.

4. December 8, no. 4 (col. 290 ed. Delehaye)

On the same day the commemoration of our holy father Sophronios, bishop of Cyprus. He was a native of the great island of Cyprus, the son of pious Christian parents. He was by natural disposition given to learning, read the Holy Scripture with care, and studied the sayings of the Lord by night and by day. He became so virtuous and pious that he was found worthy of great charismatic gifts and performed many miracles. Thus, upon the death of Damianos, the holy bishop of Cyprus, he was made archbishop of the holy church of Cyprus by all the people and the bishops. And when he had received the church, he became a champion of the poor, helped the orphans, protected the widows, brought relief to those who were heavily laden, and clothed the naked. When he had lived his life in this manner and had pleased God in every way he died peacefully.

5. December 12, no. 1 (col. 303 ed. Delehaye)

In memory of our holy father and miracle-worker Spyridon, bishop of Tremithous in Cy-prus. He lived at the time of the emperor Constantine the Great; he was simple in manner and lowly of heart. He was a shepherd. He took a wife and begot a daughter. When his wife died he became a bishop; he also became a miracle-worker. At a time of drought he caused it to rain, and he turned famine into prosperity . . . And he attended the Council of Nicaea [325] and put the heretics to shame . . . And when he had done many other things he died peacefully. His liturgy is performed in the venerable chapel of St. Peter, the chief of the apostles, which is located next to the great and holy church [Hagia Sophia in Constantinople].

6. January 19, no. 4 (col. 404 ed. Delehaye) [ΑΚΕΠ I 120]

On the same day the victory of the holy martyr Theodotos, the bishop of the city of Kyre-nia in Cyprus. He lived at the time of the emperor Licinius [308–324] and of Sabinus, the gov-ernor of the island of Cyprus. Because he had confessed Christ he was brought before the governor Sabinus himself and beaten with whips. Then he was hung up, his flesh was scraped, and he was stretched out on a fiery iron bed. But miraculously, through the grace of Christ, he was rescued from the fire. Then he had his feet pierced with nails and was forced to run. Finally he was cast into prison. When the persecution ended by decree of Constantine the Great he was released from confinement and two years later passed on to the Lord.

7. February 17, no. 3 (cols. 469–70 ed. Delehaye)

Commemoration of our holy father Auxibios, bishop of the city of Soloi in Cyprus. He came from the Old Rome, being a Greek. He followed the holy apostle and evangelist Mark, was taught the word of truth by him, was baptized, and was ordained bishop of the city of Soloi in Cyprus. When he had gone forth and had turned many towards Christ, had been found worthy of diverse gifts, and had performed countless miracles he passed on to the Lord.

8. May 12, no. 2 (cols. 675–77 ed. Delehaye)

On the same day the commemoration of our holy father Epiphanios, archbishop of Constantia in Cyprus. This man, the great and miracle-working Epiphanios, came from the land of Phoenicia, from the neighborhood of Eleutheropolis; his father was a farmer and his mother practiced weaving . . . When he had become the archbishop he endured many trials at the hands of the heretics, but he strengthened the truth by his words and drove the heretics from the church. When he visited Constantinople he was pressured by [the empress] Eudoxia to subscribe to the exile of [St. John] Chrysostom, but he refused. But when she threatened to open the idolatrous temples if he would not comply he yielded and subscribed. When [St. John] Chrysostom heard about this he wrote to him, "Brother Epiphanios, I have heard that you have consented to my exile. Let me tell you that you will not sit on your throne." And Epiphanios replied, "Athlete John, be beaten and win." And this is what happened. As Epiphanios was returning from Constantinople to Cyprus he died on board his ship, just as the great John had written to him . . . He had lived 115 years minus three months when he passed on to the Lord. His liturgy is performed in his holy house [chapel?] which is in the [Church of] St. Philemon.

9. May 26, no.2 (col. 710 ed. Delehaye) [ΣΒΠΚΙ 58.2]

St. Therapon . . . was a bishop on the island of Cyprus, came close to Christ by his blood, and achieved martyrdom . . . His precious relics were translated to the royal city [Constantinople] when the Saracens were planning to attack the island of Cyprus and to lay it waste. The saint, in a vision, said to his caretaker: "Rise swiftly, take my relics, and bring them to Constantinople; for the enemies of the Cross of Christ are about to attack this island and to lay waste these places." And he [the caretaker] swiftly did as told. And now, where he [Therapon] lies, he brings forth an abundance of miracles all the time. His cult is practiced in his holy martyrium, which is close to the Church of the Olive [?].

10. June 11, no.1 (cols. 743–46 ed. Delehaye) [ΣΒΠΚΙ 58.3]

Martyrdom of the holy and renowned apostles Bartholomew and Barnabas. Of these two Bartholomew was one of the Twelve . . . But Barnabas, who is also called Joseph in the Acts of the Apostles [4:36] and was one of the Seventy, was ordained as a companion of Peter [?]. His name means "Son of Consolation." He was of the tribe of Levi and had been born and raised in Cyprus. He was the first to preach the gospel of Christ in Jerusalem, Rome, and Alexandria, but when he came to Cyprus he was stoned and burned by the Jews and the Greeks. Mark, the apostle and evangelist, obtained the body and placed it in a cave; then he sailed to Ephesus and reported the death of Barnabas to Paul. And Mark wept for Barnabas for a long time. It is reported that he was buried together with the Gospel of Matthew, which he had copied and which was later found together with the apostle's body. From this circumstance the faithful [of Cyprus] derive the privilege whereby their island shall not be subject to any other bishop but shall be administered by its own bishop. His liturgy is performed in the venerable chapel of St. Peter, the chief of the apostles, which is located next to the holy great church [Hagia Sophia in Constantinople].

11. June 16, no.1 (col. 751 ed. Delehaye)

Commemoration of our reverend father and miracle worker Tychon, bishop of the city of Amathous in Cyprus. He had pious and Christ-loving earthly parents, who dedicated him to the service of God. And when he had learned the holy scriptures and was sufficiently versed in them he was ordained a deacon by the bishop Mnemon. When the latter had departed from life he himself was enthroned as bishop by the great Epiphanios. When he had led many from the erroneous worship of idols to faith in Christ our God and had destroyed many pagan temples and overturned the idols in them he passed on to the Lord. He had performed many miracles both while still alive and after his death. Of these one or two deserve to be mentioned as examples of the man's virtue.

12. June 23, no. 2 (cols. 765–66 ed. Delehaye) [ΑΚΕΠ I 118]

On the same day the martyrdom of the holy martyrs Aristokles the presbyter, Demetrianos the deacon, and Athanasios the reader. Of them the holy martyr Aristokles was by nationality a Cypriot, from the city of Tamassos, a presbyter of the catholic church. At the time of the emperor Maximian [Galerius, 293–311] he went on some mountain and hid in a cave, fearing the persecution that was going on. When he was engaged in prayer he was surrounded by a light brighter than the sun. And a voice came from heaven and bade him go to the metropolis of Salamis and there endure martyrdom. He went on his way and came to Ledrae [later Leukosia], to the house of the holy apostle Barnabas. And there he found Demetrianos the deacon and Athanasios the reader, who received him hospitably. He revealed to them the reason for his coming and the things which he had seen in his vision, and they eagerly chose to contend for Christ. When they had reached the city which was their destination they stood in a conspicuoius and lofty place. The governor spotted them, had them brought to him, and found out that they were Christians. First he ordered the holy Aristokles to be scourged and then he had him decapitated by the sword. And when Demetrianos and Athanasios, the holy men, persisted in confessing Christ and had suffered many tortures he ordered them to be given over to fire. Finally, when they were untouched by the fire, he ordered them to be done away with by the sword.

13. June 30, no. 1 (cols. 782–83 ed. Delehaye) [AKEΠ I 110.29β]

Barnabas, who is also called Joses in the Acts of the Apostles [Acts 4:36], is one of the seventy disciples. He copied the Gospel of Matthew by his own hand and died on the island of Cyprus.

14. June 30, no. 1 (col. 787 ed. Delehaye) [AKEΠ I 110.33γ]

Epaphrodites, who was bishop of Adriake [?].

15. August 14, no. 2 (col. 891 ed. Delehaye) [ΣΒΠΚΙ 58.4]

On the same day martyrdom of the holy martyr Marcellus, bishop of Apameia, and his seventy disciples. He lived at the time of the emperor Theodosios [379–395] and was a native of the island of Cyprus. He was engaged in secular government and was charged with the administration of the island; he amazed all by the piety and honesty with which he administered affairs. Then he transferred to the ranks of the clergy and was made bishop of Apameia in Syria.

16. August 30, no. 2 (cols. 933–34 ed. Delehaye) [AKEΠ I 118.1]

On the same day the martyrdom of the holy martyr Philonides, bishop of Kourion. This holy man lived when Diocletian was emperor [284–305] and Maximus was governor [of Cyprus]. When the martyrs with whom he had been confined, I mean Aristokles, Demetrianos, and Athanasios, had been killed, the governor issued a decree, abominable and in keeping with his own character, that the Christians should be forced and violated contrary to nature by dissolute and loathsome men. But the blessed Philonides would not endure to listen to such lawless order; he sighed deeply, wept, and prayed; then he bound up his head and covered his face with his cloak, prayed again, and leaped from a high place. Before he suffered the pain of the fall he surrendered his spirit to God, as he was borne towards the ground. An angel of the Lord forthwith bade the presbyter of this place to take up the body and to tend to it with all honors.

86. ABBREVIATED LIFE OF ST. JOHN CHRYSOSTOM (*BHG* 874d) (10th c.)

1. 40 (pp. 348–49) ed. Halkin

When this was the state of affairs a false report reached Theophilos [of Alexandria] to the effect that John had received the ascetics into communion and was ready to support them. He was intent not only on revenging himself on the followers of Dioskoros and Isidore but also on driving John from his throne. He sent letters to the bishops in every city, hiding his true purpose and pretending to fault only the books of Origen. Because of his enmity towards the others he denied in publc what he thought. He befriended Epiphanios, the saintly bishop of Constantia on the island of Cyprus, and prevailed upon him to convene a council of the bishops in Cyprus for the purpose of condemning the books of Origen. And he, because of his excessive piety, was convinced by Theophilos' letter.

2. 43–44 (pp. 354–56) ed. Halkin

43. Not much later Bishop Epiphanios came from Cyprus to Constantinople, having been persuaded by the the arguments of Theophilos and bringing with him the decree condemning the books of Origen. He landed at the Martyrium of John—this is seven milestones from the city [at Hebdomon]—disembarked from the ship, held a service, and ordained a deacon; then he returned to the city. Wishing to please Theophilos he declined John's invitation and stayed in private quarters. The next day those who harbored animosity towards John prevailed upon the great Epiphanios, when a service was held in the church which is called the Church of the Apostles, to come forward and, in the presence of all the people, condemn the books of Origen, excommunicate the followers of Dioskoros, and charge John with supporting them. These things were reported to John. And the next day, when Epiphanios had entered the church, he had the following message delivered to him through Sarapion: "Epiphanios, you do many things against church laws. First you performed an ordination in the churches under my jurisdiction, and then, without authorization from me, you held a service in them, relying on your own authority. Be on your guard lest some disturbance break out among the people and you find yourself in danger resulting from it." When Epiphanios had heard these words he discreetly withdrew from the church.

44. Apart from a few minor variations, this chapter is taken verbatim from the corresponding chapter (44) of the Life of St. John Chrysostom by George of Alexandria; see **46.2**.

87. Περὶ Νικηφόρου τοῦ ἄνακτος (On the Lord Nikephoros) (10th c.)

1. 14.1 ed. Halkin, *Inédits Byzantins* [ΣΒΠΚΙ 52]

Then he [Nikephoros II Phokas, 963–969] drove out the barbarian devils [the Arabs] who were lurking on the island of Cyprus and put them to flight [965].

88. SOUDA (10th c.)

1. Β 462 Βοῦς Κύπριος (Cypriot ox) [ΑΚΕΠ II 164.7γ]

Of the vulgar and unfeeling, since Cypriot oxen eat dung, it is said.

2. E 2742 Epiphanios [AKEΠ I 135.15]

Epiphanios, bishop of Constantia, the former Salamis, in Cyprus, wrote treatises against all the heresies, those called *Panaria* and many others. These are read by the educated for their contents and by the common folk for their proverbs. He died in old age.   (trans. P.W.W.)

3. Z 79 Zeno [AKEΠ I 36]

Son of Mnaseas or of Demios, from Kition. Kition is a city of Cyprus. He was a philosopher who founded the Stoic School. He himself is also called a Stoic because he taught in Athens in that stoa which was first called the Stoa of Peisianax and later the Stoa Poikile . . . He was called a Phoenician, because Phoenicians were the settlers of the small town. His floruit was at the time of Antigonos Gonatas [284/3–239 B.C.], in the 120th Olympiad [300–297 B.C.].

4. Θ 541 θύϊνα [AKEΠ I 110.34]

During the reign of the emperor Zeno [A.D. 474–475 and 476–491] there were found in Cyprus the remains of the apostle Barnabas, the companion of Paul. Lying on the breast of Barnabas was the Gospel of Matthew, which had leaves of thyine-wood.   (trans. P.W.W.)

5. K 497 Καταγηρᾶσαι (to grow old); Σ 122 Sardanapalus [AKEΠ I 14.33]

May you become older than Tithonos, wealthier than Kinyras, and more voluptuous than Sardanapalus, so that to you might be applied the proverb, "old men are twice children, "which is said of those who are very old. But Tithonos, when he had become exceedingly old, according to the prayer [of Eos], was changed into a cicada. And Kinyras, the offspring of Pharnake (?) and king of Cyprus, was distinguished by his wealth. And Sardanapalus, king of the Assyrians, died having spent his life in licentiousness and wantonness.

6. K 1620 Cimon [AKEΠ I 61.11]

Cimon, the son of Miltiades . . . sailed to Cyprus and Pamphylia to wage war and was victorious at the Eurymedon River with naval and land forces on the same day [467 B.C.] . . . He died at Kition in Cyprus [450 B.C.].

7. K 1651 Kinyras [AKEΠ I 14.14]

Name of a person.

8. K 2738 Cypris [AKEΠ II 20.139β]

An epithet of Aphrodite; any woman desiring to conceive. She is also called Kythereia, because she conceals lovers.

9. M 1283 Μοτοφαγία [ΑΚΕΠ II 114]

A certain sacrifice performed at Salamis in Cyprus.

10. Ξ 51 Xenophon [ΑΚΕΠ I 14.26α]

A Cypriot historian. [He wrote] *Kypriaka*. This is a history of erotic subjects, concerning Kinyras, Myrrha, and Adonis.

11. Ῥ 290 Ῥύκου κριθοπομπία (Rhykos sending barley) [ΑΚΕΠ II 163.4]

Eratosthenes says in the ninth book [of his *Amathousians*] that this king, having been taken prisoner and then returned to his own [country], sent barley to the city of the Athenians.

12. Σ 781 Soloi [ΑΚΕΠ II 155.6, no. 35]

A city of Sicily [Cilicia] and Cyprus. Hence the word "solecism," since they speak in their own barbaric tongue. Solon founded the city, whence it has its name.

13. Σ 776 Solon

Solon, the son of Exekestides, an Athenian, philosopher, lawgiver, and leader of the people . . . When the tyrant Pisistratus plotted against him he migrated to Cilicia and founded a city, which he named Soloi after himself. Others say that Soloi in Cyprus also was founded by him and that he died in Cyprus.

14. Σ 976 Spyridon [ΑΚΕΠ I 121.3β; 121.8α]

A person's name. Bishop of Trimythous, one of the cities of Cyprus, who, though a bishop, because of his lack of pride continued to shepherd his sheep . . . He performed many other wonders and was present at the Council of Nicaea.   (trans. P.W.W.)

15. Τ 1032 Triphyllios [ΑΚΕΠ I 125]

Triphyllios was a bishop, student of Spyridon, the miracle worker of Cyprus, who wrote about the miracles of our holy and marvel-working father Spyridon, as it is written in iambic verse about his life, which must be sought for as very beneficial.   (trans. P.W.W.)

16. Φ 449 Philo [ΑΚΕΠ I 136.6]

A man from Karpasia. He wrote a treatise on the Song of Songs [Song of Solomon].

17. X 623 Chytroi [ΑΚΕΠ II 155.6, #39]

This is a city in Cyprus, so called.

89. VITA OF ST. DEMETRIANOS (10th c.)

1. Ed. Grégoire, *BZ* 16 (1907) 232–33 [ΣΒΠΚΙ 42]

When he [St. Demetrianos, bishop of Kythereia, 9th or 10th c.] was still dwelling in the flesh, was pressed by old age, and was expecting that release through which the crown of righteousness is gained, there occurred a raid of Babylonian [Arab] barbarians on the island of Cyprus . . . When they had fallen upon the island, devastated many places, gathered a large number of helpless prisoners, and taken much booty, they came also to the town of the blessed Demetrianos; they plundered it and emptied it of its inhabitants and then quickly returned to the place from which they had come, having become the cause of much grief for those who were left on the island of Cyprus . . . But the great Demetrianos, having been deprived of his flock, cried loudly, lamented, and with many tears called upon the mercy of God, for the rescue of his flock, which had been scattered and destroyed by fierce wolves. No longer able to bear the pain in his heart, he followed the captives himself. He had two aims uppermost in his mind: either to share their misfortunes with them and to lighten their burden, or to free them from danger entirely and to lead them back to the land which had nourished them. And when he had reached Babylon [Old Cairo] and presented himself to its governor he cited the treaty and especially pointed out to him the savageness of the barbarians. This he did not casually, but with many bitter tears . . . But the chief of the barbarians was moved by the saint's tears, laid aside his natural savageness, and said, "Cease your excessive grief; for you will in every way gain the fulfillment of your desires." When this barbarian of whom I have spoken had learned of the reason and of the inhuman cruelty of the raiders, after two days he called the blessed Demetrianos and turned over to him both the booty and all the captives, and thus with great kindness sent them back to their own country. But the blessed saint with all the captured people reached his native land and with them glorified the God who had saved them, and they with great joy returned to their own homes.

90. CONTINUATOR OF GEORGE HAMARTOLOS or GEORGE THE MONK (10th c.)

1. *Vitae Recentiorum Imperatorum,* Migne, *PG* 109, col. 921 [ΣΒΠΚΙ 47]

In the same manner he [Leo VI the Wise, 886–912] founded in the place I have mentioned a Church of St. Lazarus and established it as a monastery for eunuchs. There he deposited the body of St. Lazarus, which he had brought from Cyprus, and that of Mary Magdalene, which he had brought from Ephesus, and dedicated the same church.

91. ABBREVIATION OF THE LIFE OF ST. JOHN CHRYSOSTOM by Theodore of Tremithous (*BHG* 872d) (ca. 1000)

1. 30 (p. 64) ed. Halkin

The emperor [Arkadios, 395–408] sent Arsakios [archbishop of Constantinople 404–405], the divine Epiphanios of Cyprus, Akakios of Beroea, Severianus [of Gabala in Galilee], and the three kinsmen of Theophilos [of Alexandria] to Pope Innocent [I, 401–417] with the following letter.
[Note: but Epiphanios is believed to have died in 403.]

92. SYMEON METAPHRASTES (d. ca. 1000)

1. Vita of St. Spyridon 2 [ΣΒΠΚΙ 51.1]

He (Spyridon) was a native of Cyprus. He was not an eloquent person, nor elegant in his ways, nor did he enjoy crowds and public life, but he was simple and quiet and, if anyone ever, kept away from business. For this reason he modeled himself entirely after the life of the patriarch Jacob, as we have said. And he was a shepherd.

2. Vita of St. Spyridon 3 [ΣΒΠΚΙ 51.1]

For this reason he, a shepherd, was appointed a shepherd and commanded to care for people rather than for sheep. And it was while Constantine the Great held the rule of the Romans that Spyridon was ordained bishop of the city of Trimithous.

3. Vita of St. Spyridon 4 [ΣΒΠΚΙ 51.1]

God chastised the island (of Cyprus) with a lack of rain, and a severe drought ensued; the drought was followed by famine, and the famine by a plague. A large part of the population had already died and others expected to die soon. This emergency required another Elijah, or someone like him, who would open the heavens by his prayers [1 Kings 17–18]. This was none other than Spyridon. For when the plague was raging and ravaging the people, he himself felt great anguish for his flock. Driven by a father's cares, he beseeched God as one benefactor would another. And God at once filled the sky with clouds from the ends of the earth. And this was a miracle, lest anyone might believe that rain came about by a natural turn of the elements: God only showed the clouds from a distance and did not allow them to reach the island until the saint again implored him. No sooner had the saint shed a flood of tears, when abundant rain broke forth. And the earth grew rich, the fruits were nourished, and the crops grew, and all troubles came to an end at the same time. And in this Spyridon was a greater benefactor than Elijah himself, if I may speak boldly.

4. Vita of St. Spyridon 12

When Constantine the Great was ruling the Roman empire—and he was the first Christian emperor—and Paulinus and Julian were consuls [325] . . . a famous council of holy fathers was gathered at Nicaea for the purpose of deposing Arius, who had impiously called the Son a creature, and to declare that the Son was of the same substance as the Father (*homoousios*) . . . And among them also was the great Spyridon, whose life and the grace that dwelt with him were more effective instruments of persuasion than the speeches of others with their inescapable syllogisms and elegant periodic sentences.

5. Vita of St. Spyridon 14–15

14. And he (Spyridon) stepped up to the man and said, "In the name of Jesus Christ, philosopher, pay attention to me and listen to what I wish to say." And the philosopher replied, "Speak, and I shall listen." Then Spyridon said, "There is one God, the creator of heaven and earth and all other things in between. He is the one who led forth the powers of heaven. He is the one who has formed man from earth and has established all things, those which are visible and those which are not. By his Word and by the Spirit heaven and earth were produced, the sea and the air took their places, living things were created, and man was formed, that great living thing and marvelous work. All things came forth, stars, lights, day, night, and all other things. This Word of God we know to be the Son and God, and we believe that he was borne by a virgin, crucified, and finally buried, but rose again, and that, having risen, he made us rise with him and gave to us eternal and everlasting life. And we say that he will come again, the incorrupt judge of our deeds, words, and thoughts. And we say that he is of one substance with the Father (*homoousios*), shares his throne, and partakes of equal honor. Do you not agree, philosopher?"
15. . . . And after a long silence he could only answer, "Yes, I think this is so."

6. Vita of St. Spyridon 17–18 and 21 [ΣΒΠΚΙ 51.2]

17. Constantine the Great [306–337] had recently died, and his sons had divided the empire. And Constantius [II, 337–361] had obtained the rule of the eastern portion and had taken up residence in the great city of Coele-Syria, namely Antioch. And a serious illness fell upon him and defied the skill and the hands of the physicians. Then he despaired of all others and prayed to him who alone can heal both souls and bodies. And as he prayed more intently he experienced a night-time vision in which an angel showed him an assembly of many holy bishops. And as the emperor gazed upon them he saw two bishops standing; they were similar to the bishops but seemed to be presidents or rulers. These the angel pointed out to him and said that they alone possessed the skill to cure his ailment. And when he awoke he wondered who they might be and could not interpret the dream. How could he, knowing neither their names nor their countries?
18. Letters were sent to all the regions of the Roman empire and the bishops were summoned. And when of those who had come none had met the test of recognition the emperor sent word also to the island of Cyprus and summoned Spyridon and his grace. But he had already learned all about the emperor through the Spirit, for grace had indicated to him all things through dreams. And when the emperor's words met with his approval he undertook the journey to him

not unwillingly. And he brought with him the man who had stood by his side in that vision which the emperor had received; his name was Triphyllios.

21. . . . He (the emperor) rose at once from his throne and approached the great Spyridon. For the desire to regain his health made him deem other things of little value. Certainly he held the imperial splendor and the greatness of the empire less important than honor to the great Spyridon . . . Then he rested his head on the saint's shoulder amidst tears and sought his prayers, knowing that they were the best medication, easily capable of curing him. And when Spyridon had placed his hands upon the emperor's head, at once the illness was taken away and the emperor regained his health.

7. Vita of St. Spyridon 30 [ΣΒΠΚΙ 51.3]

There is in Cyprus a city by the same name as Cyrene in Libya [Kyrenia]. The great (Spyridon) had reason to go there. He was accompanied by Triphyllios, his disciple, who had already been appointed to the bishopric of the city of Kallinikesiai [Leukosia], according to the dream. He decided to pass through the city of Kythrea and the mountain of Pentadaktylos, and when they came to the place called Parymne—this is a good and enjoyable place, offering many pleasures—Triphyllios was delighted by the place and desired to acquire some property there and to make it the seat of his church. These things very much occupied Triphyllios' mind, but did not at all escape Spyridon's notice, and when he recognized these things he gently rebuked his disciple, saying, "Triphyllios, why are you continually revolving these vain and empty things in your heart, desiring fields and vineyards? In truth, these things are of no value; they only seem to be and charm by their name. We have property in heaven, which cannot be taken away from us; we have a home not built by hands. Cling to those; enjoy those, or their anticipation. These things cannot be transferred from one person to another, but he who has once become master of them, remains so, in no way losing his inheritance." When Triphyllios had heard these words he not only heard them, but hid them in the chambers of his heart, repented, and begged the saint's forgiveness; and thereafter he lived such a perfect life that he became a chosen vessel of Christ, like Paul, and was found worthy of innumerable gifts.

8. Vita of St. Spyridon 35 [ΣΒΠΚΙ 51.4]

It is reported that . . . the patriarch of Alexandria . . . called a synod of all the bishops under his jurisdiction . . . The patriarch did as he had been told [in a vision], sent a letter, and summoned the saint [Spyridon]. The letter explained the reason for the summons, the vision which he had experienced, and why [the saint's] coming was essential. He [Spyridon] obeyed at once and set out on his journey as soon as he had finished reading the letter. He boarded a ship and sailed to Alexandria.

9. Vita of St. John the Almoner 1.2

He [John the Almoner] was a native of the island of Cyprus, which nourished him like a flowering and precious plant, but the famous city of Alexandria gained him for its bishop and patron. His father, Epiphanios by name, was an illustrious man who was endowed with such excellence that the government of the island was entrusted to him. His mother was a noble woman and, being married to such a man, was remarkable for her beauty of both body and soul. And John, having obtained such parents, did not bring shame to his family but was eager to add to its distinction.

10. Vita of St. John the Almoner 13.73–74

73. He [John] was a good shepherd, a holy man; I mean the patriarch. He believed in the word of Christ, the prince of shepherds, who taught, "If they drive you from one city flee to another" [Matthew 10:23]. Thus, when Alexandria was about to be surrendered into the hands of the Persians, he withdrew from it under divine guidance. He returned to his native country, Cyprus, intending to bestow his body to the place which had nourished him, for he had a premonition that his death was close at hand. Then the patrician Niketas, whom we have repeatedly mentioned, took this Persian incursion for an opportunity to beg the holy man to travel to the royal city and give the emperor the benefit of his prayers and his blessing . . . But when they had come to the island of Rhodes and the patriarch had fallen into a trance; he saw in reality, not in a dream, a shining man, like a eunuch, who held a golden scepter in his hand, approached him, and said, "The King of Kings is calling you."

     At once John summoned the patrician, related to him the vision which he had experienced and said, "You, my good friend, desired to lead me to the king who rules on earth. But he who holds heaven and earth and all things in his power was first to call me to him." Upon hearing these things the patrician was filled with sorrow and pain, but was not able to keep John back. But when he had received the benefit of John's prayers he readily sent him to Cyprus.
74. But when he had come to his own city, Amathous, he ordered secretaries to write down his testament . . . When the great man of God had made these dispositions he gave up his spirit into the hands of the living God.

93. *NOTITIAE EPISCOPATUUM ECCLESIAE CONSTANTINOPOLITANAE* (10th–13th c.)

1. *Notitia* 10.758–74 (p. 338 ed. Darrouzès) [ΣΒΠΚΙ 49]

The eparchy of the island of Cyprus has 13 cities; it was administered by governors of consular rank, i.e. by senators. These cities are named as follows:

	These are the cities of Cyprus according to the old list; now the list is as follows:
Constantia, the metropolis	[Constantia, the metropolis]
Tamasia, of superior rank	Tamasia
Kition	Kition
Amathous	Amathous
Kerbia	Kourion
Paphos	Paphos

Arsinoe	Arsinoe
Solia	Solias
Lapethos	Lapythos
Kyrenia	Kyreneia
Kythereia	Trimithous
Trimethous	Kythereia
Karpasion	Karpasion
Leukada	Leukousia
Neapolis	Nemesos.

situated in the Gulf of Pamphylia.

94. VITAE OF ST. ATHANASIOS THE ATHONITE (first half, 11th c.)

1. Vita A 91

Then the great man [Athanasios] embarked on another ship and departed for Cyprus. In a few days he crossed the sea. Then he decided again to keep Antony for a traveling companion; but the other [monk], Theodotos, he sent to the Mountain [Mt. Athos].

2. Vita A 92/93

But Theodotos returned to the Mountain [Mt. Athos], while they themselves [Athanasios and Antony] proceeded to Cyprus . . . When they had reached the island they disembarked from the ship, went to the monastery which is called the Monastery of the Priests [also known as the monastery of St. Eutyches, at Paphos], reported to the abbot, and paid him the customary respects.

3. Vita A 94–95/96

The emperor [Nikephoros II Phokas, 963–969] . . . sent out written orders to search [for Athanasios] in every place under his control.

These orders went to all the world under his control, and every place and every city were searched, and by nearly everyone, as if the search were for an imperial drachma; and the search also reached Cyprus. And the abbot of the monastery of which we have just spoken, when he learned of the emperor's orders, questioned the great man closely, asking who they were, whence they had come, and in search of what they had come.

4. Vita A 99

When he had remained by himself for a little while on the mountain he wanted to go to Cyprus. When the prevailing wind was not favorable he returned to land, and when the ship was unable to sail he undertook the journey on foot.

5. Vita B 30 [ΣΒΠΚΙ 53.1]

Father [Athanasios], accompanied only by Antony, wanted to sail with him to Cyprus. They embarked on a ship and crossed the sea.

6. Vita B 31 [ΣΒΠΚΙ 53.2]

When they had reached the island of Cyprus they went to the monastery which is called the Monastery of the Priests, reported to the abbot of this monastery, and paid him their respects. They asked him to furnish them the necessary sustenance and to accept their labor in return. "We have a great desire," they said, "to go and worship at the Holy Sepulchre, but because we fear the Saracens we are afraid to undertake the journey there." These things they requested. The abbot received them gladly and assigned them accommodations in the mountains under his control. Now the imperial decree made its way everywhere, also to Cyprus, and there was a big search for him on the island.

7. Vita B 33 [ΣΒΠΚΙ 53.3]

When he had remained on the mountain for a short time he wanted to go to Cyprus and seek out its bishop. The ship on which he was traveling reached Attaleia without difficulty. But when it was prevented from continuing the voyage by strong contrary winds he disembarked and wanted to travel on foot. And when he was in Attaleia he had the prey [?] in his hands; for there it came to the father unexpectedly according to some divine direction.

95. SKYLITZES, JOHN (floruit second half, 11th c.)

1. *Synopsis Historiarum*, Nikephoros Phokas 15 (p. 270 ed. Thurn) [ΣΒΠΚΙ 54.1]

In the second year of his reign he [Nikephoros II Phokas, 963–969] also subjected the entire island of Cyprus to Roman control, driving out the Saracens by Niketas Chalkoutzes the patrician and general [965].

2. *Synopsis Historiarum*, Constantine Monomachos 4 (p. 429 ed. Thurn) [ΣΒΠΚΙ 54.2]

At this time there occurred on Cyprus another uprising, the originator of which was Theophilos Erotikos [1043]; he was the governor of the island and always aiming at rebellion. When he heard of the disaster that had befallen [Michael V, 1041–1042] Kalaphates and of the resulting confusion he believed that he found the right time to realize his objectives. He won over the whole population of Cyprus and prevailed upon them to remove the *protospatharios* [member of the imperial hierarchy] Theophylaktos, the judge and collector of taxes, charging him with [excessively] heavy collection of taxes. But Monomachos [Constantine IX, 1042–1045] moved against him without much delay. The patrician Constantine Chage was sent against him in command of an army, seized him, subdued the whole population, and brought him before the emperor. The emperor dressed him in women's clothes, displayed him in the hippodrome when a race was taking place, stripped him of his property, and released him.

96. KEKAUMENOS (1020/1024–after 1070s)

1. Λόγος νουθετικὸς πρὸς βασιλέα (*Advice to the emperor*; appended to the author's *Strategikon*), p. 294 ed. Litavrin [ΣΒΠΚΙ 57]

The warships which have been stationed in the islands for the purpose of guard duty do nothing else but to collect from the Cyclades and from both the Greek and the Asian mainland wheat, barley, legume, cheese, wine, meat, olive oil, much money, and whatever else the islands have. They do the same on Cyprus and on Crete. You, Sir, must keep careful watch on these things and keep your forces safe and ready, not giving cause for complaint. So much on the subject of sailors and soldiers.

97. *TYPICON* (ritual ordinance) of the monastery of St. John Chrysostom at Koutsovendi (Cod. Paris. gr. 402) (after 1090)

1. fol. 56r–v (December 9), cited by Cyril Mango and Ernest J. W. Hawkins in *DOP* 18 (1964) 334, n. 58

St. Anne conceiving the mother of God; and the dedication of the holy church of our father St. John Chrysostom, which was founded in Cyprus at Mt. Koutsovendis in the year 1090; on this occasion relics of the holy martyr Prokopios, the holy martyr Jacobus the Persian, and the holy martyr Marina were deposited.

2. fol. 146r (April 26), cited by Cyril Mango and Ernest J. W. Hawkins in *DOP* 18 (1964) 334, n. 59

It is to be noted that on this day we observe the commemoration of our holy father, teacher, and *hegoumenos* [abbot] George, the founder of the holy monastery of Chrysostom in Cyprus.

98. Περὶ προβολῆς καὶ ψήφου καὶ ἐκλογῆς καὶ καταστάσεως καὶ προνομίων μητροπολιτῶν καὶ ἀρχιεπισκόπων καὶ ἐπισκόπων (*On the Nomination, Election, Appointment, and Prerogatives of Metropolitans, Archbishops, and Bishops*) (second half, 11th c.)

1. Ed. Darrouzès, p. 134

. . . according to the [eighth] canon of [the Council of] Ephesus [431] it is necessary "that for each province the rights pertaining to it from the beginning and from long ago according to long-prevailing custom be kept whole and inviolate, each metropolitan having authority to take action for the security of his province," in order that, just as Cyprus, so also every province should always on its own regulate ordinations and all other matters arising.

. . . this was also the intention of the archbishop of the City of God [Antioch] in the case of the Cypriots, for whom the canon in question was designed, judging every province not previously subject to one of the patriarchs to be equal to the archbishop of Cyprus [i.e. to be autocephalous].

99. NICHOLAS IV MOUZALON, patriarch of Constantinople 1147–1150 (ca. 1070– 1152)

1. Στίχοι Νικολάου μοναχοῦ τοῦ Μουζάλωνος [ΣΒΠΚΙ 63]

This poem is 1057 iambic trimeters long. A convenient summary of it is provided by George Hill, *A History of Cyprus* (Cambridge University Press, 1940), vol. I, pp. 303–304:

The historians on whom we depend for our knowledge of the events described in the preceding pages throw no light on the internal conditions of Cyprus during this period. But chance has preserved a remarkable poem by Nicolaus Mouzalon, archbishop of Cyprus from about 1107 to 1110, written after his resignation of the see. It testifies abundantly to the sufferings of the Cypriotes under the Byzantine officials. The quarrel between the secular and ecclesiastical powers was of course perennial, and the archbishop may have been prejudiced, and have exaggerated his shadows. But, all allowances made, enough remains to show the condition of the Cypriotes to have been miserable in the extreme (vv. 885–910): their food was such as the Baptist ate, they went naked to the day, sheltered only in caves; the fruits of their labours were were taken from them; those who could not pay their taxes were hung up, and dogs hang up beside them and pricked on to tear their flesh. If one who was wanted by the officials escaped, his neighbour was held responsible and punished in his stead. The clergy were equally oppressed (vv. 652 ff.); bishops were hanged and tortured to death, deacons sent to the galleys, relics stolen and sacred vessels used for profane purposes; all such offenses were condoned by the secular authorities. There were also black sheep among the clergy, who acted as tools of the government officials, and were encouraged and protected in their criminal courses. Thus, says the archbishop (vv. 267 ff.), he saw this lovely island, like the king's daughter all glorious within, this blessed island no island of the blessed, this Elysian field the home of a wretched people, girt around by the streams of the sea, but oppressed within by unescapable misfortunes; its inhabitants more miserable than Tantalus, reaping but eating not (oh vain labour!), gathering grapes but drinking not (oh bitter toil!).

100. NIKETAS of Ankyra (first half, 12th c.)

Λόγος ἀντιρρητικὸς πρὸς τοὺς λέγοντας μὴ δεῖν παρατεῖσθαι (*On the Right of Resignation*)

1. Ed. Darrouzès, pp. 250–52

Who of you does not know that the synkellos Stephen, now deceased, resigned from the see of Nikomedeia? [ca. 1003] And a little before him Nikephoros, who bore the name of Nicaea? And before him Epiphanios [III] who had lived an illustrious life and had presided over the illustrious church of Cyprus? [9th c.]

101. DOXOPATRES, NEILOS (first half, 12th c.)

1. Τάξις τῶν πατριαρχικῶν θρόνων (*Notitia Thronorum Patriarchalium*) Migne, *PG* 132, col. 1097; p. 20–21 ed. Finck [ΣΒΠΚΙ 61]

There are some eparchies which are not subject to the patriarchal thrones, such as the island of Cyprus, which has remained entirely autocephalous and not subject to any of the patriarchal thrones. Rather it is under its own authority because the apostle Barnabas was found there with the holy Gospel of Mark [the Gospel of Matthew in other accounts] on his chest. There are in Cyprus thirteen bishoprics, of which the one called Constantia has primacy. The others are Kition, Amathous, Kyrion, Paphoi, Arsenoe, Soloi, Lapithos, Kyrenia, Tamasos, Kythres, Trimithos, and Karpasos.

Bulgaria is similar to Cyprus in that it, too, is autocephalous, not subject to any of the patriarchal thrones, but being governed by its own authority and being ordained by its own bishops . . . Therefore to this day Cyprus and Bulgaria receive their bishops from the emperor. These are ordained by their own bishops, as has been mentioned, and are called archbishops, since they are autocephalous.

102. KOMNENE, ANNA (1148) (1083–ca. 1153/54)

1. *Alexiad* 9.2.1–3.1 [ΣΒΠΚΙ 60.1]

Within a few days, the Emperor [Alexios I Komnenos, 1081–1118] heard that Caryces had rebelled and seized Crete, and Rhapsomates Cyprus, so he dispatched John Ducas against them with a large fleet. When the Cretans learnt that Ducas had reached Carpathus [an island midway between Rhodes and Crete], which they knew was not far off, they attacked Caryces, murdered him cruelly and then surrendered Crete to the Great Duke. Ducas organized the administration of the island and left an adequate garrison for its protection, and then sailed down to Cyprus. As soon as he had run his ships ashore, he took Cyrene [Kyrenia] at first assault, and Rhapsomates, informed of this, made great preparations to oppose him. Consequently he left Levcosia [Nicosia], occupied the heights behind Cyrene and fixed his palisades there, but refused battle, for he was ignorant of war and unversed in generalship. For the right thing would have been to fall upon the Romans whilst they were unprepared. But Rhapsomates put off the battle for some time, not really for the purpose of preparing for the clash of arms as if he were not ready (on the contrary he was well prepared and could have engaged in battle at once, had he wished); but he acted like one who did not wish to risk an engagement at any time, but had taken up war as children do at play and went about it softly, and kept sending envoys to the Romans as if expecting to entice them over by honeyed words. And I fancy he did this through his ignorance of warfare. (For I have been told that he had only recently handled spear and sword and did not even know how to mount a horse and if by chance he mounted and wanted to ride, he was seized with fright and dizziness, so utterly inexperienced was Rhapsomates in military experience.) It was either for this reason or because the sudden advent of the imperial troops had overwhelmed him, that his mind was in this state of uncertainty. Consequently when he did hazard an engagement, with a kind of despondency, the result did not turn out well for him. For Butumites had won over some of the deserters from Rhapsomates' army and enlisted them in his own. A few days later Rhapsomates drew up his troops and offered battle marching slowly down the steep hillside. When the armies were only a short distance apart, a portion of Rhapsomates' army, numbering about one hundred, detached itself and galloped at full speed to attack Ducas apparently, but they turned the tips of their spears backwards and went over to him. On seeing this Rhapsomates at once turned tail and slacking his reins fled toward Nemesus [Limassol], hoping to reach that town and find a vessel which would convey him to Syria and to safety. But Manuel Butumites was following fast behind him. So hard pressed by him and foiled in his hope, he reached the mountain on the other side and sought refuge in the church, built of old, to the name of the Holy Cross. Then Butumites (to whom Ducas had assigned this pursuit) captured him there, promised him his life and took him back with him to the Great Duke. Afterwards they all moved on to Levcosia and after receiving the submission of the whole island, they secured it as far as their means permitted and sent a full account of all these doings to the Emperor by letter. The emperor appreciated their efforts and decided he must take steps to secure Cyprus. For this reason he nominated Calliparius as judge and assessor; he was (not) one of the nobles, but had a high reputation for just dealing and incorruptibility, combined with modesty. The island also needed a military governor, so he appointed Philocales Eumathius as Stratopedarch, assigning the protection of it to him, and gave him ships of war and cavalry with which to guard Cyprus, both by land and sea. Butumites conducted Rhapsomates and the other 'Immortals' who had joined him in rebellion and returned with them to Ducas, and thus made his way to the capital.

Such were the events which took place in the islands, I mean Cyprus and Crete. [1092]

(trans. Elizabeth A. S. Dawes)

2. *Alexiad* 11.4.3 [ΣΒΠΚΙ 60.2]

Then considering the severe famine (for an ox-head was being sold for three gold staters) and also because he despaired of taking Antioch, Taticius [a Byzantine general, the *Primicerius*] departed, embarked on the Roman fleet which was in the harbour of Sudi [the port of Antioch], and made for Cyprus.

(trans. Elizabeth A. S. Dawes)

3. *Alexiad* 11.7.3–4 [ΣΒΠΚΙ 60.3]

But Godfrey [of Bouillon, ca. 1060–1100] after being again elected king of Jerusalem [Defender of the Holy Sepulchre] sent his brother Balduinus [Baldwin, king of Jerusalem 1100–1118] to Edessa. Then the Emperor ordered Isangeles [Raymond of St. Giles, Count of Toulouse] to hand over Laodicea to Andronicus Tzintziluces and the forts of Maraceus [Marakes] and Balaneus [Valania] to the soldiers of [Philocales] Eumathius, at that time Duke of Cyprus; and go on further and do his best to get possession of the other forts by fighting. And this he did in obedience to the Emperor's letter [1099–1100]. (trans. Elizabeth A. S. Dawes)

4. *Alexiad* 11.7.6 [ΣΒΠΚΙ 60.4]

Immediately on arrival he [Isangeles] went up and seized the summit of the hill (which is a branch of the Lebanon) opposite Tripolis, in order to have his fortified camp there and also to divert the water which flowed down the slopes of this hill to Tripolis. He then wrote a report to the Emperor [Alexios I Komnenos, 1081–1118] of what he had accomplished, and begged to have a well-fortified stronghold built there before more troops arrived from Chorosan [Khorasan, i.e. northern Mesopotamia] and overwhelmed him. The Emperor entrusted the Duke of Cyprus with the erection of such a fort and ordered him to dispatch the fleet quickly with all requisites and also the masons to build this fort on the spot Isangeles signified to them. (trans. Elizabeth A. S. Dawes)

5. *Alexiad* 11.7.7 [ΣΒΠΚΙ 60.5]

And the other [Tancred, ca. 1075–1112, nephew of Bohemund I] did not relax the siege in the slightest; consequently when [Andronikos] Tzintziluces saw Tancred's determination, and he and his were being reduced to straits, he asked for help from there (*or* from Cyprus). But the authorities in Cyprus were dilatory, and, as he was now very hard beset both by the siege and the pressure of famine, he elected to surrender the town [Laodikeia]. (trans. Elizabeth A. S. Dawes)

6. *Alexiad* 11.8.5 [ΣΒΠΚΙ 60.6]

When the news of his [Isangeles'] death [1105] was brought to the Emperor [Alexios I Komnenos, 1081–1118], he immediately wrote to the Duke of Cyprus, and ordered him to send Nicetas Chalintzes with plenty of money to Gelielmus [Guillaume, nephew of Raymond of St. Giles] in order to propitiate him and influence him to swear an oath that he would maintain unbroken fidelity to the Emperor just as his deceased uncle Isangeles had preserved his to the end. (trans. Elizabeth A. S. Dawes)

7. *Alexiad* 11.9.3–4 [ΣΒΠΚΙ 60.7]

Butumites started with all his forces and reached the city of Attalus [III; Attaleia, modern Antalya]; there he noticed that Bardas and the chief cup-bearer, Michael, would not comply with his wishes and to prevent the whole army perhaps mutinying, and all his labour being in vain, and his being obliged to return from Cilicia without accomplishing anything, he at once wrote to the Emperor [Alexios I Komnenos, 1081–1118] full details about these men, and asked to be relieved of their company. The Emperor vividly aware of the harm that is wont to result from such beginnings, turned them and the others he suspected into another direction by writing to them to go to Cyprus with all speed and join Constantine Euphorbenus, who held the position of Duke of Cyprus at the time, and obey him in everything. On receiving the letters they gladly embarked for Cyprus. But after they had been a short time with the Duke of Cyprus, they began their usual impudence with him, in consequence of which he looked upon them askance. But the young men mindful of the Emperor's affection for them wrote to the Emperor and ran down Euphorbenus, and asked to be recalled to Constantinople. After perusing their letters the Emperor, who had sent several of the richer men (of whom he was suspicious) with these two to Cyprus, was afraid lest these might from annoyance join the two in rebellion, and straightway enjoined Cantacuzenus to go and bring them back with him. Directly Cantacuzenus arrived in Cyrenea he sent for them and took them back. This is what happened to those two, I mean Bardas and the chief cup-bearer Michael.

(trans. Elizabeth A. S. Dawes)

8. *Alexiad* 11.10.6–9 [ΣΒΠΚΙ 60.8]

The survivors of the Pisan fleet turned their attention to pillaging whatever islands they touched and especially Cyprus; Philocales Eumathius [the Stratopedarch] happened to be there and advanced against them. At this the sailors were so distraught by fear that they did not even give a thought to the men who had gone away from the ships for foraging, but left the greater number on the island, hurriedly loosed their cables and sailed away to Laodicea to Bohemund [I, Prince of Taranto] . . . When the sailors who had been left on the island to collect plunder returned and did not see their own fleet, they threw themselves into the sea in desperation and were drowned.

The commanders of the Roman fleet including Landulph [the Great Duke] himself met in Cyprus and decided to make overtures for peace. As all agreed to do this, [Manuel] Butumites was sent to Bohemund. The latter saw him and detained him quite fifteen days, then famine oppressed Laodicea, and as Bohemund was still Bohemund and not changed at all, and had not learned to speak words of peace, he sent for Butumites and said, "You did not come here for the sake of peace or of friendship, but in order to set fire to my ships. Be gone now; and you have reason to be thankful that you get away from here unharmed." So he sailed away and found the men who had sent him in the harbour of Cyprus. From his report they recognized more fully Bohemund's wicked disposition, and the impossibility of peace being made between him and the Emperor [Alexios I Komnenos, 1081–1118], so they left Cyprus and with all sails set they sailed over the watery ways to the capital. But opposite Syce [15 km. east of Anemourion, on the coast of Cilicia] a great tempest and violent sea arose and the ships were dashed on shore and half-broken, all except those Taticius commanded. Such were the events connected with the Pisan fleet. Bohemund with his extreme natural astuteness was afraid that the Emperor might proceed to seize Curicum [Kourikos; modern Korgos], keep the Roman fleet in its harbour and thus protect Cyprus and at the same time prevent his allies from Lombardy coming to him along the eastern coast. Because of these considerations he decided to rebuild the town himself and occupy the harbour. For Curicum had formerly been a very strongly fortified town, but allowed in later times to fall into ruin.

The Emperor had already thought of this and anticipated Bohemund's plan by sending the eunuch Eustathius (whom he promoted from the rank of Canicleus to Great Drungaire of the fleet) with orders to occupy Curicum with all speed. Further he was to rebuild it quickly, and the fort Seleucia as well, which was six stades distant, then leave an adequate garrison in each and appoint Strategius Strabus Duke over them, a man of small body, but of long and varied military experience. He was moreover to have a large fleet at anchor in the harbour and order them to keep a careful look-out for the men coming from Lombardy to Bohemund's aid, and also to help guard Cyprus.

(trans. Elizabeth A. S. Dawes)

9. *Alexiad* 14.2.6 [ΣΒΠΚΙ 60.9.1]

The Emperor [Alexios I Komnenos, 1081–1118] commended this advice and shortly summoned Manuel Butumites and another man who knew the Latin language and sent them to the Counts and to the King of Jerusalem, after giving them full instructions on the subject about which they were to converse with the Counts and also with Balduinus himself, the King of Jerusalem [1100–1118]. As it was imperative that they should have money to use in their mission to these Counts, because the Latins are so covetous, he handed Butumites orders for Eumathius Philocales, at that time Duke of Cyprus, telling the latter to supply them with as many ships as they needed; he also bade him give them plenty of money of all kinds, of every shape and coinage and of varying qualities to be used as gifts for the Counts. He also enjoined on the men mentioned, more especially on Manuel Butumites, that after receiving the money from Philocales, they should anchor off Tripoli and visit the Count Pelctranus [Bertrand], the son of the Isangeles [Raymond of St. Giles, Count of Toulouse] who has often been mentioned in this history, and remind him of the faith which his father had always kept with the Emperor, and hand him the Emperor's letters at the same time. And they were to say to him, "You must not shew yourself inferior to your own father, but preserve faith with us just as he did. I would have you know that I am going to Antioch to take my vengeance on that man who has violated the solemn oaths he made to God and to me. Be careful not to give him assistance in any way and do your best to induce the Counts to pledge their faith to us so that they may not for some reason or other espouse Tancred's cause." So they made their way to Cyprus and, after collecting the money there and as many ships as they wanted, they sailed straight to Tripoli.

(trans. Elizabeth A. S. Dawes)

10. *Alexiad* 14.2.12 [ΣΒΠΚΙ 60.9.2]

Meanwhile [Manuel] Butumites embarked on his Cyprian ships there (they were twelve in all) and sailed along the coast towards Ace [Acre], and there met Balduinus [Baldwin, king of Jerusalem, 1100–1118] and then reported to him all the Emperor [Alexios I Komnenos, 1081–1118] had ordered him to say; but he supplemented his speech by saying that the Emperor had already reached Seleucia.

(trans. Elizabeth A. S. Dawes)

11. *Alexiad* 14.2.14 [ΣΒΠΚΙ 60.10]

So at last the ambassadors threatened them [Bertrand's son and the bishop of Tripoli] saying, "If you do not give back the money to us, you are not true servants of the Emperor

[Alexios I Komnenos, 1081–1118] and you are proved not to observe the same fidelity to him as Pelctranus [Bertrand] and his father Isangeles [Raymond of St. Giles, Count of Toulouse] did. Very well then, you shall not have an abundant supply of necessaries from Cyprus in the future, nor shall the Duke of Cyprus come to your aid, and then you will perish by famine."

(trans. Elizabeth A. S. Dawes)

103. BASILAKES, NIKEPHOROS (12th c.)

1. *Encomium of Nicholas Mouzalon,* (ca. 1150) [ΣΒΠΚΙ 64]

Title: Speech given by a public speaker on Patriarch Lord Nicholas Mouzalon [ca. 1070–1152], who had once resigned as archbishop of Cyprus but later [1147–1150] served as patriarch of Constantinople.

8. This was the situation, and the island of Cyprus was in need of someone to proclaim [the gospel]; and there was a great effort to find a man who would lead the flock of Christ according to [the precepts of] Christ. But the swift wings of your good report were with you everywhere, and you were much "in everyman's mouth" [cf. Theognis 1.240]; and the emperor [Alexios I Komnenos, 1081–1118], not a little tickled in his ears, was utterly taken captive by the beauty of your soul [1107].

9. But you at once returned to your accustomed and beloved solitude.

12. . . . But you, my patriarch and Jacob [comparing Mouzalon with the patriarch Jacob of Genesis 25–50], instead of leading the flock of Christ to "the place of pasture" and "the water of refreshment" [cf. Psalms 23:2], I mean the sacred meadow of scripture, which sprouts with all good things and is surrounded by every wisdom, took yourself to the island of Cyprus.

104. ARISTENOS, ALEXIOS (mid-12th c.)

1. *Interpretation of the Canons*, ed. Rhalles and Potles, vol. II, p. 206 [ΣΒΠΚΙ 75.1]

Any of the bishops who have forcefully taken over another province which was not subject to them from the very beginning or have usurped some privilege of another bishopric shall not be justified in any such actions, but let them be restored to those bishops who have a legal claim to them. Every province should have clear and inviolate control of the things which rightfully belong to it. And let there be no illusion of worldly power under the pretense of divine service. And anyone who produces another document, one which is in conflict with the present rulings, shall in no way benefit from it.

[Interpreting the eighth canon of the Council of Ephesus, 431]

2. *Interpretation of the Canons*, ed. Rhalles and Potles, vol. II, p. 397 [ΣΒΠΚΙ 75.2]

This bishop of the island of Cyprus, John (for this is the New Justinianopolis), because of the raids of the barbarians, to be freed from enslavement by heathens, and to be subject clearly to the scepter of a most Christian state, left Cyprus and took up residence in the province of the Hellespont. He was given jurisdiction, formerly exercised by Constantinople, over the bishoprics of the Hellespont and the right to preside over all the bishops in that province, to run his own government, and to be ordained by his own bishops. This is as the Council of Ephesus [431] had ruled. But when Cyprus was freed from subjection to the heathens the metropolitan sees of the Hellespont returned once more to the throne of Constantinople.

[Interpreting the 39th canon of the Council in Trullo or Quinisext Council, 691–692]

105. ZONARAS, JOHN (d. after 1159?)

1. *Chronicon* 1.5 [AKEΠ I 35.1; II 149.5α; 150α]

Chetim settled the island of Chetima. This is Cyprus, so named by the Greeks because of their goddess Aphrodite, whom they call Cypris.

2. *Chronicon* 3.26

When he [Cyrus the Great] came to Babylonia he appointed satraps over the subjected nations: Arabia, Cappadocia, Greater Phrygia, Lycia, Ionia, Caria, Phrygia at the Hellespont, and Aeolis. But he did not appoint satraps over the Cilicians, Cypriots, and Paphlagonians because he thought that these had willingly served on his side. Nevertheless they, too, paid tribute . . . [539 B.C.]

After this he campaigned against Egypt. Thus he expanded his rule east as far as the Red Sea, north as far as the Euxine [Black] Sea, west as far as Cyprus and Egypt, and south as far as Ethiopia.

3. *Chronicon* 4.10 [AKEΠ I 72.3]

After he had been victorious at Issos [333 B.C.], he [Alexander] seized Damascus, where the Persians and Darius [III] himself had left their money and most of their equipment. After this Cyprus and Phoenicia, with the exception of Tyre, came into his hands.

4. *Chronicon* 6.13 [AKEΠ II 163.11α]

Helena [Queen of Adiabene, first century A.D.] had a desire to come to Jerusalem and to worship at the temple of God . . . When she found many there perishing from famine she had grain shipped from Alexandria; she also purchased at great expense a shipment of figs from Cyprus and distributed it to the needy.

5. *Chronicon* 9.18 [AKEΠ I 92.1α]

When he [Antiochos III] learned that Ptolemy [V Epiphanes] had died and since he very much desired to seize Egypt, he left his son Seleukos [the later Seleukos IV Philopator] with a force at Lysimacheia (Thracian Chersonese), while he himself set out on the march. But when he learned that Ptolemy was alive he stayed away from Egypt and attempted to sail to Cyprus, but was prevented by a storm and returned home. [196 B.C.]

6. *Chronicon* 9.25

Then Antiochos [IV Epiphanes] was afraid and raised the siege [of Alexandria, 168 B.C.]. Thereupon the Ptolemies [VI Philometor and VIII Physkon] (for thus they were both called), freed from outside fear, again took to quarreling. Then they were reconciled again by the Romans; the terms were that the older one should hold Egypt and Cyprus and the other one the region around Cyrene. For these regions then belonged to Egypt. But the younger one, taking offense at the slight, came to Rome and obtained Cyprus from the Romans. But the older one made an agreement with the younger one, giving him certain cities instead of Cyprus and committing himself to pay him money and grain.

7. *Chronicon* 10.23 [ΑΚΕΠ I 109.2α]

At that time he [Quintus Labienus Parthicus, the son of Titus Labienus, Caesar's second-in-command] escaped, but later he was captured by Demetrios [39 B.C.]. The latter was a freedman of the previous Caesar [Julius Caesar] and had been sent to Cyprus by Antony [Mark Antony, to serve as governor; see *RE* IV 2803, no. 52].

8. *Chronicon* 11.22 [ΑΚΕΠ I 116.1]

The Jews in Cyrene rebelled and were killing the Romans and the Greeks, and those in Egypt and Cyprus similarly were killing an equal number. But Trajan subdued them, having sent an army against them. [A.D. 116/117]

9. *Chronicon* 15.6.11–12

After a few days this tyrant [Constantine V Kopronymos, emperor 741–775] went to the forum with his patriarch [Constantine II, 754–766] and with the like-minded bishops, confronted the whole population, and forbade the veneration of the holy icons, calling those who venerate them idolaters, and pronounced anathema on the venerable Germanos [I, patriarch of Constantinople 715–730], on George of Cyprus, the patriarch of Constantine [Constantia], and on the great John of Damascus, a man outstanding in wisdom and virtue. [754]

10. *Chronicon* 15.9. 8

The patriarch Niketas [I] the eunuch had presided over [the church of] Constantinople for fourteen years when he died [780]. Paul of Cyprus [Salamis], a reader and orthodox [in belief] was ordained patriarch [Paul IV].

11. *Chronicon* 16.13 [ΑΚΕΠ I 113.5; ΣΒΠΚΙ 59.1]

He [Leo VI the Wise, emperor 886–912] erected another church to St. Lazarus [in Constantinople]. Hither he transferred the sacred body of the saint, which he had removed from Cyprus, and also that of Mary Magdalene [890].

12. *Chronicon* 16.25.10 [ΣΒΠΚΙ 59.2]

Cyprus, which had been in the hands of the Saracens, was restored by him [Nikephoros II Phokas, emperor 963–969] to Roman [Byzantine] rule [965].

13. *Chronicon* 17.22.20–22 [ΣΒΠΚΙ 59.3]

The affair of [the general George] Maniakes ended under such circumstances [1043]. But another tyranny was launched in turn; the originator of this one was [the general] Theophilos Erotikos. He had observed, at the time of the second Michael [Michael V Kalaphates, 1041–1042], the nephew of the first [Michael IV the Paphlagonian, 1034–1041], that the empire had been entrusted to women [the empresses Theodora and Zoe]. Thus he beguiled the Cypriots (for he was their governor at the time) and attempted an uprising. But [Constantine IX, 1042–1055] Monomachos wasted no time in destroying him. He sent a force against him which defeated him and easily returned the island to subservience.

14. *Chronicon* 18.25.16–17 [ΣΒΠΚΙ 59.4]

The island of Crete and then Cyprus defected [1092]; the former was held by Karykes, who rose against the emperor [Alexios I Komnenos, 1081–1118], but Cyprus by Rhapsommates. But these, too, did not for long remain outside the reach of Roman [Byzantine] rule.

15. *Interpretation of the Canons,* ed. Rhalles and Potles, vol. II, pp. 204–205 [ΣΒΠΚΙ 74.1]

The chief priest [patriarch] of the church of Antioch [John I] took it upon himself to perform the ordination of bishops in Cyprus, on the grounds, perhaps, that Cyprus anciently had been subject to the duke of Antioch; for a general had been sent there [to Cyprus] by the duke of Antioch. Therefore some Cypriot bishops approached this synod [the Third Ecumenical Council, Ephesus, 431], claiming, both orally and in writing, that by long-standing practice the bishop of Antioch had no right to ordain bishops in Cyprus. The synod granted the bishops audience and decided that the Cypriot bishops had an unrestricted and inviolate right, according to the canons of the Holy Fathers and the ancient practice. For the 35th canon of the Holy Apostles [the 85 *Apostolic Canons,* compiled ca. 380 and forming the last chapter (47) of the *Apostolic Constitutions*] and the third canon of the Council of Antioch [341] decreed that the bishops must not be so bold as to perform ordinations in provinces which are not subject to them. If they do, their actions will be invalid and they will be deposed. And the sixth canon and the seventh canon of the First Ecumenical Council [Nicaea, 325] provide that that the ancient practices also apply to the chief priests [patriarchs]. In accordance with these canons the venerable Fathers of this council, too, have ruled that the bishops of Cyprus should ordain their own bishops in that island. And the same ruling shall apply everywhere, and no bishop shall seize a province which has not from the beginning, that is from ancient times, been subject to him or his predecessors. But if anyone, they declare, has taken over a province which does not belong to him he shall surrender it to those who have been forcefully deprived of it. Let the canons not be violated; let the bishops not employ divine service as a pretext or use it as a cover, and let them not be possessed by the vanity of wordly power. And let us not, by serving those who have no right, lose the freedom which our Lord has given us by shedding his own blood for the freedom of men. Therefore the holy synod voted to guard the rights of each province according to ancient practice, and it gave permission to the metropolitans to receive [copies of] the rulings. And if any record or document be produced which is not in full agreement with the present rulings it shall be invalid.

[Interpreting the eighth canon of the Council of Ephesus, 431]

16. *Interpretation of the Canons,* ed. Rhalles and Potles, vol. II, p. 396 [ΣΒΠΚΙ 74.1]

In the third synod [the Third Ecumenical Council, Ephesus, 431] it was voted by the holy fathers who attended this synod that the bishops of Cyprus should perform their own ordinations of bishops. For the man who was then bishop of Antioch [John I] was attempting to make Cyprus subject to himself and to ordain bishops in Cyprus. This privilege and this canon were granted by the vote of the synod [the Council in Trullo or Quinisext Council, 691–692] to the churches of Cyprus without introducing anything new; furthermore the new city which is called Justinianopolis shall have the same rights as Constantinople. For just as the Asian, Pontic, and Thracian provinces are subject to the throne of Constantinople, so it was granted to this throne [the throne of Justinianopolis] to preside over the province of the Hellespont; and the bishop of Kyzikos is to be subject to it and to be ordained by it; for this city, I mean Kyzikos, is in the province of the Hellespont. Whether the decision concerning Kyzikos has ever been put into practice I do not know. So far that part of the decision which pertains to Kyzikos is not in force, and the bishop of Cyprus has no rights over other places and cities on the Hellespont.

[Interpreting the 39th canon of the Council in Trullo or Quinisext Council, 691–692]

106. ACTS OF THE SYNOD OF 1157 [ΣΒΠΚΙ 65]

1. P. 318 ed. Sakkellion

We have come to the imperial city from provinces nearby and far away, and we are all gathered in the Holy Spirit, by the will and decision of our God-governed emperor [Manuel I Komnenos, 1143–1180], under the presidency of his inspired power, and in the presence of the senate and also of the patriarchs, that is the patriarchs of Constantinople and of Jerusalem, who have joined with his power in making decisions on this issue, and of the patriarch-elect of the heavenly city of Antioch. Nor have our archbishops, that is the archbishops of Bulgaria and Cyprus [John the Cretan, 1152–1171], been left out of this decision, and we now in full agreement [reading ὁμοφρονοῦντες for ὁμοφρονοῦντας] ratify these rulings.

2. P. 321 ed. Sakkellion

Our two patriarchs are in full agreement on this matter, and also our archbishops of Bulgaria and Cyprus [John the Cretan, 1152–1171] and the remaining assembly of priests have come to the same conclusion and do not disagree one with another on any point in this matter. So it was appropriate also that the patriarch-elect of the great heavenly city of Antioch, Soterichos Panteugenos, being in attendance at the council, should be questioned; and then the desired information was readily found.

3. Pp. 323–24 ed. Sakkellion

And I, [John the Cretan, 1152–1171] archbishop of Cyprus, declare this: As far as this man [Soterichos Pantageunos] is concerned I am a newcomer. Therefore at first I did not fully understand what blasphemies he reportedly uttered, that is against the true doctrine of the church. But on the basis of what I have heard him saying today, before this imperial and holy tribunal, I declare that he not only is entirely unsuitable for the office of patriarch but also has become entirely unworthy of the rank of deacon, which he thinks he still holds, so that this, too, must be taken from him.

[Note: Soterichos Pantageunos held that the eucharistic sacrifice is offered only to the Father, rather than to the three persons of the Trinity.]

4. P. 325 ed. Sakkellion

On the 13th of May, a Monday, in the fifth indiction. Under the presidency of our God-crowned emperor the Lord Manuel [I] Komnenos [1143–1180], in the palace of Blachernai, and all his officials being in attendance on his holy majesty, except the *protonotarios* [chief of the notaries]: the grand *droungarios*, the *protasekretis* [head of the chancery], and the *nomophylax* [head of the law school]. Our patriarchs, except for the patriarch of Antioch, joined him in making a decision. So did I, archbishop of Bulgaria, without the archbishop of Cyprus [John the Cretan, 1152–1171], who was not present. We, all the bishops listed above, are in agreement.

5. Pp. 327 ed. Sakkellion

If I sign after the blessed archbishop of Bulgaria in the divine and necessary order of the church, no prejudice to the throne of Cyprus shall result from my signature, since I—so I maintain—occupy a higher rank on various legal grounds. Therefore, although I agree with the decisions contained in this volume, I reserve the rights of the throne [of Cyprus] for myself. I welcome these decisions and vow to abide by them faithfully until I die. John, the least among monks and archbishop of Cyprus.

[Note: a descending order of rank is being followed.]

107. ACTS OF THE SYNOD OF 1170 [ΣΒΠΚΙ 66]

1. Pp. 479–80 ed. Petit

At the time of the Most Holy and Ecumenical Patriarch the Lord Michael [III of Anchialos, 1169–1177], on the 30th of January, a Friday, in the third indiction, under the presidency of our God-crowned holy emperor the Lord Manuel [I] Komnenos [1143–1180] . . . [a synod was held]. The following were in attendance with his imperial majesty: our holy lord and Ecumenical Patriarch the Lord Michael, the holy patriarch of Jerusalem the Lord Nikephoros [II] the blessed archbishop of Bulgaria the Lord Constantine, and the blessed archbishop of Cyprus the Lord John [the Cretan, 1152–1171].

2. Pp. 481–82 ed. Petit

Hence his holy Majesty the emperor has summoned today my own modesty [μετριότης, a self-assumed title of humility], the holy patriarch of Jerusalem the Lord Nikephoros [II], and the blessed archbishops Constantine of Bulgaria and John of Cyprus, and additionally the entire divine and holy assembly of priests residing in this imperial city.

3. P. 485 ed. Petit

The bishop of Selymbria [on the Thracian side of the Propontis] said: "On the basis of what I have heard [Constantine] the bishop of Kerkyra [Corfu] saying today before the imperial tribunal and in the presence of two most holy patriarchs [Michael of Constantinople and Nikephoros [II] of Jerusalem] and the two most blessed archbishops of Bulgaria [Constantine] and of Cyprus [John], I find him liable not only to deposition, but also to the curse of anathema, as he is opposing the correct and divine doctrine itself."

4. P. 486 ed. Petit

The blessed archbishop of Cyprus, John, anxious to do nothing prejudicial to the precedence of his throne by stating his own decision before [Constantine] the blessed archbishop of Bulgaria, said: "I hear the bishop of Kerkyra [Corfu], before the holy imperial tribunal, making pronouncements which are contrary to the principles to which he had previously agreed at the time when sanction was given to the interpretations of the Gospel verse 'My father is greater than I am' [John 14:28]. Therefore it is my judgement that he should be deposed."
[Notes: 1. An ascending order of rank is being followed. 2. The interpretation of the verse quoted is critical to the orthodox doctrine of the Trinity. The bishop of Kerkyra held that on this occasion Christ was speaking not in his own person, but as a representative of all mankind.]

5. P. 487 ed. Petit

I, John, by God's grace archbishop of Cyprus, have taken my place in order and have signed, without prejudice to the throne of Cyprus from the fact that I am signing below and after [Constantine] the blessed archbishop of Bulgaria.

[Note: a descending order of rank is being followed.]

108. TZETZES, JOHN (ca. 1110–1180/85)

1. *Historiae* or *Chiliades* 3.964–65 [ΑΚΕΠ I 81.4]

Timarchos, father of Cypriot Nikokles,
was described by Aristotle as having two rows of teeth.
[Timarchos, king of Paphos; cf. Aristotle, fr. 527 ed. Rose]

2. *Historiae* or *Chiliades* 3.993–1002 [ΑΚΕΠ I 47.1]

Artybios the Persian had raised a horse
to be a fellow-fighter in battle.
But when he sailed to Cyprus
and met Cypriot Onesilos in battle
he fell to the ground before Onesilos.
His horse, seeing its master fallen,
reared up and fought against Onesilos,
pounding his shield with its front feet.
And it would have nearly killed the Cypriot king
if his shield-bearers had not cut off its feet with their swords.
[Artybios, Persian general; Onesilos, king of Salamis; 498 B.C.; cf. Herodotus, *Histories* 5.104 and 110–12]

3. *Historiae* or *Chiliades* 6.367–68 [ΑΚΕΠ I 66.14β]

And this Andocides sold his cousin
to the Cypriot king for some wheat.
[Between 414 and 407 B.C.; cf. Andocides, *De reditu suo* 11–12 and 20–21]

4. *Historiae* or *Chiliades* 7.556 and 559–62 [ΑΚΕΠ I 115.1β]

And the Sibyl told . . .
how Lebounios will come to Cyprus.
And thus she spoke about Cyprus and about Antioch,
"Alas, poor Cyprus, a huge wave will cover you;

but you, poor Antioch, will perish by weapons of war."
[cf. *Oracula Sibyllina* 4. 140–44]

5. *Historiae* or *Chiliades* 7.564–67 [AKEΠ I 5]

Concerning the coming of Kilix to Cyprus,
thus spoke the wisest of women:
"The time will come when wide-eddying Pyramos,
extending the shore, will reach holy Cyprus."
[Kilix, brother of Kadmos and eponymous founder of Cilicia; Pyramos, a river in Cilicia;
cf. *Oracula Sibyllina* 4.97–98; Strabo, *Geography* 1.3.7 and 12.2.4; and Apollodorus, *Library*
3.1.1]

6. *Historiae* or *Chiliades* 11.649–52 [AKEΠ I 66.46]

To Evagoras, king of Cyprus, he [Isocrates] wrote
exhortations and words of advice, and to Nikokles.
And after the death of Evagoras he addressed to his son,
who is called Demonikos, many exhortations.
[cf. Isocrates, *Evagoras*, *Nicocles*, and *Demonicus*; also Scholia to Isocrates]

7. Scholia to Lycophron, *Alexandra* 447: Σφήκειαν εἰς Κεραστίαν [AKEΠ II 149.2]

Cyprus was previously called Sphekeia, as Philostephanus [of Cyrene, 3rd c. B.C.; *FHG*
III 30, fr. 10] reports in his work *On Cyprus;* the name is derived from the inhabitants, who were
called Sphekes [wasps]. But it is also called Kerasteia, as Androcles [or Menander; *FHG* IV 448,
fr. 7] reports in his work *On Cyprus*, because it was inhabited by men having *kerata* [horns]. But
Xenagoras in his work *On Islands* [*FHG* IV 527, fr. 8; *FGrH* IIB 240, fr.26] says that it was
called Kerasteia because it has many projecting headlands, which are called *kerata*.

8. Scholia to Lycophron, *Alexandra* 448: Ὑλάτου τε γῆν [AKEΠ II 85.1α]

Hyle is a city in Cyprus in which Apollo Hylates is worshipped. "Of Hylates" means "of
Apollo." For Hyle is a place near Kourion in Cyprus and sacred to Apollo; therefore people call
the god Hylatos.

9. Scholia to Lycophron, *Alexandra* 448: Σάτραχον [AKEΠ II 162, no. 6α]

The Satrachos is a city and a river of Cyprus; some write it "Setrachos," with "e."

10. Scholia to Lycophron, *Alexandra* 586: Κηφεὺς δὲ καὶ Πράξανδρος [AKEΠ I 24α]

Kepheus was from Achaea and Praxandros was from Sparta; they came to Cyprus, as
Philostephanos [of Cyrene, 3rd c. B.C.; *FHG* III 31, fr.12] says.

109. KINNAMOS, JOHN (after 1143–after 1185)

1. *Epitome* 1.10 (pp. 22–23 ed. Meineke) [ΣΒΠΚΙ 72.1]

When he [the emperor John II Komnenos, 1118–1143] learned that Raymond [of Poitiers] prince of Antioch [1136–1149] had rebelled, he marched straight back to Cilicia [1142], he intended that Cilicia and Antioch along with Attaleia [Antalya in Pamphylia] and Cyprus should be granted to Manuel [his son, the future emperor Manuel I] for his portion.

(trans. Charles M. Brand)

2. *Epitome* 2.3 (p. 35 ed. Meineke) [ΣΒΠΚΙ 72.2]

Since the sea did not favor them, the Romans cruised off that region for ten days; when they ran short of water, they unexpectedly ran ashore on the mainland, drove back the foe, plundered two coastal forts, and filled their ships with as much wine and riverwater as possible. Meeting with a favorable breeze, they set sail for Cyprus.

These disasters constrained Raymond to travel the road to Byzantion [1145].

(trans. Charles M. Brand)

3. *Epitome* 2.18 (pp. 83–84 ed. Meineke) [ΣΒΠΚΙ 72.3]

So this was done there. The emperor promoted a certain Nicholas, by surname Mouzalon, to the patriarchal throne [1147]; he had previously belonged to the priestly order, but after he had possessed the throne of the Cypriots' church he then voluntarily resigned from it. But no sooner did he take up administration than every mouth was roused against him. They claimed he had unlawfully mounted the throne, because he had previously abandoned the priesthood along with the church assigned to him. At first he was stubborn and unwilling to resign the throne. But once the emperor had made a determination on the matter, he [Mouzalon] perceived that he had been allotted the losing side; without waiting to be examined again, he abandoned the throne and continued to live as an individual. In his stead was designated Theodotos [1151–1153], who was thoroughly practiced in ascetic discipline.

(trans. Charles M. Brand)

4. *Epitome* 4.17 (pp. 178–79 ed. Meineke) [ΣΒΠΚΙ 72.4.1]

Since the emperor [Manuel I Komnenos, 1143–1180] did not accord him [Reginald of Châtillon] what he wanted, this Reginald tried to frighten him, brandishing many threats; asserting that he required money, he acted as follows [1156]. After he had constructed ships, he made sail for Cyprus, attacked those there in piratical fashion, and carried off an abundance of wealth. At first, however, the emperor's nephew John [Komnenos the *protosebastos*] who then governed the land, and Michael Branas and whoever else was stationed there for its defense, repelled and manhandled him. Then when Branas was pursuing him more impetuously than was necessary at Leukosia [Nicosia], John went forth to to join him, and so both were captured by Reginald.

(trans. Charles M. Brand)

5. *Epitome* 4.17 (p. 181 ed. Meineke) [ΣΒΠΚΙ 72.4.2]

Reginald, as we previously said, felt extreme poverty and determined to ravage Cyprus.

(trans. Charles M. Brand)

6. *Epitome* 6.1 (p. 250 ed. Meineke) [ΣΒΠΚΙ 72.5]

The emperor [Manuel I Komnenos, 1143–1180] honored Andronicus [his cousin, the later emperor Andronikos I], who as stated had returned from Russia [Tauroskythai], with every kindness, presented the man with quantities of gold, and sent him to Cilicia to settle matters there [1166]. In order that he might be able to engage in lavish expenditures, he granted him the taxes of Cyprus.

(trans. Charles M. Brand)

110. MANASSES, CONSTANTINE (ca. 1130–ca. 1187)

1. *Hodoiporikon* (*Journey to Jerusalem*) 2.56–65 [ΣΒΠΚΙ 67]

When I was thus suffering badly, the renowned Alexios Doukas, who was then governing Cyprus, took pity on me; he is a generous and gentle man, of royal lineage. To make a long story short and to speak forcefully, by the order, will, and judgement of both I was taken to renowned Cyprus, so that I might find purer air and shake off the illness that was upon me. [1161]

2. *Hodoiporikon* (*Journey to Jerusalem*) 2.84–90 and 98 [ΣΒΠΚΙ 67]

And now I dwell in much-sung Cyprus, the shiny land, the fertile land, which is κύπειρος [?] to others, but Cyprus to me. For what is the dimness of the lower stars compared to the brightness of the sun which nourishes all? Or what is all of Cyprus and all that it has compared to the city of Constantine itself? . . . I dwell in a land in which words are scarce.

3. *Hodoiporikon* (*Journey to Jerusalem*) 3.16–21 [ΣΒΠΚΙ 67]

When I had fallen into a sea of maladies and when my body was racked by all manner of troubles I was taken to the great island of Cyprus, so that I might shed the load of my sufferings. Again I encountered dangers of a different sort, and the roughness of the wave made sport of me.

4. *Hodoiporikon* (*Journey to Jerusalem*) 4.1–16 [ΣΒΠΚΙ 67]

O, my hands, be strong and move for me; my feet, get up and leap for me. O, tongue, break loose a song of gratitude; and you, my thrice-suffering heart, rejoice.
Behold, I see most clearly the blessed Byzantium, most beloved of all. But what is this? Have I been deceived again? Do I live in Cyprus, the evil-smelling bitterness, or in the stifling city of Ptolemy [Alexandria], or in Nazareth, which is hateful to me? Do I in vain picture you,

golden city? Is this a dream and the laughter of night, or did I clearly see you while awake, not in a dream? But this is not Paphos and the land of Kition, it is not the poor city of Tremithous; it is not a hot stream of air, making it difficult to breathe.

5. *Hodoiporikon* (*Journey to Jerusalem*) 4. 42–43 [ΣΒΠΚΙ 67]

We found Cyprus terrified by many disturbances and fierce terrors.

6. *Hodoiporikon* (*Journey to Jerusalem*) 4. 56–6 [ΣΒΠΚΙ 67]

The count of Tripolis [Raymond III], therefore seething with anger, that rash man, breathing insolence . . . assembled a force, appointed commanders, and came to plunder the land of Cyprus [1161]. He is a most unreasonable man, and I do not know who in the emperor's realm might overcome him.

7. *Hodoiporikon* (*Journey to Jerusalem*) 4.95–108 [ΣΒΠΚΙ 67]

It was the day of the awesome feast, usually called Pentecost, and we were all assembled in church, attending the evening service. I happened to be standing near the door, when another man walked in, a Cypriot by birth, but surpassing all Cypriots in folly. He approached, stepped up, and stood next to me; he stank of wine, and he stank of garlic. And I, my nostrils filled with the foul odor . . . became dizzy and began to faint. [1162]

8. *Hodoiporikon* (*Journey to Jerusalem*) 4.152–58 [ΣΒΠΚΙ 67]

I left the town of Tripolis and the land of Cyprus, the very worst of fortresses. Yea, the island of Cyprus is a solid fortress, a wall of iron, a cage of stone, a Hades without escape, having no exits. Anyone unfortunate enough to be held on Cyprus would not easily escape from there.

111. EUSTATHIOS of Thessalonike (ca. 1115–1195/96)

1. *Commentary on Dionysios Periegetes* 508 [ΑΚΕΠ I 14.18; 32.1; II 10.9; 149.3; 152.1α; 153.2; 163.26]

[Dionysios says] that Cyprus does not rank behind any other island, that it is washed by the Bay of Pamphylia and the Bay of Issos, and that there is no other island further east. He also says that it is a city beloved by Aphrodite . . . Some people say that Cyprus derives its name from Kypros, the son of Kinyras, or else from a flower which grows there abundantly and is called kypros. But others say that it was once called Kryptos, because it was hidden by the sea; such a story is also told about Delos, and about Rhodes by Pindar [*Ol.* 7.56]. But Lycophron [3rd c. B.C. tragic poet; *Alexandra* 447] reports that it was once called Sphekeia and Kerastia. But the

Cypriots are the most fortunate of islanders; for it is said that they once ruled the sea. The circumference of the island is 6420 stadia, following the bays.

2. *Commentary on Iliad* 1.18 (27.39–42)

There are other mountains called Olympus. Thus in the Peloponnese, as [Dionysios] Periegetes records; and in Cyprus a mountain, shaped like a breast, between Kition and Amathous, is called Olympos. And another ridge on Cyprus was also so named; on it was a temple of Aphrodite Akraia [Aphrodite of the Cape *or* of Heights], which was forbidden to women.

3. *Commentary on Iliad* 2.499 (267.1–2)

There are other cities named Erythrai in Ionia, Libya, Locris, and Cyprus—the present-day Paphos, it is said—and in Boeotia.

4. *Commentary on Iliad* 2.557 (285.11–12) [ΑΚΕΠ I 20.13]

There is also Salamis in Cyprus, which Teucer founded after the fall of Troy and named Salamis after his native country.

5. *Commentary on Iliad* 2.625 (305.25–35)

Such also is the phrase "to Cyprus—to Paphos," for Cyprus is the whole and Paphos is a part of it . . . And Hipponax [fr. 75 Diehl, *Anthologia Lyrica Graeca*] employs this figure in his phrase "bread from Cyprus and wheat from Amathous"; for Amathous is a part of Cyprus. And Alcman [fr. 35 Diehl, *Anthologia Lyrica Graeca*] writes "leaving lovely Cyprus and sea-girt Paphos." And Aeschylus [fr. 463 Nauck, *Tragicorum Graecorum Fragmenta*] writes "having all the fame of Cyprus and Paphos"; for Paphos is encompassed within Cyprus, just as Chalcis and Eretria are in the phrase "they held Euboea and Chalcis and Eretria."

6. *Commentary on Iliad* 5.708 (596.44–45)

There was also, it is said, a city named Hyle in Locris and another in Cyprus, from which Apollo Hylates derives his name, according to Lycophron [3rd c. B.C. tragic poet; *Alexandra* 447–51].

7. *Commentary on Iliad* 6.488 (657.41–42)

Herodotus [*Histories* 4.162] reports that Pheretime, the wife of the lame Battos, when she came to Salaminian, that is Cypriot, Euelthon, asked him for an army for a certain war.

8. *Commentary on Iliad* 7.199 (676.24–25)

Concerning Salamis [it is to be said], that it lies off the coast of Attica and is renowned. It has been pointed out elsewhere that there is also a Salamis in Cyprus.

9. *Commentary on Iliad* 9.152 (743.22–23)

[Stephen of Byzantium, s.v. Αἴπεια, mentions] Aipeia, a city in Laconia . . . There is, he says, another city [by that name] in Cyprus and yet another in Crete.

10. *Commentary on Iliad* 10.409 (813.47–49) [ΑΚΕΠ I 37]

. . . the Kitians, not those of Phoenicia, but those of Cyprus; their city Kition is so named, it is said, after some woman named Kition.

11. *Commentary on Iliad* 11.20–23 (827.33–828.5) [ΑΚΕΠ I 14.1α; 14.2; 41.1α]

Kinyras—that is the common Doric or Homeric form of the name; the Ionic form is Kinyres—was the son of Theias, according to some; he was king of Cyprus and very rich. When the Achaeans came to him he received them hospitably and even promised to send supplies to Troy. But it is said that he failed to do so, was cursed by Agamemnon, and died in a musical contest with Apollo, as he was a master of music. Therefore Kinyras was named after the κινύρα [a stringed instrument]. And his daughters, fifty in number, leapt into the sea and were changed into halcyons.

Others say that he swore at Paphos to send fifty ships to Menelaos, but sent only one. The others which he sent were fashioned of clay and contained earthen images of man; thus he contrived to keep his oath with an army of clay. Beside the so-called Cypriot guest-friendship shown the Achaeans one must note also the Delian one, of which Lycophron [3rd c. B.C. tragic poet; *Alexandra* 447] reports that it was much more splendid than that of the Cypriots . . .

Noteworthy is also that Homer appears not to have known the guest-friendship of Kinyras, only his reputation from hearsay. For he had learned, so he says, the great fame of Cyprus, and so forth. But of Cyprus' great wealth and other good fortunes the historians report. That Amasis [pharaoh of Egypt ca. 569–525 B.C.] was the first to force Cyprus to pay tribute is reported by Herodotus [*Histories* 2.182]. From him we also learn that "Kinyres" is of the Ionic dialect, since he calls a surging river κυματίης rather than κυματίας [*Histories* 2.111]. And such.

And Homer says that Kinyras gave to the king [Agamemnon] a breastplate to be a guest present. For the great report had reached Cyprus that the Achaeans were about to sail to Troy in their ships; so he [Kinyras] gave to the king this gift to please him. Thus he established by gifts his friendship with the Greeks, and clearly he was not paying compensation for failing to participate in the campaign . . .

But the great fame of the Greek hosts is shown by the fact that the Cypriots sent gifts first, not after the Trojan expedition, but when the Greeks were about to sail.

12. *Commentary on Iliad* 13.582 (947.48–54) [ΑΚΕΠ I 66.43β]

It is to be noted that the terms ἄναξ (lord) and ἄνακτες (lords) may refer not only to kings, as in this case to Helenos, hero and lord, but that the expression is applied in other contexts to different things. On Cyprus, it is reported, there was a well-known class of men known as lords. These received daily, it is said, from the "listeners" reports of whatever they had heard; this was done for the control of the island's affairs. Such listeners could also be called πευθῆνες (informers), from πεύθω (to inform), from which πύστις (information) is derived.

13. *Commentary on Iliad* 15.641 (1035.44–48) [ΑΚΕΠ II 164.5α]

Therefore the comic poet Antiphanes [4th c. B.C.; fr. 175 *FAC* II] is reported to have suitably said . . . "In Athens there are owls, in Cyprus there are various doves, and on Samos Hera has a breed of golden birds, the beautiful and much-admired peacocks."

14. *Commentary on Iliad* 17.307 (1108.13–14)

Then consider also that the poet has substituted the part for the whole, that is Panopeus for Phocians; this happens also in the expression "to Cyprus—to Paphos" and in other places.

15. *Commentary on Iliad* 21.12 (1220.33–42) [ΑΚΕΠ II 164.3]

Then he [Homer] compares the Trojans fleeing into the river with locusts which are fleeing into a river from a fire-storm which the farmers have lit, driving them from their fields . . . It is to be noted that some people, departing from this point and drawing weighty conclusions from insufficient evidence, claim that the poet was a Cypriot and, for the same reason, that he knew that the island is at times troubled by locusts, just like Cyrene and Barce in Libya. But if anyone should be persuaded by these arguments that the poet, because he knows the misfortune of the island of Cyprus, is for this reason believed to be Cypriot, [let me point out that] the poet is a man of many countries and records the customs and misfortunes of many cities.

16. *Commentary on Iliad* 22.499 (1283.29–31) [ΑΚΕΠ II 79.2α]

He [Athenaeus, *Deipnosophists* 2.69d–e] says that those who use lettuce continuously lose their sexual potency. Therefore the plant and others [of similar kind] are hated by Aphrodite, according to the Cypriot myth which holds that Adonis had fled into a bed of lettuce when he was killed by a boar.

17. *Commentary on Iliad* 23.826 (1332.3–6) [ΑΚΕΠ I 39.4 and 82.1]

It is obvious that Solos is also the name of a city, the citizens of which are the Soleis. But there was also Soloi in Cyprus, which is recorded by King Eunostos. (He has the same name as Eunostos, the daemon of mills, to whom reference has been made elsewhere.) But how "solecism" is a synthesis of this "Solos" or "Soloi" is found in the writings of [Dionysios] Periegetes. It seems that the lawgiver Solon also derives his name hence.

18. *Commentary on Odyssey* 1.184 (1409.6–18) [ΑΚΕΠ I 18.3; II 173.1α]

On Cyprus, too, according to some, there is a city named Temese, and it, too, produces bronze. Nevertheless the geographer does not identify Homeric Temese and Brentesion [Brundisium] with each other, but writes separately concerning Temese and separately concerning Brentesion . . . Concerning Temese he writes that the first city of Brettia [Bruttium] is Temese, later called Tempsa, a foundation of the Ausoni . . . But of Temese in Cyprus the ancients believed that it should correctly be pronounced Tamasos, with "a"; hence also the expression "Tamasian krater," which is found in Lycophron [3rd c. B.C. tragic poet; *Alexandra* 854]. There, according to the geographer, the corrosion of the bronze has medicinal value and the copper sulphate derived from it is used as ink.

19. *Commentary on Odyssey* 8.360–65 (1600.30–50) [ΑΚΕΠ II 12β]

When the adulterers just mentioned had been freed from their bonds they rose forthwith. He went to Thrace; for Thrace is Ares' home, because its people are very warlike, as is apparent in many places. But Aphrodite, because of the Cypriots' charm, came to Paphos on Cyprus; there she had a sanctuary and an altar on which sacrifices were made to her. There the Graces washed her and anointed her with the immortal oil which is on the gods who live forever . . . And he calls Aphrodite laughter-loving because of her smile . . . But "to Paphos" he adds habitually, for the sake of accuracy, to make clear where on Cyprus the laughter-loving [goddess] went.

20. *Commentary on Odyssey* 17.443 (1826.46) [ΑΚΕΠ I 16.1]

If Kinyras, in the *Iliad* [11.19–20], was king of Cyprus, now he is no longer alive and Dmetor, just mentioned, seems to be king.

21. *Commentary on Odyssey* 18.29 (1835.48) [ΑΚΕΠ I 19]

A crop-destroying pig [ληιβοτείρης], one that destroys another man's crops, one which had its tusks removed by the owner of the place. This was the law on Cyprus, they say.

112. BALSAMON, THEODORE (d. after 1195)

1. *Interpretation of the Canons*, ed. Rhalles and Potles, vol. II, pp. 205–206 [ΣΒΠΚΙ 76.1]

Before the great city of Antioch was lost by the empire of the Romans a resident duke used to be sent by the emperor, and he in turn used to send a general to Cyprus, treating it as a dependency of Antioch. But the Cypriot bishops conducted their own affairs and performed their own ordinations. At that time the bishop of Antioch attempted, so it seems, to perform ordinations in the churches of Cyprus, on the grounds that a general was being sent to the island by the duke of Antioch. The matter was taken by the Cypriot bishops to the Council of Ephesus [431], and the council granted them audience. The council then ruled that the Cypriot bishops should perform their own ordinations, according to the canons and the ancient practice. The same thing shall apply also, so the council ruled, to the other dioceses and provinces, and no bishop shall be able to take over another province which has not been subject to him since the beginning. Furthermore those who do such a thing and by force and [unlawful] authority hold on to another bishop's territory shall surrender it, lest the canons be violated and lest, under the pretense of divine service, the illusion of worldly power or of vanity make its appearance among the bishops. And the council allowed each of the metropolitans to receive a copy of this canon for his security. And no other document or imperial decree that is produced by anyone shall be valid if it is in conflict with this canon. To wit the second canon of the Second Council [Constantinople, 381–382], the 28th canon of the Fourth Council [Chalcedon, 451], the 39th canon of the Sixth Council [actually the Council in Trullo or Quinisext Council, 691–692], and their provisions. And note that the churches of Romania [the Byzantine Empire], with the exception of some, are subject to the throne of Constantinople.

[Interpreting the eighth canon of the Council of Ephesus, 431]

2. *Interpretation of the Canons*, ed. Rhalles and Potles, vol. II, pp. 396–97 [ΣΒΠΚΙ 76.2]

From the eighth canon of the third council [Ephesus, 431] it is evident that, at the request of a certain bishop of Cyprus named Rheginos, a ruling was made to the effect that the church of Cyprus should be autocephalous and that the bishop of Antioch should be forbidden to perform ordinations in Cyprus. The present canon, issued at the request of another archbishop of Cyprus, John, pertains also to the decisions made at Ephesus and names the church of Cyprus New Justinianopolis; it rules that it should have the same rights as the church of Constantinople. Likewise the churches of the provinces of the Hellespont and the church of Kyzikos. And their bishops are to be ordained by the archbishop of Cyprus. But today none of these churches is subject to the archbishopric of Cyprus, nor does it [the archbishopric of Cyprus] have the rights of Constantinople. We must find out how this came about.

[Interpreting the 39th canon of the Council in Trullo or Quinisext Council, 691–692]

113. Τὰ πραχθέντα ἐπὶ τῇ καθαιρέσει τοῦ πατριάρχου ἐκείνου τοῦ Μουζάλων (*Acts of the Deposition of the Patriarch Mouzalon*) (second half, 12th c.)

1. Ed. Darrouzès, p. 310

Nicholas IV Mouzalon (patriarch of Constantinople 1147–1151) addressing the emperor Manuel Komnenos (1143–1180):

You have adduced yesterday a multitude of arguments to the effect that I, having resigned the bishopric of Cyprus [ca. 1110], am not able to hold holy office.

2. Ed. Darrouzès, p. 312

The emperor addressing the patriarch:
Do you claim that you received it [the priesthood] long ago when you were sent to be a shepherd to the people of Cyprus, and that it remains in your possession, as it was not surrendered when you resigned from the bishopric?

3. Ed. Darrouzès, p. 326

The emperor addressing an assembly of bishops:
Thus the bishop of Cyprus, by resigning from his office, has returned to the status of an unconsecrated and unprepared person, and thus he does not have the qualifications to be a bishop.

4. Ed. Darrouzès, p. 330

The bishops addressing the emperor:
And we, mighty emperor, having received authority from the Spirit through the holy canons, decree that this man, not being able to receive holy orders a second time and therefore, without holy orders, not being able to perform divine tasks, be driven from his throne; also, since he has disregarded the divine laws and, in his vanity, has surrendered the bishopric of Cyprus and has dared to ascend to the highest throne, that of Constantinople, be excommunicated for the rest of his life.

114. GLYKAS, MICHAEL (second half, 12th c.)

1. *Annals,* ed. Becker, pp. 594–95 (Migne, *PG* 158, col. 593) [ΣΒΠΚΙ 62.1]

When Theophilos Erotikos, who was in command in Cyprus, learned what had happened to [Michael V, 1041–1042] Kalaphates and that things were in a state of confusion, he prevailed upon the Cypriots to stage a rebellion [1043]. But the emperor sent a force against him and seized him. Then he displayed him at a triumph in the hippodrome, dressed in women's garb, confiscated his property, and released him. At this time also the Patriarch Alexios died, and Michael Keroulares [Cerularius, 1043–1058], the monk, was appointed in his stead.

2. *Annals,* ed. Becker, p. 620 (Migne, *PG* 158, col. 617) [ΣΒΠΚΙ 62.2]

At that time [1092] Cyprus and Crete both contemplated defection, but were quickly brought under control again; in Cyprus it was Karykes who had risen up, and in Crete it was Rhapsamates [Rhapsommates].
[But cf. Zonaras, no. 14 (*Chronicon* 18.25.16–17)]

115. VITA OF ST. THERAPON (12th c.)

1. *AASS* Maii VI.681 [ΣΒΠΚΙ 69]

Where this saint came from, who his parents were, when he lived, or under whom he was martyred, having found the crown of martyrdom, we are unable to say, since all record of him has been lost in time. That he chose a monk's life is shown by his icons, which depict him in that manner. That he became bishop of the island of Cyprus, was brought close to Christ by his blood, and won the athlete's contest, that we have learned from the tradition which was handed down and that we believe, having been taught, without benefit of written record, by our forebears. His precious relics were taken to Constantinople when the Saracens were planning to attack the island of Cyprus and when the saint himself in a vision had given instructions for his *translatio*. And now, where he lies, he brings forth an abundance of miracles all the time.

116. VITA OF ST. TRIPHYLLIOS (12th c.)

1. *AASS* Iun. II, p. 683–85 [ΣΒΠΚΙ 70]

3. When he [Triphyllios] was steadily advancing, aided by the prayers of his teacher [Spyridon], he became, at the midpoint of his life, an excellent shepherd of Christ to give care to souls. By divine will he was appointed to the see of the metropolis which used to be called Kallinikessiai but now is called Leukosia [modern Nikosia]. This is the largest and most beautiful among the cities of Cyprus, clearly occupies the first rank, and prospered by his prayers when, by divine will, he was chosen to preside over this city and beyond. Thus, not incidentally, we learn of the vision seen by the emperor Constantine the Great when he was suffering from some malady of his head and was seeking a cure from God. This vision pointed out Triphyllios to the emperor; so the emperor sent for the bishop, and he appeared before his throne as quick as the vision and announced the cure.

4. When he had ascended to the throne by the apostolic laws and under the holy hands of Spyridon, he followed in the footsteps of his teacher, teaching, expounding the holy scriptures, fortifying souls with spiritual bread, and offering to those who were thirsty a drink of living water [cf. John 4:10–11 and 7:38], which he was able to draw from the rivers of the spirit. And this not intermittently for a period of some days, but every day he offered daily bread spiritually, as the Lord has commanded us to ask [Matthew 6:11; Luke 11:3], leading the spoken word to higher thought. This is the origin of the practice, which has become custom and is followed here from the fall equinox to the spring equinox . . . Let one man speak and interpret, but let the others be silent [cf. 1 Corinthians 14:27]. Thus the teachings of St. Triphyllios will take deep root . . .

5. Who could say how many miracles he performed in the course of his life? He was indeed a successor to Spyridon both in his character and in the miracles which he performed . . . He lived in poverty and readily, by his own hand, gave everything to those in need; he dug up those covered up [reading συγχωαθέντας, not συγχωρηθέντας] by the earthquake, dressed them, and gave to them from his substance, being a noble man and having descended from noble parents. He devoted himself to continuous fasts and prayers, so that he might become an example to his

flock. He built a convent for women, using his mother's funds, and persuaded his mother [Domnika] to put on the monastic habit . . . He also built the present sacred precinct, large enough to accommodate the entire city, and there, too, is his tomb . . .

7. When the Arab people, in the days of Herakleios [610–641], were practicing piracy and ravaging many of the islands, God allowed the outrages committed by these people also to reach Cyprus. Thus they came and did what they usually do. When they came to the tomb of the saint and laid their unholy eyes upon it they were driven by the hope of finding gold within it . . . And when they had easily advanced further in their hopes they saw the great man (what miracle after the passage of so many years!) as if he were asleep, and his tomb giving forth a sweet odor. Then they took him up and, yielding to their madness, cut the sacred head from the body with a sword. Forthwith his blood flowed forth, and God himself, I believe, fashioned for him, in addition to his other crowns, a crown of martyrdom, which he, possessed by the love of Christ, had been seeking to obtain but which the bright fire of the piety of Constantine the Great towards Christ had denied him [by ending the persecutions]. Then they dragged his body in front of the tomb, piled up a pyre, and attempted to keep up a fire. But the body did not seem to yield to the fire until one of the barbarians, looking on, shouted: "In the name of Jesus your Christ allow yourself to be burned by the fire." And I, the one who has compiled this record, am a witness of this: I have seen his sacred head half-burnt and the pieces of his body showing the effect of the fire, and these are displayed for veneration each May 3, which by chance is the very day on which the infidels desecrated his tomb. [But the saint's feast day is June 12 or 13.]

[Note: this text appears to be badly corrupted and poorly edited. The translation here offered remains necessarily tentative.]

117. Περὶ μεταθέσεων (On Transfers) (12th c.)

1. p. 177 ed. Darrouzès [ΣΒΠΚΙ 71.1]

26. During the reign of Constantine Pogonatos, when the Saracens had seized Cyprus, the metropolis of Kyzikos, together with its bishoprics, was given to the archbishop of Cyprus.

[Note: Constantine IV, who reigned 668–685, is not usually called *Pogonatos*. The emperor at the time of the Council in Trullo, 691–692, which ruled in this matter, was Justinian II.]

2. p. 183–84 ed. Darrouzès [ΣΒΠΚΙ 71.2]

57. Nicholas Mouzalon, when he had become archbishop of Cyprus, resigned the throne of Cyprus and was granted the monastery of Kosmidion, over which he presided for some time; then he became patriarch of Constantinople.

During the reign of Manuel [I] Komnenos [1143–1180] Nicholas Mouzalon—previously having become archbishop of Cyprus and then having resigned, according to many the holy office itself, but according to many others only the administration of its affairs—was 28 years later transferred to the patriarchate of Constantinople.

118. KEDRENOS, GEORGE (12th c.)

1. *Compendium Historiarum* (Migne, *PG* 121, col. 56) [ΑΚΕΠ I 14.17γ]

Aphrodite is indeed called intelligent and artful. She married Adonis, who was the son of Kinyras and a philosopher himself. It is reported that they lived together practicing philosophy until [his] death.

2. *Compendium Historiarum* (Migne, *PG* 121, col. 101) [ΑΚΕΠ I 4; II 118α]

The Egyptians were the first to to invent geometry, while the Chaldaeans invented astrology, and the Arabs and Phrygians the observation of birds. But the Chaldaeans or the Cypriots invented the practice of sacrificing to the gods (they are known by either name, being by nationality Persian). The Babylonians invented astronomy through Zoroaster, and the Egyptians received it from them. The Medes and the Persians invented magic, witchcraft, and the use of drugs.

3. *Compendium Historiarum* (Migne, *PG* 121, col. 548) [ΑΚΕΠ I 121.7]

But so that God might show [at the Council of Nicaea] that the Kingdom of God is founded not in speech but in power, one of the holy fathers, by name of Spyridon, bishop of Trimithous, very simple in nature and unaccomplished in speech, asked that permission be given to him to speak to the philosopher. But the fathers, knowing the simple and untrained nature of the man, tried to prevent him. But he, not holding back, stepped up to the man and said . . .

4. *Compendium Historiarum* (Migne, *PG* 121, col. 564) [ΑΚΕΠ I 129.2]

In the 28th year [of the reign of Constantine the Great, i.e. in 334] a great famine arose in the East.

5. *Compendium Historiarum* (Migne, *PG* 121, col. 565) [ΑΚΕΠ I 129.5]

When an earthquake struck Cyprus [in the 28th year of the reign of Constantine the Great, i.e. in 334], the city of Salamis was ruined and a considerable number [of people] perished.

6. *Compendium Historiarum* (Migne, *PG* 121, col. 565) [ΑΚΕΠ I 128α; ΣΒΠΚI 55.1]

In the 29th year [of the reign of Constantine the Great, i.e. in 335] Dalmatius was proclaimed Caesar. And Kalokairos, who had seized power in Cyprus, was burned alive by Dalmatius [actually by Dalmatius the Elder, censor] in Tarsos of Cilicia.

7. *Compendium Historiarum* (Migne, *PG* 121, col. 632) [ΣΒΠΚΙ 55.2]

The great Epiphanios of Cyprus came to Hebdomon [a suburb of Constantinople] and performed ordinations and held services without authorization of John [Chrysostom].

8. *Compendium Historiarum* (Migne, *PG* 121, col. 633) [ΑΚΕΠ I 135.12α; ΣΒΠΚΙ 55.3]

When Epiphanios was returning to Cyprus and had learned from God that his end was near, he is reported to have said to those who accompanied him: "I am in a hurry, yes, in a hurry; I leave to you the palace, the city, and the theater." He also predicted that John [Chrysostom] would die and gain victory in exile; and John, in turn, predicted that Epiphanios would die on board his ship. These things the blessed men learned beforehand by divine inspiration, lest anyone might suppose that there was enmity between them.

9. *Compendium Historiarum* (Migne, *PG* 121, col. 673) [ΑΚΕΠ I 110.34α; ΣΒΠΚΙ 55.4]

At this time [in the fourth year of the reign of Zeno, i.e. in A.D. 478] the body of St. Barnabas the apostle was found in Cyprus under a cherry tree [a carob tree according to other accounts]. On his breast the apostle had the Gospel of Matthew, written by his own hand. For this reason Cyprus later became a metropolis, and because it functioned not under Antioch but under Constantinople. But Zeno deposited the Gospel in his palace, in the Church of St. Stephen in Daphne.

10. *Compendium Historiarum* (Migne, *PG* 121, col. 825) [ΣΒΠΚΙ 55.5]

In this year [649] Mabias [Muawiyah, governor of Syria, to become the first caliph of the Umayyad dynasty in 661] waged war upon Cyprus with 1700 ships and took Constantia and the entire island.

11. *Compendium Historiarum* (Migne, *PG* 121, col. 844) [ΣΒΠΚΙ 55.6]

In his sixth year [691] Justinian [II, 685–695 and 705–711] foolishly broke the peace with Abimelech [Abd al-Malik of the Umayyad dynasty, 685–705]. For he unreasonably wanted to repopulate the island of Cyprus and he rejected the money sent to him by Abimelech, on the grounds that it was minted in an unfamiliar way.

12. *Compendium Historiarum* (Migne, *PG* 121, col. 888) [ΣΒΠΚΙ 55.7]

The fleet of the Saracens sailed from Alexandria to Cyprus, where the Roman fleet was stationed. The Roman general launched an attack, sealed the mouth of the harbor, and utterly destroyed all [the enemy ships], allowing only three to escape to deliver the message. [747]

13. *Compendium Historiarum* (Migne, *PG* 121, col. 896) [ΣΒΠΚΙ 55.8]

Then, following the example of his teacher [Constantine V, 741 and 743–775], Lachano-drakon assembled all the monks from the Thrakesian theme at Ephesus and spoke to them: "Let anyone who wishes to obey the emperor and us put on a cloak and take a wife right now. But those who do not comply will be blinded and exiled to Cyprus." And at once deed followed word.

14. *Compendium Historiarum* (Migne, *PG* 121, col. 900)

In the fifth year [of the emperor Leo IV, 775–780] Niketas [I, 766–780], patriarch of Constantinople . . . died, and Paul [IV, 780–784], the venerable reader from Cyprus, was appointed.

15. *Compendium Historiarum* (Migne, *PG* 121, cols. 917–20) [ΣΒΠΚΙ 55.9]

Ἀαρών [Harun al-Rashid, of the Abbasid dynasty, 786–809] . . . sent a fleet against Cyprus, destroyed the churches, resettled the Cypriots, took a lot of booty, and thus broke the peace. [806]

16. *Compendium Historiarum* (Migne, *PG* 122, col. 97)

In the same year, the second year of his reign, Nikephoros [Phokas, 963–969] returned the entire island of Cyprus to Roman control, driving out the Saracens by the patrician Niketas Chalkutzes. [965]

17. *Compendium Historiarum* (Migne, *PG* 122, col. 281)

At this time [1043] there occurred in Cyprus another revolt, the originator of which was Theophilos Erotikos. He was the governor of the island and a man always fond of stirring up trouble. When he learned of the end of [Michael IV] Kalaphates and of the general confusion he believed that the right moment had come to implement his plan and stirred up the whole population of Cyprus . . . But [Constantine IX] Monomachos lost no time in putting him down. For he sent as commander of the force the patrician Constantine Chage, who made the whole population of Cyprus submit, seized Theophilos, and sent him to the emperor.

119. VITA OF ST. ZENO (12th c.)

1. *REB* 25 (1967) 147–52 [ΣΒΠΚΙ 68]

Commemoration of our holy father Zeno, bishop of Kourion.
This holy father of ours Zeno came from Amathous. Because of his reputation for a righteous way of life he was appointed bishop of Kourion. When a council of holy fathers was

assembled at Ephesus [431] to take action against the impious Nestorios, who was blaspheming the Theotokos by denying that she was the Holy Virgin, then this thrice-blessed man, moved by divine zeal, also came to Ephesus. And before all others he denounced Nestorios and expelled him from the Church like a diseased limb. And he taught all men to proclaim the Theotokos truly and mightily and to call her the Virgin-forever. But when the patriarch of Antioch attempted to bring Cyprus under his jurisdiction and to perform ordinations there, Zeno convinced him that Cyprus should not be under him but should remain free and independent as before and from the beginning.

And when he had returned to his own country he passed on to the Lord. And even after his death he does not cease to perform miracles . . . And ever since then he affects many healings and countless miracles for those who approach his holy tomb with all their heart, for the glory and praise of our Lord Jesus Christ, to whom honor and veneration are due forever and ever. Amen.

120. STEPHEN (12th c.)

1. Scholia to Aristotle's *Rhetoric* 1399a, 4 (ed. Cramer, *Anecd. Gr. Paris.* I, pp. 292–93; ed. Rabe, p. 302) [ΑΚΕΠ I 66.13ε]

The father of Nikokles was Evagoras. Isocrates wrote an epitaph for Evagoras and sent it to Nikokles, celebrating the man in his work. Conon, the Athenian general, also fled to him [Evagoras] while the Spartans were in power [404 B.C.] Evagoras subdued them and made it possible for Conon to return to his own country [393 B.C.].

121. *ETYMOLOGIUM MAGNUM* (12th c.)

1. s.v. Ἀῷος [ΑΚΕΠ I 2α; II 160, no. 2]

Phileas [of Athens, 5th c. B.C.?] says that Aoos was the first king and was the son of Eos and Kephalos. After him also a mountain in Cyprus is called Aoon, and from this mountain spring two rivers, Seraches and Plieus. Parthenios [of Nicaea, 1st c. B.C.] has called one of these rivers Aoos, because it flows toward the East.

2. s.v. Κύπρος [ΑΚΕΠ II 149.5γ]

Because it has fertile and rich soil.

122. ACTS OF THE SYNOD OF 1209 [ΣΒΠΚΙ 78]

1. Pp. 141–44 ed. Chatzepsaltes

The record of the deliberations of the synod which met in the year 6717 [annus mundi = A.D. 1209], the 12th indiction, Kyritzes Manuel serving as *chartophylax* [keeper of the records].

In the month of June, on the fourth day, the 12th indiction, under the presidency of our holy lord the Ecumenical Patriarch Michael [IV Autoreianos, 1208–1214], in the vestibule of the church of the august monastery of Hyakinthos [at Nicaea], which had been given to his holiness as a residence [while Constantinople was under Latin occupation].

The following holy bishops were in attendance: Theodore of Sardis, Philip of Nikomedeia, John of Nicaea, Theodore of Laodikeia [western Asia Minor?], Nicholas of Mokissos [Justinianopolis, Cappadocia], Nicholas of Crete, Manuel of Thebes, Constantine of Madytos [Thracian Chersonese], George of Apameia, Michael of Nazianzos [Cappadocia], John of Abydos, Constantine of Kallipolis, George of Achyraous [Mysia], George of Maroneia [Thrace], George of Paros, Leo of Lemnos, and Nikephoros of Lopadion [northwestern Asia Minor]; and also pious rulers . . .

Sabbas, the pious bishop of the holy see of Paphos on the renowned island of Cyprus, has today approached our holy synod and reported on the condition of the holy churches there since the Latin power supplemented the Roman power. And he said that when the Latins had captured the island the churches remained in their usual order and so did the clergy, as long as Sophronios the blessed archbishop was counted among the living.

But some time later Sophronios departed this life and passed on to the Lord. Thus the island was again administered solely by the other bishops there and deprived of its [spiritual] leader while silence enveloped the vacant throne and while the island waited for word from heaven above, that is for an archbishop to be nominated by his imperial highness and to be sent to the island, according to the traditional practice and with God's approval.

When this did not happen and many years went by during which the island did not have the benefit of the archbishop's care, a gathering took place of all the priests, all the monks, and the better sort of the people, and especially of whatever local bishops were left on the island, with the permission of the ruler of the land, the noble king, namely the king of Jerusalem [Aimery *or* Amaury, 1194–1205]—for he appreciated men of faith, integrity, and devotion to piety and spoke foreign languages. Then they found Esaïas, the holy archbishop of Lydda [in Palestine], wandering about the island of Cyprus at that time. He was a fugitive from his own church at Lydda and from the rule of the foreigners, the Arabs, so that he could not function in his see. Then, by universal agreement, all placed him on the throne of the great Barnabas and accepted him as their shepherd [ca. 1203–1205].

Thus he was installed in the archbishopric of Cyprus and ordained other bishops, namely [Neilos] the *protothronos* [ranking bishop] of the holy see of Damasia [Tamasos] and the bishop of Paphos. The latter is the one who has reported these things publicly and who has declared that he is petitioning our modesty [μετριότης, a self-assumed title of humility] and the holy synod, on behalf of the archbishop, his own person, the other bishops, and all the Christian people of Cyprus, that his rights be preserved. The archbishop of Cyprus, so the bishop of Paphos explained, was at his appointment appointed to a place that had long been important and he had not been invited to absent himself from Lydda for the purpose of a transfer when he was walking about in the archbishopric of Cyprus, and the needs of the moment were pressing and precluded strict adherence to the rules.

Thus our modesty, the brethren here assembled, and this pious bishop of Paphos, who has reported to us, understand that the afore-mentioned Esaïas, the archbishop of Cyprus, has not assumed office by his own volition but by the common judgement of the bishops and at the urgent request of all the Christian people on the island; at the same time we recognize the importance of administration and what in this case set aside the strict rules, there being need for an orderly administration to be re-established. Therefore we have, by action of the synod, accepted and adopted this action of the Cypriots and have ruled that this archbishop of Cyprus, the blessed Esaïas, be enrolled with his brethren and fellow-servants, and have spiritually embraced those who were ordained by him.

Therefore the same blessed Esaïas, our beloved spiritual brother and fellow-servant, shall have all the rights and privileges of the archbishop of Cyprus, and shall appoint, if necessary, other bishops in any bishoprics there that fall vacant, according to the established canonical rules, and shall exercise all the other functions that are given to the bishops, since he is the true archbishop of Cyprus. If any of the bishoprics there should fall vacant and something should prevent the appointment of other bishops, then the bishops who are there shall preside in the territory of the churches thus vacant.

This account has been excerpted from the daily minutes of the synod and confirmed by the signature and seal of the honorable *chartophylax* of the great church of God, Manuel Kyritzes; given in the month and in the indiction indicated of the year 6717.

The signature: the *chartophylax* of the holy great church of God, Manuel Kyritzes.

123. NEOPHYTOS ENKLEISTOS (1134–after 1214)

1. *Encomium of Theosebios* 8 [AKEΠ I 114; II 131]

To be married and yet to maintain one's chastity intact is a great and difficult-to-obtain prize. Among the very few who have attained it I mention the great Konon, who was converted and baptized in the days of the apostles and who heard about self-control and chastity. With words of divine sound he persuaded his newly wedded wife, and they agreed to keep their chastity undiminished. When they were asked about their childlessness they gave barrenness as a reason and thus kept a secret from all. Then he was elevated to a bishop's throne, was witnessed performing many miracles, was a champion of the truth, clung to the salvific message, and taught it. Later he was decorated with the crown of martyrdom and passed on to the Lord.

2. *Encomium of Gennadios* 5 and 7 [AKEΠ I 134.6]

He (Gennadios) took him (Neilos, a monk) for a travel companion and disciple and came to Jerusalem. There he worshipped intently at the life-bearing tomb of Christ, performed his holy devotions and prayers, and in no way, as he was there, did he accept death. But he quickly returned to Cyprus and when his ship had anchored in the harbor of the city of Paphos he chose not to remain in the city, but left his disciple there, while he went to the mountain on which once the great Hilarion had established the Hesychastic and ascetic struggle against the demons . . .

Gennadios [I, 458–471] is the archbishop of Constantinople, who on his own volition gave up the throne and entrusted the secret to me (Neilos), the least (of men). We left the city secretly under cover of night and came to Jerusalem. From there, after we had performed our devotions, we traveled to Cyprus, where he left me in the castle of Paphos. "I shall go," he said, "to see the place in which the great Hilarion once became a Hesychast, and then I shall return." This much I know. But in what manner he returned from there and how he died, I do not know.

3. *Letter Concerning the Misfortunes of the Land of Cyprus*, 1196 [ΣΒΠΚΙ 73]

A cloud veils the sun, and a mist mountains and hills, and these for a while shut out the warmth and bright ray of the sun; and us too, for now twelve years, a cloud and mist, of successive calamities which have befallen our country, wrap round.

For Jerusalem having fallen under the rule of the godless Saladin [1187], and Cyprus under that of Isaac Comnenus [1184], fights thenceforth and wars, tumult and turbulence, plunder and dread events, covered the land in which these men ruled, worse than cloud and mist. For lo! the life-giving sepulchre of our Lord, and the other holy places, for our sins have been given to the Musalman dogs, and at this great calamity every Godloving soul weeps: as it is written [Psalms 46:6], "the nations raged, the kingdoms were moved," the sovereigns of Germany and England, and of nearly every nation are moved, I say, on behalf of Jerusalem, and have done nothing. For Providence was not well pleased to thrust out dogs, and to bring wolves in their room.

And now for twelve years the waves swell up even worse: and he, our beloved spiritual son, to whom forsooth we write these things, enduring not to see and to hear the horrors, and partly to suffer them, after many questionings and contrivances, by a divine impulse fled from their bloodstained hands with all his people, and having approached [Isaac II] Angelus, the sovereign of Constantinople [1185–1195], was honourably welcomed by him, and from him received the dignity of "Augustus." And I, in fulfilment of my promise, lo! by the grace of God, write the rest as I promised, setting forth to those who may read these our present difficulties. Which difficulties, when they shall end, no one among men knoweth, but He only who rebuketh the sea and the winds, and they are still.

Strange things and unheard of have befallen this land, and such that all its rich men have forgotten their wealth, their fine dwellings, families, servants, slaves, their many flocks, herds, swine, cattle of all kinds, grainbearing fields, fertile vineyards and variegated gardens, and with great care and secrecy have sailed away to foreign lands, and to the queen of cities. And those who could not fly—who is fit to set forth the tragedy of their sufferings? The searches, the public prisons, the exaction of money squeezed from them, thousands upon thousands! But these, by the just judgment of God, were allowed to befall us on account of the burthen of our sins, that we might be humbled, and perchance be deemed worthy of forgiveness.

England is a country beyond Romania [the Byzantine Empire] on the north, out of which a cloud of English with their sovereign, embarking together on large vessels called *smacks*, sailed towards Jerusalem. For at that time the monarch of the Germans [Frederick Barbarossa], it is said with 900,000 soldiers, was making his way to Jerusalem; and passing by the land of Iconium [Asia Minor] and coming through the eastern countries, his troops perished from the length of the journey, and from hunger and thirst. And their sovereign, as he was riding, was drowned in some river [in Cilicia, 1190]. But the English king [Richard the Lionheart], the wretch, landed in Cyprus [1191], and found it a nursing mother: had it not been so, he too perchance would have suffered the fate of the German. But how Cyprus was taken, this too I will briefly relate.

When it became necessary that the most pious sovereign Manuel Comnenus [I, 1143–1180], of happy memory, should send a garrison to the royal stronghold in Armenia, he sent one of his kin, quite a youth, Isaac by name, who after guarding the fortresses for some years engaged in war with the Armenians. He was taken captive by them and sold to the Latins. They held him for many years bound with chains, for his uncle, the Emperor Manuel, was dead, leaving his realm to his son Alexius [II Komnenos, 1180–1183], also a child. Whereupon his uncle Andronicus [I Komnenos], who reigned with him, killed the boy and seized the kingdom [1183–1185]. But at the entreaty of the assembly he sent a very large ransom, and bought the said Isaac out of the hands of the Latins. Isaac came to Cyprus, took it, and was proclaimed king. He ruled over it for seven years [1184–1191], and not only utterly despoiled the land, and perpetually harassed the lives of its rich men, but every day he hounded and oppressed its nobles, so that all lived in distress, and sought how by any means they might protect themselves against him.

While things were so, lo, the Englishman lands in Cyprus, and forthwith all ran unto him! Then the king, abandoned by his people, gave himself also unto the hands of the English. Him the English king bound in irons, and having seized his vast treasures, and grievously wasted the land, sailed away to Jerusalem, leaving behind him ships to strip the country and to follow him. But king Isaac of Cyprus he shut up in chains in a castle called Marcappus [Markab on the coast of Syria]. The wicked wretch achieved nought against his fellow wretch Saladin [sultan, 1175–1193], but achieved this only, that he sold our country to the Latins for two hundred thousand pounds of gold. Whereon great was the wailing, and unbearable the smoke, as was said before, which came from the north. He that would tell of them at length, the time shall fail him.

The state of our country now is no better than that of the raging sea under a great storm and tempest. Nay it is worse than a wild sea. For a calm succeeds the wildness of the sea, but here day by day the tempest increases, and its fury knows no end. Unless indeed it hear "Hitherto shalt thou come, but no further: and here shall thy proud waves be stayed" [Job 38:11]. In the book of Leviticus [26] are clearly written the evils which have come upon us, to wit, wars and defeats; our seed is without fruit, the labour of our hands the enemy hath devoured it, and our strength is become a thing of nought, and we few in number, and an alien people hath waxed many in our land. Ye have walked contrary unto Me, saith God, and I will walk contrary unto you also in fury [Leviticus 26: 27–28]. Even so it is. For unless a man shall fall sick, and halt, neither will the physician apply cutting with bitterness and burning. It is manifest that had we not grievously angered our all-good Physician, and walked contrary unto Him, He would not have been contrary disposed unto us, chastening us for our salvation.   (trans. C. D. Cobham)

4. Ἐγκώμιον εἰς τὸν τίμιον καὶ ζωοποιὸν σταυρόν (Encomium of the Venerable and Life-giving Cross), fol. 37r–v

For seven years [1184–1191] this land was held rebelliously and governed by Isaac Komnenos and suffered to no end. Then, when he had been removed, the land was sold by the persecutor, Englinos [Richard the Lionheart], to the Franks for 200,000 measures of gold. And they have held it in slavery and plundered it for another five years, and no one yet knows the end of it. It is now the year 6704 [annus mundi], indiction 14 [A.D. 1196], the month of August, when this account was written, with God's help. I could say much about these things but do not want to. I have spoken these things out of regard for the mercy of God, because he did not just die for us, but was counted among the transgressors [Isaiah 53:12; Mark 15:28; Luke 22:37].

5. *Oratio de Terrae Motibus* 10 (ed. Delehaye)

Having collected from many sources this brief account of earlier dreadful earthquakes, I feel compelled in the present work also to collect and report briefly the events which I have seen with my own eyes or simply heard. For early on in my confinement in the Enkleistra, in the fourth hour of the night, such a strong earthquake suddenly shook the earth [ca. 1159] that I almost fell flat on my face, from my bed to the ground. Such a quake occurred up to seven times during the night, and fourteen churches in the whole district of Paphos collapsed, including the great church of the Immaculate Theotokos, in the fortress of Paphos, which the people call the Limeniotissa. Then most people supposed that I had been killed by the precarious nature of the cliff and the cave of the Enkleistra. For all things were then confused and insecure. Thus some people came to me early in the morning. When they saw that the stones which I had placed to form a vault around the entrance of the cave had not fallen they glorified God and asked to learn the reason for the earthquake.

6. *Typike Diatheke* (*Ritual Ordinance,* A.D. 1214) ch. 1 (ed. Tsiknopoullos, p. 73)

Since he who directs life has extended my life span and fifty-five years have passed, the need for a new ordinance has arisen.

7. *Typike Diatheke* (*Ritual Ordinance,* A.D. 1214) ch. 3 (ed. Tsiknopoullos, pp. 74–75)

No one knew these thoughts of mine except God, who was my guide. When I was eighteen years old my parents were anxious to arrange a marriage for me. For seven months they were seeing to the things which usually go along with weddings and to the earnest-money. But while they were busily thinking about the wedding, I was busily thinking about a means of escape. Then, with God's consent and good help, I secretly left my father's house and made my escape to the monastery of [St. John] Chrysostom at Mount Koutzovendis, a place which those wishing to seek me out were least likely to reach.

8. *Typike Diatheke* (*Ritual Ordinance,* A.D. 1214) ch. 4 (ed. Tsiknopoullos, p. 76)

I arrived at the fortress of Paphos . . . I was taken to the guards of the station, seized like a fugitive, and cast into prison for one night and one day.

9. *Typike Diatheke* (*Ritual Ordinance,* A.D. 1214) ch. 5 (ed. Tsiknopoullos, p. 77)

In the year 6667 [anno mundi; A.D. 1159], the seventh indiction, on June 24, the feast day of the birth of the blessed *Prodromos* [John the Baptist], I came to the cave just mentioned; I was then twenty-five years old. I searched out the quiet of the place until the month of September. Having found the place lonely and deserted, I began to dig the cave and to widen it and to take down its weak spots. This I did for a whole year until the following September, the feast of the Exaltation of the Holy Cross [September 14].

10. *Typike Diatheke* (*Ritual Ordinance,* A.D. 1214) ch. 7 (ed. Tsiknopoullos, p. 78)

As a guardian, with the help of God, take care, I beg you, of this holy Enkleistra of mine. And if greed and injustice on some strong man's part should befall it and trouble the brethren, quickly, with the help of God, establish justice, like someone empowered by God, and your reward, from God, will be the salvation of your soul. Then you will be remembered for ever by this holy Enkleistra of mine as a benefactor, guardian, and brother.
[This is addressed to the Frankish king of Cyprus, Hugh I, 1205–1218.]

11. *Typike Diatheke* (*Ritual Ordinance,* A.D. 1214) ch. 10 (ed. Tsiknopoullos, p. 80)

Behold, fifty-five years have passed since this Enkleistra was established [1159+55 = 1214].

12. *Typike Diatheke* (*Ritual Ordinance,* A.D. 1214) canon 7 (ed. Tsiknopoullos, pp. 95–96)

When our country was subjected to awful slavery by the Latin race God's care kept us free. Therefore we too, brethren, must keep ourselves free from sin.

124. CHONIATES, NIKETAS (1155/57–1217)

History or *Annals*

1. *The Reign of Manuel Komnenos,* pp. 137–38 ed. van Dieten [ΣΒΠΚΙ 77.1]

This emperor [Manuel I Komnenos, 1143–1180] was very concerned about the cities and fortresses of Cilicia, over which the shining and renowned Tarsus presides as metropolis. Consequently, after many illustrious governors of noble blood had been assigned there, the lot finally fell to Andronikos Komnenos, who was both of the highest nobility and the handsomest of men [1166]. There he collected the tribute from Cyprus, which provided his operating expenses. He conceived a hatred for Thoros [II, king of Lesser Armenia], who, in turn, thoroughly despised him, and declared war on Thoros, often opposing him in battle. (trans. H. J. Magoulias)

2. *The Reign of Manuel Komnenos,* pp. 160–61 ed. van Dieten [ΣΒΠΚΙ 77.2]

Manuel [I Komnenos, 1143–1180] . . . appointed the grand duke Andronikos Kontostephanos commander of the fleet . . . Not long afterwards, Kontostephanos set sail (it was the eighth day of the month of July [1169]) . . . Kontostephanos gave orders for the ships to make their way to Cyprus . . . He came ashore on Cyprus, made his arrival known to the king [Amalric

I of Jerusalem, 1162–1174], and inquired as to his intentions, whether he should await the king there or continue on his way to Jerusalem . . . After a long delay, he [Amalric] signaled Andronikos to hasten to Jerusalem to take counsel with him and decide what joint action they should effect.

(trans. H. J. Magoulias)

3. *The Reign of Andronikos Komnenos,* pp. 290–92 ed. van Dieten [ΣΒΠΚΙ 77.3]

This Isaakios [Komnenos] appointed by his granduncle, Emperor Manuel [I Komnenos, 1143–1180], governor of Armenia and Tarsus and general of the troops stationed in these parts, met the Armenians as adversaries in battle and was taken captive. He was incarcerated in a fortress for many years, during which time Emperor Manuel died. Later ransomed by the Hierosolymitai, who are called friars [the Templars], he deemed it fitting to return to his homeland to enlist Andronikos's [Andronikos I Komnenos, 1183–1185] help in repaying the ransom money on the advice of Theodora, with whom, as we have often said, Andronikos had sexual relations; this Isaakios was her nephew. Constantine Makrodoukas, the husband of Isaakios's maternal aunt, and Andronikos Doukas, Isaakios's kinsman and fast friend from childhood, urged Andronikos to receive Isaakios favorably and to pity him his lengthy exile.

But this Isaakios, who imagined his homeland to be as distant as the stars, did not wish to submit to Emperor Andronikos, and he paid no heed to the advice of kinsmen or cherished companions of his youth. Aspiring to power, he passionately desired to become emperor himself, and unable to bow to the yoke of rulers, he ill-advisedly used the monies, provisions, and auxiliary forces sent to him from Byzantion to canvass for the throne. Therefore, with a large force he sailed down to Cyprus, where he first represented himself as the lawful ruler commissioned by the emperor [c. 1183]. Producing for the Cypriots imperial letters which he himself had composed, he read aloud counterfeit imperial decrees ostensibly representing his responsibilities and did those other things which those who are deputed by others to govern are required to do. Not long afterwards, he exposed himself as a tyrant, revealing the cruelty which he nurtured and behaving savagely towards the inhabitants.

Such was the disposition of this Isaakios that he so far exceeded Andronikos in obdurateness and implacability as the latter diametrically surpassed those who were notorious as the most ruthless men who ever lived. Once he felt secure in his rule, he did not cease from perpetrating countless wicked deeds against the inhabitants of the island. He defiled himself by committing unjustifiable murders by the hour and became the maimer of human bodies, inflicting, like some instrument of disaster, penalties and punishments that led to death. The hideous and accursed lecher illicitly defiled marriage beds and despoiled virgins. He irresponsibly robbed once prosperous households of all their belongings, and those indigenous inhabitants who but yesterday and the day before were admired and rivaled Job in riches, he drove to beggary with famine and nakedness, as many, that is, whom the hot-tempered wretch did not cut down with the sword . . .

When Emperor Andronikos heard of these events, in no way whatever could he be restrained, for he saw that which of old had terrified him was now about to befall him . . . He sought some means by which Isaakios might be apprehended and his anticipated destroyer sent from this life; he was afraid lest Isaakios sail from Cyprus and overthrow his tyrannical rule, knowing full well that Isaakios would be warmly received by all, since the evil from afar seems less grievous than that which is at hand, and the greater evil which awaits us appears less oppressive than that which afflicts us in the present. It seems to be a human trait to be content with any brief and incidental relief from suffering.

(trans. H. J. Magoulias)

4. *The Reign of Andronikos Komnenos*, p. 340 ed. van Dieten [ΣΒΠΚΙ 77.4]

Andronikos surmised from what he heard that the letters [of an oracle] designated the Isaurian; he contended that this was Isaakios Komnenos, who ruled as tyrant over Cyprus and whom he suspected of aspiring to his throne, since he had sailed from Isauria to Cyprus.

Isaakios was an evildoer as no other, a ruinous Telchine [malevolent daemon], a flooding sea of calamities, an Erinys [avenging deity] raging furiously against the erstwhile happy and prosperous inhabitants of this island. I express my sympathy in words for those who experienced this common disaster.

(trans. H. J. Magoulias)

5. *The Reign of Andronikos Komnenos*, p. 347 ed. van Dieten

Demetrios Poliorketes [336–283 B.C.] of ancient times [had a most ardent and passionate love for] Lamia, whom Ptolemy [I Soter, ca. 367/66–283/82 B.C.] took captive when campaigning in Cyprus [306 B.C].

(trans. H. J. Magoulias)

6. *The Reign of Isaakios Angelos*, pp. 369–70 ed. van Dieten [ΣΒΠΚΙ 77.5]

As Isaakios Komnenos still ruled as tyrant over Cyprus [1184–1191] and was not disposed to keep his hands off the revenue payments that were promised to the emperor, or to bend his knee to him, or to moderate the horrors which he wickedly inflicted on the Cypriots, ever contriving novel torments, the emperor [Isaac II Angelos, 1185–1195] decided to fit out a fleet against him. Seventy long ships were made ready: the designated commanders were John Kontostephanos, who had arrived at the threshold of old age, and Alexios Komnenos, who, although of good stature, courageous, and a second cousin to the emperor, had had his eyes put out by Andronikos and thus was considered as unfit for battle by all those participating in the campaign. His appointment was deemed by many as an inauspicious omen.

The voyage to Cyprus was without danger, with a favorable wind gently filling the sails, but immediately after entering the harbors, a storm broke out that was more furious than any at sea. Isaakios, ruler over Cyprus, engaged them and put them to flight. The most formidable pirate on the high seas at that time, a man called Megareites, unexpectedly came to the aid of Isaakios and attacked the ships, which he found emptied of men, for they had disembarked to join in the land war. The captains of the triremes performed no brave deed but readily surrendered themselves into the hands of the enemy. Isaakios handed them over to Megareites to do with them as he wished. He took them to Sicily, where he recognized the tyrant of that island [William II, king of Sicily 1169–1189] as his lord. Isaakios, after defeating the Romans, enlisted many in his own forces, and many he subjected to savage punishments, for he was an inexorable tormentor; among these was Basil Rentakenos, whose legs he cut off at the knees with an ax. This man was most skilled in warfare and had served as a teacher to Isaakios as Phoenix of old instructed Achilles to be a speaker of words and a doer of deeds. The most wrathful of men, Isaakios's anger ever bubbled like a boiling kettle; when in a rage, he spoke like a madman with his lower jaw aquiver, and not knowing how to reward his pedagogue with bright gifts, he subjected him to such retribution. He allowed the ship's crews to go wherever they wished, and they came to their homes as though returning after a long time from a distant shipwreck, as many, that is, as did not succumb to one of the three evils of sea, hunger, and death.   (trans. H. J. Magoulias)

7. *The Reign of Isaakios Angelos*, p. 418 ed. van Dieten [ΣΒΠΚΙ 77.6]

The king of the English [Richard the Lionheart] put out to sea, sailed to Cyprus, and seized both the island and her tyrant, taking captive the inhuman and implacable destroyer, Isaakios Komnenos [1191]; at first the king put him in chains and shortly afterward removed the accursed wretch and presented him to one of his English-speaking countrymen. Before he sailed on to Palestine, he left troops behind in Cyprus, which he had already claimed as his own; later he dispatched cargo ships to the island and received the necessities of life from there as tribute. And when he left Palestine, he gave Cyprus [May 1192] to the king of Jerusalem [Guy de Lusignan, 1186–1192; king of Cyprus 1192–1194] as though it were his own province, so that he might relax there during the cessation of hostilities and rule the Cypriots, who were attached by him to the Lord's sepulcher, and the island as joined to the borders of Palestine. And so in this fashion did these events take place.   (trans. H. J. Magoulias)

8. *The Reign of Alexios Angelos*, pp. 463–64 ed. van Dieten [ΣΒΠΚΙ 77.7]

Having become both master and destroyer of the island of Cyprus, he [Isaakios Komnenos] was taken captive by the king of England [1191], who was sailing to Palestine across the sea, and presented to one of his compatriots as a slave who wants whipping. It was bruited about everywhere that the rogue suffered a most miserable death, but, as proved later, his demise was only a false rumor; freed from his fetters and released from prison, though this should not have taken place, he made his way quickly to Kaykhusraw, the ruler of the city of Ikonion [Kay-Khusraw I, Seljuk sultan 1189–1194], and welcomed by the latter as his guest, he rekindled his old passion for the throne. Emperor Alexios [III Angelos, 1195–1203], encouraged by Empress Euphrosyne, who was closely related to Isaakios, dispatched many letters recalling him. He stubbornly refused and was vexed at the letters' contents, for he said that he had learned only how to rule, not how to be ruled; how to lead others, not how to obey others.

He wrote many letters to leading men of Asia, proposing no forbidden action nor any seditious act against the established authorities but promising rewards to all those who obeyed him should he succeed in becoming emperor. But just as the goal that he pursued earlier had remained unattainable and in vain had he formed plots which God did not design, so now he was also guilty of futilely contriving to achieve the impossible. Neither did the Turk pay him heed as he wished (he wanted the Turk to follow him in campaign against the Romans with all his forces and to execute all his commands), nor did any of those to whom he wrote in secret lend an attentive ear, but like asps they all stopped up their ears to his incantations.

Who, having pursued a bloodthirsty beast, does not see it a short time later springing and making a kill? Or who, having made friends with a venomous serpent, even becoming attached to it and nurturing it in his bosom, is not mortally wounded when it bites and disgorges its venom? However, Isaakios Komnenos gave up the ghost shortly thereafter and joined those other tyrants whom the hand of the Lord utterly destroyed.

(trans. H. J. Magoulias)

9. *Events Which Befell the Romans Following the Fall of Constantinople, by the Same Choniates*, pp. 639–40 ed. van Dieten [ΣΒΠΚΙ 77.8]

Then Kaykhusraw, the ruler of Ikonion, advanced with an army against Attaleia [spring 1206], imagining that he would take the city without a blow since she was incapable of saving herself. Aldebrandinus, the city's ruler, and his chief ministers, informed of Kaykhusraw's impending attack, dispatched envoys to Cyprus and received from there an auxiliary force of infantry numbering two hundred Latins. When the battle was at hand and the Turkish forces had surrounded the city, the Latin troops closed ranks, and, taking the Turks by surprise, they came to the defense of the Attaleians. So terrified were the barbarians that many of the troops were slain, and Kaykhusraw retreated, having besieged Attaleia no more than sixteen days.

(trans. H. J. Magoulias)

125. GERMANOS II, patriarch of Constantinople (1223–1240)

1. First letter to the clergy of Cyprus, 1223

The Greek text of this very long letter is found in ΣΒΠΚΙ 79. A useful summary is provided by Hackett 91:

The Cypriots were now expressly forbidden to give the required tokens of fealty and submission. But to the other two demands, since they seemed of trivial importance and, on the showing of the delegates themselves, prompted merely by motives of avarice and greed, the Patriarch and his advisers urged the Orthodox pastors to offer no opposition.

The synodical letter embodying these decisions bore the signature and seal of Theodore Stilbe, the Chartophylax of the Œcumenical See. It concluded with the following exhortation:

"Imitate, O brethren of Cyprus, the Church of Constantinople, and let your clergy imitate ours. Our flocks, too, have long been separated from their pastors and forced to dwell with ravening wolves. Yet they have suffered the wolves to howl and have confounded them by their calmness, while at the same time keeping inviolate the sacred trust of their ancestral faith."

2. Second letter to the clergy of Cyprus, 1229

The Greek text of this long letter is found in ΣΒΠΚΙ 80. A useful summary is provided by Hackett 91–93:

This first letter was, after an interval of six years, followed in 1229 by a second. Germanos begins by commending his Orthodox brethren in Cyprus, both Syrians and Greeks, for the readiness, with which they had received and acted on his former counsels. He nexts declares the Roman Church to have fallen away from the ancient standards, both in its disregard of the rights of others, as laid down by canons and Councils, and in its unauthorized addition to the creeds of Christianity. In its attempts at universal dominion it had not hesitated to try and subvert the other Patriarchates. Its ambition had at last prompted it to place the Pope in the place of Christ, the true Head of the Church. The later Pontiffs had by their actions repudiated their predecessors, who through their representatives had assented to the canons and decrees of the General Councils, and had treated them as they did the Greeks. The Italians had introduced a new faith and new dogmas, and had invented different canons. Let them, therefore, seek a different Christ and different Apostles. The Patriarch asserts that his object, in bringing these matters briefly to the notice of his readers, was that they might recognise how great was the evil in yielding spiritual submission and obedience to the peculiar tenets of the elder Rome. He, therefore, strictly enjoins them to shun the society and ministration of those ecclesiastics who, from whatever motive, have submitted to the Latins and acknowledged the supremacy of the Pope. He assures them that they had better pray privately at home than join in public worship with those, who have ranged themselves on the side of their persecutors. Such offenders, too, were only to be restored to communion after a public confession of their error before the Latin Archbishop and a return in their allegiance to the Patriarch and the Holy Synod. Clerics, moreover, who remain constant to the Orthodox Church, are absolved from canonical obedience to their bishops, who have submitted, and are not to fear any sentence of excommunication pronounced by them. All such sentences are not only invalid, but rather recoil upon their authors, who have created scandal among the people of God by trampling under foot the discipline of the canons, receiving trespassers and busybodies, and giving them their hands, a sign of obedience and servitude. Even though such persons may contend that they have not surrendered their ancestral customs, nor acted contrary to the canons, yet their defence will be of no avail, as the canons subject to excommunication those bishops, who invade the dioceses of others, and anathematise those, who introduce any innovation into Christianity. After an exhortation to the Orthodox to continue steadfast in the faith, the letter concludes by invoking the divine protection upon all ecclesiastics, both Greek and Syrian, and by praying that they may keep their minds free from the new error concerning the faith, and that the laity may remain warm partisans of Orthodoxy.

126. NEOPHYTOS, archbishop of Cyprus (first half, 13th c.)

1. Letter to the Emperor [ΣΒΠΚΙ 81]

I, archbishop of the island of Cyprus, the servant and supporter of your God-crowned, mighty, and holy majesty, make bold to call upon your inspired power, our holy lord, most pious and excellent emperor of the Romans and our natural ruler of all the world [John III Vatatzes, 1222–1254].

As a thirsty deer yearns for the springs of water, so I similarly desire to appeal to you and to cast myself often in adoration at your holy and undefiled feet. And from your majesty's august command I learn of your majesty's God-granted and long-lasting health. But a personal visit is impossible for me, and it is not easy to overcome the matter of distance by sea and by land; and there are various other circumstances, arising from a great mound of sins, which stand in the way, and I am unable to do anything because of the violence and influence of those who are now our masters. Be assured, our holy lord and ruler, of your great fame and renown. The pious name of your holy majesty is heard and voiced-about in all the holy churches of God in Cyprus of the Romans, throughout the whole island. In our divine services and daily observances an everlasting and indelible [monument] is erected [to you], clearly, without opposition, and loudly, as from the beginning and by the divine providence which observes all things. And we constantly pray that your majesty may live for many years in good health, happily, and safely and may erect trophies and memorials in triumph over seen and unseen enemies who oppose your power.

Let your inspired majesty be assured, most pious emperor of the Romans and our ruler, that in Cyprus I, your servant and supporter and with me the oppressed fathers and bishops, wait for nothing unless it be because of the indelible memory of your majesty and of all the Christians of the island. But the blessed lord and ruler the ecumenical patriarch [Germanos II, 1223–1240], for some reason which I do not know, does not allow us to be at rest, but daily he disturbs us and all the people with his letters. But your holy majesty knows that this throne of Barnabas, the first of the disciples and apostles of Christ, is not subject to the ecumenical patriarch but is autocephalous and [its occupant] is appointed by the emperor. And I, your servant and supporter, have received my appointment from the thrice-blessed orthodox ruler and emperor. And I have been found worthy to behold and to revere your holy majesty, which I beseech as my natural ruler to receive me as far as justice permits. For the error of bodily submission [to the papacy], which I admittedly committed, our lord the ecumenical patriarch and his holy synod have given me forgiveness, with the concurrence of the church and the lay people of the island. And in the matter of my brethren the well-known monks who were put to death [by the Latin authorities in 1231] I call the judgement of the *ephoros* to witness that their death happened not through my word, nor through my deed, nor according to my intention, nor by my will. But they themselves willingly suffered death, when they had spoken to those in power harsh words which they were not at all willing to hear, concerning the faith of men, and thus their condemnation occurred. But the blessed lord the ecumenical patriarch receives letters from those whom I have lawfully chastised, [asking him] to publish notices and restrictions against me rashly throughout the land and to disturb the entire island. And if it is your majesty's will that I should leave the island, give an order by an imperial decree, and I shall leave the island without a hearing. But if this is not the will of your holy majesty, then we petition you to accept us as your servant and supporter. For we can no longer endure the provocations.

May the divine providence, which controls all things and is kind to men, keep your inspired majesty in long life and in happiness. The entire holy synod of Cyprus offers its humble respects to your imperial majesty, which God may grant a long life. I, your unworthy servant, boldly have submitted this.

127. JOEL (1204–1261)

1. *Chronographia* (pp. 95–96 ed. Iadevaia) [ΑΚΕΠ I 110.34β; ΣΒΠΚΙ 84]

The body of the Apostle Barnabas was found on the island of Cyprus under a carob tree; on its breast lay the Gospel of Matthew, written by Barnabas himself. And for this reason the

Cypriots do not recognize Antioch as their metropolis. The Gospel just mentioned was deposited by Zeno in the palace [478] and is read annually in the Chapel of St. Stephen on Thursday of Holy Week.

128. BLEMMYDES, NIKEPHOROS (1197–ca. 1269)

1. Γεωγραφία συνοπτική (*Concise Geography*) *GMM* II 462 [ΣΒΠΚΙ 85]

Cyprus, which was once called Kerastes, is situated in the East, in the Gulf of Pamphylia.

129. SKOUTARIOTES, THEODORE (ca. 1230–after 1282)

1. Σύνοψις Χρονική, p. 147 ed. Sathas

The emperor Leo [VI the Wise, 886–912] built [in Constantinople] an exceedingly beautiful church of St. Lazarus, having transferred the remains of St. Lazarus [from Cyprus] and those of Mary Magdalene [from Ephesus]. Shortly after having deposited these remains in that church he passed away.

2. Σύνοψις Χρονική, pp. 261–62 ed. Sathas [ΣΒΠΚΙ 86.1]

I wish to include in my account also those events which happened in Cilicia, lest they be overlooked although they are rather significant. The emperor Manuel [I Komnenos, 1143–1180] was very much concerned over the cities of Cilicia, among which Tarsos as the metropolis occupies the first rank. When many noble men had come there the choice fell upon Andronikos [Komnenos, 1166]. He, when he had arrived there and had collected the tribute of Cyprus for his expenses, frequently fought against Torouses [Thoros II, king of Lesser Armenia] but never accomplished anything noteworthy.

3. Σύνοψις Χρονική, p. 274 ed. Sathas [ΣΒΠΚΙ 86.2]

From there [the Hellespont], having a favorable wind, having loosed his cables, and having spread his sails, he [Andronikos Kontostephanos] sailed to Cyprus. In the course of this voyage he encountered six ships which the emir of Egypt had sent on an intelligence mission; he captured two of them, but the others, having kept their distance, escaped. [1169]

When he had landed in Cyprus he made his arrival known to the king [Amalric I of Jerusalem, 1162–1174] and asked to learn his will, whether he [Andronikos] should await him [Amalric] in Cyprus or go on to Jerusalem. But the king was unable to give his consent because he had made promises to the emperor and had agreed to give his full cooperation; so he decided to stall. Finally he advised the grandduke to come to Jerusalem so that they might meet there and devise a joint course of action.

4. Σύνοψις Χρονική, pp. 341–42 ed. Sathas [ΣΒΠΚΙ 86.3]

That is how those things happened. Then there was a man by name of Isaac, the son of a daughter of the *sebastokrator* Isaac [a brother of the emperor Alexios I Komnenos, 1081–1118] and a kinsman of the emperor Manuel [I Komnenos, 1143–1180]. This Isaac, when his grand-uncle the emperor Manuel had put him in charge of Armenian affairs and appointed him to govern Tarsos and the surrounding cities, made war on the Armenians facing him, was taken prisoner, and was confined under guard. Finally he made his way home from the Jerusalemite Brethren [the Templars], when the emperor Andronikos [I Komnenos, 1183–1185] agreed to pay the ransom at the behest of Theodora Komnene, who was Andronikos' mistress and whose nephew Isaac was. Andronikos was persuaded to receive Isaac by Constantine Makrodoukas, who was the bed-partner of his aunt on his father's side[?], and by Andronikos Doukas, who had been his companion since childhood and was closely related. This Isaac, then, was not willing to take orders from [the emperor] Andronikos but wanted the power of government for himself. So he used the travel funds which had been sent to him from Byzantium to seize power. Then, with a large band of men, he sailed to Cyprus. At first he pretended to the Cypriots that he was governing by a decree of the emperor; he displayed an imperial letter, which he had written himself, and imperial orders which, of course, spelled out what he was to do. But before long he showed himself to be a tyrant and dealt with the inhabitants in an inhuman manner. In his harshness he so far outstripped Andronikos as Andronikos himself outstripped those who had ever been known for their iniquity. He stained himself by the hour with the murder of innocent people, inflicted penaties and fines which resulted in death, sullied himself, wanton as he was, with unlawful unions and the rape of virgins, and robbed well-to-do families of every livelihood.

5. Σύνοψις Χρονική, p. 354 ed. Sathas [ΣΒΠΚΙ 86.4]

He [the emperor Andronikos I Komnenos, 1183–1185] summoned Seth, who from his youth had been trained in such things and who for this reason reportedly had been blinded by the emperor Manuel [I Komnenos, 1143–1180], and inqired who would succeed him [reading παραληψόμενος for παραλειψόμενος] as emperor . . . From what he had heard Andronikos suspected an Isaurian and [thought] that this was Isaac [Komnenos], who was then the tyrant of the island of Cyprus [1184–1191]. And he asked also for the time when [this would occur] and learned that it would be within a few days of the Exaltation of the Cross [September 14], and it was now the beginning of September. But when Andronikos heard the response about the time he said, "the oracle is nonsense; for where will Isaac be able to sail to from Cyprus in just a few days, and [how will he be able to] seize the power from me?"

6. Σύνοψις Χρονική, p. 371 ed. Sathas [ΣΒΠΚΙ 86.5]

When Isaac Komnenos was tyrant of Cyprus [1184–1191] the emperor [Isaac II Angelos, 1185–1195] decided to send a fleet against him. Seventy warships were outfitted and two commanders chosen: John Kontostephanos, a man of advanced age, and Alexios Komnenos, who was younger and a second cousin of the emperor, but had been blinded by Andronikos [I Komnenos, 1183–1185] and seemed to many to be unfit for the task and an inauspicious omen. They encountered no danger during the voyage to Cyprus, but thereafter, after they had landed in Cyprus, they met with disaster. For Isaac engaged them and put them to flight. Then a pirate on the seas, called Megareites, attacked the ships, which he found empty, as the men had debarked to join the land war. Megareites seized the ships without any difficulty; the captains surrendered to their opponents when they encountered the Cypriots. And Isaac gave them to Megareites to do with as he pleased. After a while they were taken to Sicily and its ruler [William II, king of Sicily 1169–1189], whom Megareites recognized as his lord. Isaac defeated the Romans and enlisted many in his own forces, while he inflicted punishments on many others, being an inexorable tormentor. Among the latter was Basil Ryndakenos [or Rentakenos], whose legs he cut off at the knees. This man was excellent at war and had once been Isaac's teacher in military matters. Isaac dismissed the ships' crews and allowed each man to go where he pleased; and these men with difficulty reached their own country, as if from some shipwreck, that is those who were not lost to the sea, hunger, or death.

7. Σύνοψις Χρονική, p. 398 ed. Sathas [ΣΒΠΚΙ 86.6]

The English king [Richard the Lionheart] landed in Cyprus, made himself master of it, and captured Isaac, its ruler [1191]. First he kept him in chains, then he exiled him from the island and presented him like a sacrificial victim to one of his [Richard's] countrymen. And he himself sailed to Palestine; but he left an armed force behind in Cyprus, dealt with the island as if it were his, and collected provisions from it. And as he left Palestine [May 1192] he presented Cyprus to the king of Jerusalem [Guy de Lusignan, 1186–1192; king of Cyprus 1192–1194] so that he might rule the Cypriots as if they had been allotted by him to the Holy Sepulchre and as if the island were included in the boundaries of Palestine.

8. Σύνοψις Χρονική, p. 430 ed. Sathas [ΣΒΠΚΙ 86.7]

Then there appeared another rebel, a certain John, a Cypriot in origin, Spyridonakes by last name [governor of the theme of Smolena], ugly in appearance, and quite old.

The emperor [Alexios III Angelos, 1195–1203] was beset at this time by yet another difficulty, namely the usual trouble with his feet. So he divided his army in two forces. The one he turned over to his son-in-law Alexios Palaiologos to lead against Spyridonakes; the other he sent against John Eonopolites [sic], who was opposing the *protostrator* [Manuel Kammytzes]. He put both of them to flight and made them fugitives. [ca. 1201]

130. GREGORY (*earlier* George) **of Cyprus, patriarch of Constantinople 1283–1289** (1241–after 1289)

1. Autobiography, pp. 177 ed. Lameere [ΣΒΠΚΙ 88]

The island of Cyprus was the native country of the man who compiled this book. His fathers and his fathers' fathers and all his ancestors were men of wealth and position in their country, until the Greeks of the island became subject to the barbarians from Italy. And when they [his fathers] had become subject and shared the common misfortune they were moderately well-off and respected, so that he decribed them as neither poor, common, and without distiction, nor prominent and very rich. He was born, then, on the island and raised by his parents until it was time for him to attend grammar school. [Later] . . . he was sent for further education to Kallinikisiai [Leukosia; modern Nicosia].

2. Letter to the King of Cyprus (1285), pp.193–94 ed. Lameere [ΣΒΠΚΙ 89]

Exalted King,

Exalted King of Jerusalem and renowned Cyprus, beloved son of our modesty [μετριότης, a title of assumed humility], Lord Henry [II, Lusignan, 1285–1324], our modesty wishes you from God the keeping of his commandments, success in every God-pleasing deed, and help in discharging the duties of your office according to his pleasure. The noble knight of your royal office, the Lord John Graterollas, has received here the letter of your royal office and has communicated it to me. From this letter my modesty has learned that you have taken upon yourself the office of your father [Hugh III, Lusignan, 1267–1284], with the help of God. And I have given many thanks to God himself that, just as your father was a good man and had a good reputation with all men, so a good son has become his successor and heir.

What else should I write to you but this: consider the virtue of your father and take him who has begotten you as a role model for your life and for the exercise of your office. Then, just as he was in every way admired by others, so you, too, will be admired. Above all conduct yourself towards the Romans under your government as he did, and also the kings before you. For all of them [the kings] loved them [the Romans], cared for them, and did not allow any injustice or tyranny to be inflicted upon them. Observe these principles, and you will have us for all the days of our life as your true friends, and we shall pray for you at all times. And may God, who oversees all, grant to your royal office a praiseworthy life.

Gregory, by God's grace Archbishop of Constantinople, the New Rome, and Ecumenical Patriarch.

131. GOUDELES, THEODOSIOS (13th c.)

1. Encomium of St. Christodoulos 12–13 (pp. 148–51 ed. Branouses) [ΣΒΠΚΙ 87]

As has been mentioned before, [Megareites] the chief pirate of the tyrant of Sicily [William II, 1169–1189], together with the man who was called by him the duke of the tyrant's fleet, was sent to collect tribute. (This chief pirate's home town happened to be Megara, a city in Attica, and for this reason he was called Megareites by family name, but all the common people, those who had no accurate knowledge of Greek, erroneously called him Margarites, not Megareites.) When he had crossed the Ionian Sea he decided to sail to the island of Cyprus. Upon landing there he found the situation there thoroughly confused and Byzantine affairs generally returning to their earlier state beyond his hope.

For the Byzantine government was in the hands of Isaac [II, 1185–1195] of the family surnamed Angeloi; this man claimed a family relationship, being a second cousin, through a daughter [Theodora, a daughter of Alexios I Komnenos, married to Constantine Angelos], to Alexios [II] Komnenos, who had ruled the empire at one time [1180–1183] and whom we have previously mentioned [see genealogical table with **123**.3]. This Isaac overthrew the ruling family which had governed the Romans before him and which was related to him, and instead of tyrant he was called the lawful emperor of the Romans first by all the residents of Byzantium and then even by the Byzantine army and the whole Byzantine government and all the cities subject to its control. Now it is this Isaac who decided to send a fleet to the *Kittieis* (which is another term for the Cypriots). The objective was to depose his namesake, the tyrant Isaac [Komnenos, 1184–1191], from power, with or against his will.

This Isaac [the tyrant of Cyprus] was on his father's side from the family of the Doukai [Κομνηνῶν is an erroneous emendation; it was his mother's surname, which he chose to adopt]; and Isaac, at one time the *sebastokrator*, had honored him because he cared for his daughter [Isaac's mother]. (This Isaac [the *sebastokrator*] was the son of John [II Komnenos, 1118–1143], who was born in the purple and a most excellent emperor, and the brother of the renowned Manuel [I Komnenos, 1143–1180], who in his own time reigned for 37 years and six months minus only a few days.) But this was not to be the end of the troubles which we heaped up on ourselves . . .

What then were the things which happened there? In the beginning the forces of our country [of the emperor] had the upper hand, and the rebel [Isaac], the enemy of our country and of Byzantine rule, fled, sought refuge in one of the Cypriot castles, entrusted his safety to those in the castle, and obviously was already thinking that the end was near. But then good fortune, I do not know whence, came to him, and bad fortune to us; for the commanders of the Sicilian fleet appeared from somewhere with the entire army which had crossed with them and joined with Isaac [the rebel]. They filled our men with terror, at once turned them to flight, and fell upon then from the back. Then our forces [the emperor's forces] were decisively defeated; many died and even more were captured. With them also the sailors, who had become involved, were by force led away. The emperor Isaac's commanders were these: [Alexios Komnenos] a cousin on his father's side, who was commonly called his nephew and whom the tyrant Andronikos [I Komnenos, 1183–1185] had blinded; and a man by the surname of Kontostephanos and the first name of John, a man of good family and of advanced age and related by marriage, through his wife's true sister [?] to the emperor Alexios [?] and the first son of John [II Komnenos, 1118–1143], who was born in the purple and was emperor of the Romans, as previously mentioned. Isaac, the man who had subjected Cyprus to his control, captured these men and sent them through Megareites to the Sicilian [William II, 1169–1189] as his share of the booty, and with them some other men, both distinguished and undistinguished. He [Megareites] took them, placed them on the tyrant's ships, together with considerable loot, and departed from the island.

132. IVERON MONASTERY (Mt. Athos) (13th c.)

1. MS. 4501 (381), folio 101r (quoted by Lampros, *Catalogue* II, p.104. par. 14) [ΣΒΠΚΙ 82]

At the time when our holy patriarch Germanos [II, 1223–1240] resided at Nicaea, Neophytos, the archbishop of Cyprus, our lord, and all his priests submitted to the pope [Gregory IX, 1227–1241].

133. CHRONICA BYZANTINA BREVIORA (13th c.)

1. 25 (vol. I, p. 199 ed. Schreiner) [ΣΒΠΚΙ 83]

1191: In the month of May, in the year 6698, in the eighth indiction, the Latins came to Cyprus.

1204: On April 1, in the year 6711, in the sixth indiction, the Latins surrounded Constantinople.

1231: On May 19, on a Wednesday, in the year 6739, the monks Ioanikos and Konon and those with him were put to death by fire.

1238: On July 22, in the year 6746, our submission [to Pope Gregory IX] took place.

1222: On May 11, on a Wednesday, in the sixth hour, in the year 6730, God's wrath sent a great earthquake upon us.

134. GALENOS, JOHN, DEACON (13th c.(?))

1. *Allegories to Hesiod's Theogony* 188–90 [ΑΚΕΠ II 1.1]

It is rightly said that the genitals of Ouranos were cast or fell on Cyprus and that for that reason the place is very fruitful and conducive to sexual activity. Here, too, Aphrodite emerged from the sea and came ashore, and at her feet all manner of plants sprang forth. The land of Cyprus is endowed with a certain charm, desirable and pleasing to the soul. So say all who have seen the place and have learned why its women are very lascivious and ready to engage in intercourse. When men are nourished by wheat they produce foam, that is seed-giving power, that is semen; and by this the woman, that is the power of love, is nourished. He [Hesiod] says that she [Aphrodite] first brought this power to Kythera and then to Cyprus.

135. XANTHOPOULOS, NIKEPHOROS KALLISTOS (before 1256?–ca. 1335?)

1. *Historia Ecclesiastica* 8.15

Unable to bear his [a philosopher's] vain words a simple old man (it is said that it was the famous and great Spyridon) engaged him in a contest of words . . . When he had been given permission he said, "In the name of Jesus Christ, philosopher, listen. There is one God, the creator of heaven and earth and all things both visible and invisible . . . Do you believe these things?

Answer me," he said. Upon these words the philosopher was speechless, and then he said that he believed. [at the Council of Nicaea, 325]

2. *Historia Ecclesiastica* 8.42 [ΑΚΕΠ I 121.3; 121.6γ; ΣΒΠΚΙ 90.1]

Quite a few [of the Fathers attending the Council of Nicaea] still bore on their bodies the marks of having confessed Christ. Among the bishops there were Paphnoutios of the Upper Thebaid and Spyridon of Tremithous in Cyprus . . .

So great was the grace of the Holy Spirit which fell upon St. Spyridon that his reputation matched his virtue. He was a farmer, married, and the father of children, but on this account no less concerned than anyone with the things of God. So great was his holiness that he became a bishop, and his see was Tremithous, which was one of the cities on the island of Cyprus. He was so humble that he herded (his own) sheep and at the same time was an excellent shepherd of men.

3. *Historia Ecclesiastica* 8.42 [ΑΚΕΠ I 125.3]

Once, when a council was taking place, one of those in attendance was the renowned Triphyllios, bishop of Ledra [Leukosia], who was an accomplished orator and spent most of his time in Berytus (Beirut) to practice law. When, with the permission of the bishops and in the presence of Spyridon, he was teaching the people, he was asked to recite the saying which Christ spoke to the paralytic, "Take up your bed (κράββατος) and walk" [Matthew 9:6]. But he used the word σκίμπους instead of κράββατος. Thereupon Spyridon took offense and said, "Are you better than he who said κράββατος, and are you ashamed to use his words?"

4. *Historia Ecclesiastica* 9.15 [ΣΒΠΚΙ 90.2]

Here [in Palestine] Hilarion was first active . . . He came so close to God through his virtue that even now he heals many of those who suffer incurable illnesses and drives out demons, earning for himself the gratitude of those who approach his tomb, not only of the Cypriots, among whom he was first buried, but also of the Palestinians, among whom he later dwelled. The reason for this is this: since he had lived and died in Cyprus, he was given burial there and was held in high regard by its people. Then Hesychas, who had become the foremost of his disciples, cleverly stole the saint's body and took it to his monastery in Palestine.

5. *Historia Ecclesiastica* 11.39 [ΣΒΠΚΙ 90.3]

Epiphanios, who much later took the government of the church of Salamis of Cyprus, was outstanding by his virtue . . . then also among the Cypriots, whose bishop he became . . . But before [reading πρὶν ἤ for Πρινή] he came to Cyprus, at this time he lived in Palestine.

6. *Historia Ecclesiastica* 12.30 [ΣΒΠΚΙ 90.4]

If anyone has a desire to learn about such heresies, whence and how they arose and among whom they took hold, we advise him to become familiar with the *Panarion*. This book was published by Epiphanios, who presided over the church of Cyprus.

7. *Historia Ecclesiastica* 12.34 [ΣΒΠΚΙ 90.5]

Thus in Cyprus and in Caesarea of Cappadocia on Saturday and on Sunday, in the evening after the lighting of the lamps, the bishops and the elders interpret the holy scriptures to the people . . . Among other peoples, we know, a bishop functions in his office not only in the city but in each village. This custom used to prevail especially among the Arabs, the Cypriots, the Novatians in Phrygia, and those who followed Montanus.

8. *Historia Ecclesiastica* 12.46 [ΣΒΠΚΙ 90.6]

Also at this time Epiphanios, who was the bishop of Cyprus, was active . . . I have learned that Epiphanios died on board his ship. His companions put his body in honey, lest by chance something unseemly might happen to it, and brought it safely to Cyprus. [403]

9. *Historia Ecclesiastica* 13.4 [ΣΒΠΚΙ 90.7]

Out of sympathy for his wife [Eudoxia] and children Arkadios [395–408] was kindled to anger . . . And then he stripped him [the eunuch Eutropios] of all his honor, confiscated all his property, and made him an exile in Cyprus. A short time later it was charged that, at the time when he had attained the highest honor [the consulship], he had used decorations beyond his rank, decorations which only the emperor is allowed to wear. Then he was brought back from Cyprus . . . and put to death by decapitation. [399]

10. *Historia Ecclesiastica* 13.12 [ΣΒΠΚΙ 90.8]

He [Theophilos of Alexandria] thought that it would greatly benefit his purposes if he could enlist Epiphanios, bishop of Salamis in Cyprus, as a supporter of his cause; for Epiphanios was highly thought of by those over whom he presided, noted for his way of life, and renowned for his uprightness. So Theophilos at once sent a message to Epiphanios and made him a friend, although he had at first been at odds with him on the grounds that he worshipped the divine in human form . . . Epiphanios had harbored for a long time a dislike for the writings of Origen; besides he was a simple man and lived an exceedingly pious life. Thus he was easily persuaded by Theophilos' offer. So he at once assembled the bishops of Cyprus and forbade them to read the writings of Origen. The decisions of the synod he dispatched to others, including the bishop of Constantinople.

11. *Historia Ecclesiastica* 16.37 [ΑΚΕΠ I 110.34γ; ΣΒΠΚΙ 90.9]

During his reign [the reign of Anastasios I, 491–518] the body of the Apostle Barnabas was found on Cyprus, lying under the kind of tree which is called a carob tree. On his chest lay the divine and holy Gospel of Matthew the Evangelist, written by Barnabas' own hand. On these grounds, too, the Cypriots claim to have their own autocephalous metropolis and not to belong to Antioch to which they were once subject. Later Justinian [I, 527–565] reinforced this ruling in order to enhance the standing of his wife Theodora, who was a native of Cyprus. He did the same for his own native city, Achrido, which he called the First Justiniana.
[Note: other sources report that the relics of St. Barnabas were found during the reign of Zeno, 474–491.]

12. *Historia Ecclesiastica* 17.28

Justinian [I, 527–565] granted an extraordinary honor to his native city of Achrido, raising it to the rank of an archbishopric, declaring its church autocephalous, and calling it the First Justiniana. Likewise he made the church of the island of Cyprus the Second Justiniana and an archbishopric, granting it the same favors as Achrido; this he did in honor of his wife, the empress Theodora, who hailed from there.
[Note: Justinian's place of birth was Tauresium, a village in Thrace.]

13. *Enarratio de episcopis Byzantii et de patriarchis omnibus Constantinopolitanis*, Migne, *PG* 147, cols. 461D–464A

The monk Nicholas Mouzalon became archbishop of Cyprus, but, as many said, resigned the holy office itself, while others said that he only gave up the administration of affairs [ca. 1110]. Later, when he had not functioned in his office for thirty-seven years, under the emperor Manuel [I Komnenos, 1143–1180], he served as bishop of Constantinople for three years and four months [1147–1151]. On the grounds that he had resigned in a questionable way he was forced out of office by those who broke away from him; many of these were bishops, and some of these he had himself ordained.

136. AKOLOUTHIA OF ST. PHILO (of uncertain date)

1. *Akolouthia* 45 (p. 3)

On the twenty-fourth of January we observe the commemoration of our holy father Philo, bishop of Karpasia and miracle worker [4th/5th c.].

2. *Akolouthia* 49 (p. 4) [ΑΚΕΠ I 136.2]

Like a bright star, blessed Bishop Philo, you have risen from the shiny city of the Karpasians. You have enlightened their minds, inspired by God and by the power of the Holy Spirit, and established yourself as their most worthy shepherd. Also you have overthrown the altars of the idols; you have saved a most impious emperor from error; you miraculously took away the illness of the empress and prepared her to receive holy baptism; you filled all with your light; you built holy churches; and you proved yourself a holy herald of the consubstantial Trinity.

[Note: It is not clear which emperor and which empress are meant.]

3. *Akolouthia* 34 (p. 17) [ΑΚΕΠ I 136.3]

Hail, child of pious Cypriots; hail, you who have saved many from error; hail, bright light and teacher of the Cypriots; hail, blessed shepherd of the Karpasians.

137. MENAION (A collection of liturgical texts, one book for each month) (of uncertain date)

1. February 9 (p. 102 ed. 1970) [ΑΚΕΠ I 112; II 130]

On the same day the commemoration of the holy martyrs Marcellus, bishop of Sicily, Philagrios, bishop of Cyprus, and Pankratios [Pancras], bishop of Tauromenion [Taormina, in Sicily] . . .
These were disciples of St. Peter the Apostle . . . Likewise Philagrios, archbishop of Cyprus, taught in the name of Christ, endured many trials for the true faith, and passed on to the Lord.

2. February 17 (p. 175 ed. 1970)

On the same day commemoration of our holy father Auxibios.

3. February 19 (p. 190 ed. 1970) [ΑΚΕΠ I 120.1]

On the same day the commemoration of the holy martyrs Maximus, Theodotos, Hesychios, and Asklepiodote . . .
These, in the presence of the governor, refused to deny Christ. Therefore they were subjected to the torment of many trials: first they were hung up on a wooden rack and scraped with iron claws; then they were carried and dragged from city to city and exposed to wild beasts . . . Then they were, all together, stoned, dragged to a wooded place, and killed by the sword.

4. May 12 (pp. 115–16 ed. 1970)

On the same day the commemoration of our holy father Epiphanios, archbishop of Constantia in Cyprus. This man, the great and miracle-working Epiphanios, came from the land of Phoenicia, from the neighborhood of Eleutheropolis; his father was a farmer and his mother practiced weaving . . . When he had become the archbishop he endured many trials at the hands of the heretics, but he strengthened the truth by his words and drove the heretics from the church.

When he visited Constantinople he was pressured by [the empress] Eudoxia to subscribe to the exile of [St. John] Chrysostom, but he refused. But when she threatened to open the idolatrous temples if he would not comply he yielded and subscribed. When [St. John] Chrysostom heard about this he wrote to him, "Brother Epiphanios, I have heard that you have consented to my exile. Let me tell you that you will not sit on your throne." And Epiphanios replied, "Athlete John, be beaten and win." And this is what happened. As Epiphanios was returning from Constantinople to Cyprus he died on board his ship, just as the great John had written to him . . . He had lived 115 years minus three months when he passed on to the Lord. His liturgy is performed in his holy house [chapel?] which is in the [church of] St. Philemon.

5. June 11 (pp. 74–75 ed. 1970)

On the eleventh day of the same month, commemoration of the holy apostles Bartholomew and Barnabas . . . Of these two Bartholomew was one of the Twelve . . . But Barnabas, who is also called Joseph in the Acts of the Apostles [4:36] and was one of the Seventy, was ordained as a companion of Paul. His name means "Son of Consolation." He was of the tribe of Levi and had been born and raised in Cyprus. He was the first to preach the gospel of Christ in Jerusalem, Rome, and Alexandria, but when he came to Cyprus he was stoned and burned by the Jews and the Greeks. Mark, the apostle and evangelist, obtained the body and placed it in a cave; then he sailed to Ephesus and reported the death of Barnabas to Paul. And Mark wept for Barnabas for a long time. It is reported that he was buried together with the Gospel of Matthew, which he had copied and which was later found together with the apostle's body. From this circumstance the faithful [of Cyprus] derive the privilege whereby their island shall not be subject to any other bishop but shall be administered by its own bishop.

6. June 16 (pp. 105 and 108 ed. 1970) [ΑΚΕΠ I 133.1]

Commemoration of our holy father Tychon, bishop of Amathous in Cyprus . . .

He had pious and Christ-loving parents, who dedicated him to [the service of] God. When he had learned the holy scriptures and had become well-versed in them he was first appointed to read the sayings and teachings [of Christ] to the people. Then, because he was worthy in all regards and because of his pure and blameless life, he was ordained a deacon by Mnemonios, the bishop of Amathous. Upon the latter's death he himself was seated on the bishop's throne by the great Epiphanios. When he had turned many from the error and vanity of idolatry to faith in Christ our Lord, had torn down many idolatrous temples, had raised holy churches, had adorned them with holy offerings, and had sanctified them, he passed on to the Lord. He has wrought many miracles, both in this life and after his death.

7. June 23 (p. 147 ed. 1970)

On the same day the martyrdom of the holy martyrs Aristokles the presbyter, Demetrianos the deacon, and Athanasios the reader.

8. June 30 (p. 218 ed. 1970)

Barnabas, who is also called Joses in the Acts of the Apostles [Acts 4:36], is one of the seventy disciples. He copied the Gospel of Matthew by his own hand and died on the island of Cyprus.

9. September 17 (p. 212 ed. 1970)

On the same day the commemoration of the holy martyrs Maximus, Theodotos, and Asklepiodote.

10. September 17 (p. 214 ed. 1970)

On the same day the commemoration of the holy martyrs Herakleides and Myron, bishops of Tamassos in Cyprus.

11. October 17 (p. 173 ed. 1970) [ΑΚΕΠ I 113.5β]

On the same day the commemoration of the *elevatio* of the sacred relics of the saintly and righteous Lazarus . . .
The blessed, famous, and most faithful emperor Leo [VI the Wise, 886–912], in holy zeal and as if by inspiration, was the first to build a most beautiful church to the saint. Then he sent [agents] to the island of Cyprus and found the holy relics in the city of Kition, in the ground, after nearly a thousand years had passed, in a marble chest. On this chest an inscription, in a foreign language, was inscribed: "Lazarus, who was raised after four days and was Christ's friend." Right away he [Leo] took the venerable treasure, placed it in a silver casket, and brought it to Constantinople [890].

12. December 8 (pp. 109–10 ed. 1970)

On the same day the commemoration of the Holy Apostles, of the Seventy . . . Epaphroditos, whom the same Apostle [Paul] mentions [Philippians 2:25–30 and 4:18], was bishop of Adrake [?] . . . All these served well, were shepherds in holiness, and governed the churches assigned to them and the people. When they had endured many trials and tests for the sake of Christ they were put to death by the idolaters; they committed their souls to the Lord, for whose sake they willingly suffered death.

13. December 8 (p. 110 ed. 1970)

On the same day the commemoration of our holy father Sophronios, bishop of Cyprus. He was a native of the great island of Cyprus, the son of pious Christian parents. He was by natural disposition given to learning, read the Holy Scripture with care, and studied the sayings of the Lord by night and by day. He became so virtuous and pious that he was found worthy of great charismatic gifts and performed many miracles. Thus, upon the death of Damianos, the holy bishop of Cyprus, he was made archbishop of the holy church of Cyprus by all the people and the bishops. And when he had received the church, he became a champion of the poor, helped the orphans, protected the widows, brought relief to those who were heavily laden, and clothed the naked. When he had lived his life in this manner and had pleased God in every way he died peacefully.

14. December 12 (p. 170 ed. 1970)

In memory of our holy father and miracle-worker Spyridon, bishop of Tremithous in Cyprus. He lived at the time of the emperor Constantine the Great; he was simple in manner and lowly of heart. He was a shepherd. He took a wife and begot a daughter. When his wife died he became a bishop; he also became a miracle-worker. At a time of drought he caused it to rain, and he turned famine into prosperity . . . And he attended the Council of Nicaea [325] and put the heretics to shame . . . And when he had done many other things he died peacefully. His liturgy is performed in the venerable chapel of St. Peter, the chief of the apostles, which is located next to the great and holy church [in Constantinople].

138. Ὀνομασία Μηνῶν (*The Names of the Months*) (of uncertain date)

1. Ed. Cramer, *Anecd. Gr. Oxon.* III, pp. 402–403 [ΑΚΕΠ II 166]

The names of the month . . . beginning with March . . . On Cyprus: Aphrodisios, Kaisarios, Plethytatos, Apogonikos, Sebastos, Archiereus, Ainikos, Autokratorikos, Esthios, Iounios, Demarchexasios, Romaios.

139. Περὶ Σιβύλλης (*On the Sibyl*) (of uncertain date)

1. Ed. Cramer, *Anecd. Gr. Paris.* I, p. 334 [ΑΚΕΠ I 115.1α]

Alas, unfortunate Cyprus, a huge wave will cover you, and the roused sea in stormy days.

140. SCHOLIA to Aelius Aristides (of uncertain date)

1. *Panathenaicus* 163.9 ed. W. Dindorf (I 268 and III 246–47); 178 ed. J. H. Oliver: ὃς μόνος ἤρκεσε τὴν Λακεδαιμονίων ὕστερον δυναστείαν καταλῦσαι [ΑΚΕΠ I 66.21α]

When Conon came to Athens he perceived that the Athenians were angry at him because of his earlier defeat [at Aegospotami, 405 B.C.]; so he fled to Evagoras, king of Cyprus . . . When Evagoras became an ally of the king [Artaxerxes II of Persia] Conon joined him. He met the Spartans in battle, defeated them decisively at Knidos [394 B.C.], returned to Athens, and rebuilt its walls [393 B.C.]. For the Spartans had taken down the walls at an earlier time when they were in power and had imposed the thirty tyrants on the people of Athens [404 B.C.]. (AC)

Conon was one of the ten generals. When he perceived the anger of the Athenians he came to Evagoras, king of Cyprus, and spent some time with him. At a later time the Spartans, having defeated the Athenians, waged war in Asia. Then Evagoras became an ally of the king [of Persia], and Conon joined him. When he had defeated the Spartans [at Knidos, 394 B.C.] he came to Athens and rebuilt the walls of Athens. He broke the power of the Spartans at Knidos. Isocrates tells the story in his *Evagoras*. (BD)

141. SCHOLIA to Aeschylus (of uncertain date)

1. *Persians* 894: Σαλαμῖνά τε τᾶς νῦν ματρόπολις τῶνδ᾽ αἰτία στεναγμῶν [AKEΠ I 20.5]

He means Salamis in Cyprus, the mother city of which is, of course, the island of Salamis in Attica, the cause of these laments. For the people of Salamis in Cyprus came from Salamis in Attica. This is the story: Ajax died by his own hand at Troy, and his brother Teucer returned to his native Salamis, but was rejected by his father Telamon and driven from Salamis, on the grounds that he had not prevented his brother from killing himself. Thus he came to Cyprus and founded a city, which he called Salamis after the one in Attica. (A)

142. SCHOLIA to Aristophanes (of uncertain date)

1. *Plutus* 1075: πάλαι ποτ᾽ ἦσαν ἄλκιμοι Μιλήσιοι [AKEΠ I 66.26α]

Some say that this was spoken to the Cypriots who wanted to have allies.

143. SCHOLIA to Demosthenes (of uncertain date)

1. *Against Leptines* (20) 68.157: πρῶτον μὲν τοίνυν Κόνωνα σκοπεῖτε

[After the Battle of Arginusae, 406 B.C.] the people [of Athens] condemned some of the ten generals to exile, others to death. But they, knowing what evil would come upon them, had fled before the judgement. One of them was Conon, who came to Evagoras, the ruler of Cyprus [after the Battle of Aegospotami, 405 B.C.]. And Evagoras endeared Conon to the king of Persia [Artaxerxes II].

2. *Against Stephanus* A (45) 64: Σόλων [AKEΠ I 39.6]

Solon, son of Exekestides, was an Athenian, a philosopher, a lawgiver, and a statesman. He lived at the time of the 47th Olympiad [592–589 B.C.]. When Pisistratus plotted against him he emigrated to Cilicia and founded a city, which he called Soloi after himself. Others say that Soloi in Cyprus is also named after Solon and that he died in Cyprus.

144. SCHOLIA to Dionysios Periegetes (of uncertain date)

1. 509: Ἄστυ Διωναίης Ἀφροδίτης [ΑΚΕΠ I 1; 11.1; 14.11; II 149.4β]

An Egyptian named Hyon settled it and named it Kerastis ("the horned"); he had a son named Keptes, who died childless. Kephalos, the son of Pandion and Herse, dwelt in Asia and had two sons, Aoos and Paphos. The latter crossed over [to Cyprus] and founded the city of Paphos. His son Kinyras landed on the island, as did Pygmalion, a Phoenician, whose daughter Thymarete Kinyras married, producing Oxyporos and Adonis . . . Cyprus lies to the east of Rhodes . . .

145. SCHOLIA to Euripides (of uncertain date)

1. *Andromache* 889: ἡ Σπαρτιᾶτις Ἑρμιόνη [ΑΚΕΠ I 17.1; *FGrH* IIIB 382, fr.12]

Helen, the daughter of Tyndareus, gave birth only to her [Hermione] in the house of her [Hermione's] father Menelaos. Lysimachos [of Alexandria, ca. 200 B.C.] and some others report that Helen was also the mother of Nikostratos. But the compiler of the history of Cyprus calls him Pleisthenes, with whom also Aganos, whom she conceived from Alexander [Paris], arrived in Cyprus.

146. SCHOLIA to Hesiod (of uncertain date)

1. *Theogony* 192: πρῶτον δὲ Κυθήροισι [ΑΚΕΠ II 155.6, no. 18]

Kythera is a city of Cyprus. It is named Kythera from hiding and concealing what is shameful, that is love-making. Or else from making love on the beach; for they are next to the sea.

2. *Theogony* 991: νηοπόλον νύχιον [ΑΚΕΠ II 47.4]

A guardian at night, that is unseen, secret. But Aristarchos [of Samothrace, 217–145 B.C.] writes μύχιον, that is one who is in charge of the innermost chamber [of the temple] on Cyprus. Another explanation: νυκτεριόν [nightly], because the rites of Aphrodite are performed at night.

147. SCHOLIA to Homer (of uncertain date)

1. *Iliad* 5.422: ἦ μάλα δή τινα Κύπρις Ἀχαιιάδων ἀνιεῖσα [ΑΚΕΠ ΙΙ 20.139α]

This [Cypris] is an epithet of Aphrodite. Those before us did not understand its meaning; for, having been led astray by Hesiod, they believed that "Cypris" means, as Hesiod says, "Cyprus-born," because she was born in sea-girt Cyprus [*Theogony* 199] . . . What confused Hesiod and the others is the passage in Book 8 [of the *Odyssey*] which reads: "Laughter-loving Aphrodite came to Cyprus, to Paphos; there she has a sanctuary and an altar on which sacrifices are made" [lines 362–63].

2. *Iliad* 11.20: τόν ποτέ οἱ Κινύρης δῶκε ξεινήιον εἶναι [ΑΚΕΠ Ι 14.1]

a. He [Kinyras] was the son of Theias and king of Cyprus. Being very rich, he was host to the Greeks who came there and promised to send supplies for them to Troy. The story has it that he failed to keep his promise and was cursed by Agamemnon; also that he was destroyed by Apollo because he had challenged the god in a musical contest, and that his daughters, fifty in number, leaped into the sea and were changed into halcyons.
b. The Cypriots kept apart from the Greeks, neither contributing to their expenses nor campaigning with them. But they gained the friendship of the Greeks by means of gifts. For they did not give the gifts in lieu of campaigning with them, but, it is said, to please the king; for his great fame had reached Cyprus.

3. *Iliad* 21.12: ὡς δ᾽ ὅθ᾽ ὑπὸ ῥιπῆς πυρὸς [ΑΚΕΠ ΙΙ 164.3α]

Because of this source some speak of "the poet of Cyprus"; for at times Cyprus is bothered by locusts, like Cyrene and Barce.

4. *Iliad* 23.130: χαλκὸν ζώννυσθαι [ΑΚΕΠ ΙΙ 170.1]

Aristotle [fr. 519 ed. Rose] speaks of the war dance of Achilles. The Achaeans brought this practice to Cyprus. For, when kings were buried, their army came out in a war dance.

5. *Odyssey* 1.184: ἐς Τεμέσην [ΑΚΕΠ Ι 18.1]

A city in Oinotria [the southernmost portion of Italy], which is now called Tempson or Brentesia. (Q) Temese is a city in Cyprus; according to some a city in Italy which is now called Brendesion and Tempsa. (Cod. Vind. 56)

6. *Odyssey* 8.362–63: ἡ δ᾽ ἄρα Κύπρον ἵκανε φιλομμειδὴς Ἀφροδίτη
ἐς Πάφον, ἔνθα τέ οἱ τέμενος βωμός τε θυήεις. [ΑΚΕΠ ΙΙ 12.2γ; 55.5]

This verse led Hesiod [*Theogony* 199] into the error of saying that Aphrodite was Cyprus-born. (Cod. Vind. 56)

At Paphos there is no statue of Aphrodite, only a sacred precinct and an altar. Homer speaks from knowledge when he says of Paphos that "there she has a sanctuary and an altar on which sacrifices are made to her." (ET)

7. *Odyssey* 17.442–43: αὐτὰρ ἔμ᾽ ἐς Κύπρον ξείνῳ δόσαν ἀντιάσαντι,
   Δμήτορι Ἰασίδῃ, ὃς Κύπρου ἶφι ἄνασσεν. [ΑΚΕΠ I 14.3; 16.2; 16.3]

Because Cyprus always had many kings at the same time, Menander in the parabasis of his *Misumenos* [fr. 335 *FAC* IIIB] also says: " I am from Cyprus, where I fared quite well; for I was in the service of one of the kings." (HQ)

When Kinyras had died Dmetor became king of Cyprus. In the *Iliad* [11.20] Kinyras is not called king of Cyprus, but simply a Cypriot. (BQ)

8. *Odyssey* 18.29: ληϊβοτείρης [ΑΚΕΠ I 19α]

A pig destroying the crop, that is another man's field. If a pig is found feeding on another man's crop it has it tusks removed. (V)

It was the law that, when a pig was found feeding on another man's crop, it had its tusks removed. (Q)

Of a pig feeding on a crop. If a pig was found on another man's field it was subject to being seized by the owners of the place. This was the law among the Cypriots. (BH)

148. SCHOLIA to Isocrates (of uncertain date)

1. *Evagoras* (9) 1: Ὁρῶν, ὦ Νικόκλεις [ΑΚΕΠ I 66.44α]

And we say that Evagoras seems to have died a long time earlier [374/73 B.C.]. And Isocrates, sending a speech now, deemed it inappropriate to compose a lament and to call to mind the laments which it was proper to perform at the time of the death itself.

2. *Nicocles* (2), Hypothesis [ΑΚΕΠ I 20.19; 68.6]

Nikokles was the son of Evagoras and traced his descent from Teucer and Telamon . . . He was king of Salamis, a city in Cyprus, which is now called the city of Constantine [Constantia] and is the metropolis of all of Cyprus. It is to him that Isocrates addresses his exhortation on how rightly to exercise kingship. But Hermippos [of Smyrna, follower of Callimachus, floruit 3rd c. B.C.] says in his work on Isocrates, quoting a certain Evander who wrote in the manner of the sophists, that Isocrates sent his speech to Nikokles after having received twenty talents from him, at the time of Evagoras' death [374/73 B.C.], as if to say that Isocrates wished to be helpful to Nikokles after his father's death.

3. Anonymous vita of Isocrates 13–14 [ΑΚΕΠ I 67]

A certain Hipponikos, it is widely believed, was a Cypriot by nationality and a friend of the sophist Isocrates. At his death this man left behind a son also named Hipponikos. Isocrates knew him as a boy and saw that he needed much instruction in rhetoric. So he wrote some guidelines, wishing to instruct him on how to live.

149. SCHOLIA to Lycophron (of uncertain date)

1. *Alexandra* 586: Κηφεὺς δὲ καὶ Πράξανδρος [ΑΚΕΠ I 24β]

Kepheus was from Achaea and Praxandros was a Spartan; they came to Cyprus, as Philostephanos [of Cyrene, 3rd c. B.C.; *FHG* III 31, fr.12] says.

2. *Alexandra* 831: καὶ τὸν θεᾷ κλαυσθέντα Γαύαντος τάφον [ΑΚΕΠ II 70]

Adonis is also called Gauas by the Cypriots.

150. SCHOLIA to Pindar (of uncertain date)

1. *Nemean* 4.76 (46): ἔνθα Τεῦκρος ἀπάρχει [ΑΚΕΠ I 20.2]

This means: then the son of Telamon ruled in Cyprus. For Teucer, when he had returned to Salamis after the fall of Troy and was suspected by Telamon of being responsible for the death of Ajax, fled and settled on Cyprus, establishing his rule there, as Lycophron [tragic poet, 3rd c. B.C.; *Alexandra* 450] reports.

2. *Nemean* 8.28 (17): σὺν θεῷ γάρ τοι φυτευθεὶς ὄλβος ἀνθρώποισι παρμονώτερος [ΑΚΕΠ I 14.30]

He says: prosperity is more abiding for men when it is generated and given with the blessing of God. Such prosperity made Kinyras on the island of Cyprus wealthy and happy in his wealth. Of him Homer [*Iliad* 11.20] says: which [a breastplate] Kinyras had once given him [Agamemnon] as a guest gift.

3. *Nemean* 8.32c (19): ἵσταμαι δὴ ποσὶ κούφοις, ἀναπνέων [ΑΚΕΠ I 14.43]

In other words: those who wish to make a long speech, such as tragic actors, take a deep breath so that their voice might suffice them when they speak. Many and diverse stories, he says, have been recorded about Kinyras; therefore I take a deep breath before I speak.

4. *Pythian* 2.27a–e (15): κελαδέοντι μὲν ἀμφὶ Κινύραν πολλάκις φᾶμαι Κυπρίων [ΑΚΕΠ I 14.16; 14.37; 42; II 92; 165]

a. The Cypriots have songs about Kinyras, but I sing about you. He was a son of Apollo, or of Paphos, according to some.

b. It is not known why he introduces Kinyras into the praises of Hiero [I of Syracuse], unless it be because he had been appointed priest to two goddesses. Hiero and his brothers were sons of Deinomenes, who brought the sacred rites from Triopion in Cyprus [actually a headland of Caria] to Sicily. It is this Kinyras from whom the Kinyridai in Cyprus derive their holy office.

c. Or thus: There are those who say that Deinomenes, Hiero's father, was of Cypriot origin. Therefore now, when he celebrates Hiero, he remembers Kinyras . . .

d. This means: Often in their songs the Cypriots celebrate Kinyras, but my song celebrates you and the Cypriots.

e. The point of this phrase is: The songs of the Cypriots celebrate Kinyras, but my song celebrates you and the Cypriots.

5. *Pythian* 2.28 (16): φᾶμαι Κυπρίων, τόν [ΑΚΕΠ I 14.13]

The king of Cyprus [Kinyras], whom Homer mentions [*Iliad* 11.20]. A son of Eurymedon and a nymph of Paphos. He was a priest of Cyprian Aphrodite.

6. *Pythian* 2.31a–d (17): ἱερέα κτίλον Ἀφροδίτας [ΑΚΕΠ I 14.39]

a. A companion and trusted friend is called "tame." And Pindar himself [fr. 238 ed. Snell] uses "domesticate' in the sense of "tame": ἔνθα ποῖμναι κτιλεύονται κάπρων λεόντων τε (There herds of boars and lions are being tamed).

b. Or thus: He does not say that Kinyras was the lover of Apollo, but that he was loved by the god because he was celebrated by the musicians.

c. And another explanation: Homer [*Iliad* 3.196 and 13.492] calls the lead ram of a flock "tame" . . . Now Pindar calls the priest "tame."

d. A *ktilos* of Aphrodite, meaning a companion and friend of the goddess.

7. *Pythian* 2.127 (69): τὸ Καστόρειον [ΑΚΕΠ II 170]

. . . Aristotle [fr. 519 ed. Rose] says that Achilles was the first to perform a war dance on the pyre of Patroklos; this war dance reportedly is called a *prylis* by the Cypriots, so that the dance receives its name from the pyre.

151. SCHOLIA to Plato (of uncertain date)

1. *Republic* 8.553C: τιάρας τε καὶ στρεπτοὺς καὶ ἀκινάκας παραζωννύντα

The τιάρα is the so-called κυρβασία. It is a headdress that only the kings of the Persians wore upright, but the generals bent-over . . . Theophrastus in his *On Kingship* [fr. 602 ed. Fortenbaugh] says that the κίταρις is Cyprian.

152. SCHOLIA to Theocritus (of uncertain date)

1. *Idylls* 1.109a: ὡραῖος χὥδωνις [ΑΚΕΠ I 14.23]

He [Adonis] was the son of Kinyras, the son of Apollo, and of his [Kinyras'] daughter Smyrna. She lay in love with her own father because of the anger of Aphrodite, having undone her hair and having boasted that not even Aphrodite had such hair. She deceived her father, dressing like a servant girl and lying in love with him. Later, when she had carried and given birth to Adonis, she was discovered and in her shame prayed to be changed into the like-named tree [the myrrh-tree].

2. *Idylls* 15.100/101: δέσποιν᾽ ἁ Γολγώς τε καὶ Ἰδάλιον ἐφίλησας [ΑΚΕΠ I 28.1; II 83]

Golgoi is a city in Cyprus, named after Golgos, the son of Adonis and Aphrodite. And Idalion is a city in Cyprus.

153. SCHOLIA to Tzetzes (of uncertain date)

1. *Historiae* or *Chiliades* 1.86 (p. 546 ed. Leone): Κνίδο

Knidos is in the area of Kos. In ancient times the power of Cyprus extended thus far and beyond.

154. MACHAIRAS, LEONTIOS (ca. 1380–after 1432) [ΑΚΕΠ I 129.3 and 130]

Leontios Machairas, a Cypriot with Frankish connections, wrote a *Chronikon Kyprou*, which ranks among the more important Greek sources for the mediaeval history and culture of Cyprus. This *Chronikon* begins with a survey of earlier Cypriot history, provides a detailed account of the years 1359–1432, and concludes with brief notices, by an anonymous continuator, which carry the account forward to the year 1458. Readers are referred to the bilingual edition of R. M. Dawkins, *Recital Concerning the Sweet Land of Cyprus Entitled "Chronicle,"* 2 vols., Oxford: Clarendon Press, 1932.

155. BUSTRON(E) (Βουστρώνιος, Μπουστροῦς, or Πουστροῦς), GEORGE (d. after 1501)

George Bustrone, a Hellenized Frank, was closely associated with James II, the last king of Cyprus, whom he served as an ambassador in 1458. His chronicle, a continuation of the chronicle of Leontios Machairas, records events in the history of Cyprus between 1456 and 1501. An edition of both chronicles, by Konstantinos N. Sathas, was published in Venice in 1873. See the translation by R. M. Dawkins, *The Chronicle of George Boustronios 1456–1489*, Melbourne University Press, 1964.

156. EPHRAIM, Patriarch of Jerusalem (Ephraim the Athenian) (d. 1771)

Ephraim was a native of Athens but lived at various times on Patmos, in Cyprus, and in Constantinople. In 1766 he became patriarch of Jerusalem, where he died in 1771. His numerous writings include the celebrated Περιγραφὴ τῆς ἱερᾶς σεβασμίας καὶ βασιλικῆς μονῆς τοῦ Κύκκου (*Description of the Holy, Venerable, and Imperial Monastery of Kykkos*), which was published in Venice in 1751.

157. KYPRIANOS, archimandrite (d. ca. 1804)

Kyprianos was a native of Cyprus, but lived for many years in Trieste and then in Venice. His highly regarded Ἰστορία χρονολογικὴ τῆς νήσου Κύπρου (*Chronological History of the Island of Cyprus*) was published in Venice in 1788; it saw a new edition in Nicosia in 1902.

Index of Authors and Works
Numbers refer to sections

Index of Scriptural References
including non–canonical writings
Numbers refer to sections and subsections

Index of Greek Words and Phrases
Numbers refer to sections and subsections

Ἀαρών, **118.15**
Αἴπεια, **111.9**
ἀγήτωρ, **29.1**
ἀερία, **29.2**
ἀκάμαντα, **29.3**
ἄναξ, ἄνακτες, **111.12**
ἀρὰς ἐπισπεῖραι, **29.4**
ἀχαιομάντεις, **29.6**
βομβοία, **29.7**
βοῦς Κύπριος, **29.8–9, 88.1**
βύβλιοι, **29.10**
γένεσις Κύπρου, **29.12**
γῆς ὀμφαλός, **29.13**
δημίην Κύπριν, **29.14**
διδόναι, **39.2**
δίπτυον, **29.15**
εἶδον ἄλιον, **33.15**
ἔλεια, ἔλα, **29.21**
ἐῷα, **29.25**
ἡμιπέλεκκον, **29.27**
θύϊνα, **88.4**
κάρβα, **33.16**
κάρπωσις, **29.28**
καταγηρᾶσαι, **88.5**
Κεδρασεύς (?), **69.1**
κινύρα, **111.11**
κῖρις, **62.1**
κίταρις, **67.16, 151.1**
κίτταρις, **29.31**
κιχητός, **29.32**
κράββατος, **22.2, 135.3**
κριθοπομπία, **29.46, 88.11**
κτίλος, κτιλεύω, **150.6**
κυμαθίας, κυματίης, **111.11**
Κυπρία πάλη, **29.34**
κυρβασία, **151.1**
ληιβοτείρης, **111.21, 147.8**
μετριότης, **107.2, 122.1, 130.2**
μνάσιον, **29.38**
μοτοφαγία, μοττοφαγία, **29.39, 67.12, 88.9**
μυρίκη, **29.41**
μύχιον, **146.2**
νησαίη λίθος, **67.13**
νυκτεριόν, **146.2**
νῦν ἡ ψυχή μου τετάρακται (Athanasios), **49.1**
ὀρτός, **29.42**
πάρνοπες, **67.14**
περιόρια, **29.44**

πευθῆνες, **111.12**
πεύθω, **111.12**
πύστις, **111.12**
Ῥοίκου (Ῥύκου) κριθοπομπία, **29.46, 88.11**
σάπιθος, **29.47**
σκίμπους, **22.2, 135.3**
Σολοιτύπος, **29.48**
τιάρα, **67.16, 151.1**
τρέμιθος (τέρμιθος), **33.34**
τρόμος, **33.34**

Index of Names and Subjects
Numbers refer to sections and subsections

N